# COGNITIVE BEHAVIORAL THERAPY WITH CHILDREN

This new edition of *Cognitive Behavioral Therapy with Children* links together the methods of cognitive behavioral therapy (CBT) practiced in academic centers with those practiced in the community. This book addresses the challenges community practitioners face when pressured to use CBT with youth who live with mental health disorders, but whose circumstances differ from those in research settings. Practitioners will learn how to overcome therapeutic obstacles. This new edition contains an expanded discussion on cultural considerations relevant to assessment and treatment as well as a new chapter on training others in CBT for children.

**Katharina Manassis, MD,** founded and led a program in anxiety disorders at Toronto's Hospital for Sick Children. She has published over 80 papers in professional journals regarding childhood anxiety disorders and has written five related books for parents and professionals, including *Keys to Parenting Your Anxious Child* and *Case Formulation with Children & Adolescents*. She has her own private practice and is a Professor Emerita in the Department of Psychiatry at the University of Toronto.

# COGNITIVE BEHAVIORAL THERAPY WITH CHILDREN
## A GUIDE FOR THE COMMUNITY PRACTITIONER

*Second Edition*

## Katharina Manassis

**Routledge**
Taylor & Francis Group

NEW YORK AND LONDON

Second edition published 2016
by Routledge
711 Third Avenue, New York, NY 10017

and by Routledge
2 Park Square, Milton Park, Abingdon, Oxon, OX14 4RN

*Routledge is an imprint of the Taylor & Francis Group, an informa business*

© 2016 Taylor & Francis

First edition published by Routledge 2009

*Library of Congress Cataloging-in-Publication Data*
A catalog record for this book has been requested

ISBN: 978-1-138-85029-3 (hbk)
ISBN: 978-1-138-85030-9 (pbk)
ISBN: 978-1-315-72476-8 (ebk)

Typeset in New Baskerville
by Apex CoVantage, LLC

THIS BOOK IS DEDICATED TO THOSE
I HAVE TAUGHT, TO THOSE WHO
HAVE TAUGHT ME, AND TO JULIA
AND MARTIN, MY OWN CHILDREN.

# Contents

# Preface

## A TALE OF TWO CASES

A few years ago, I was invited to present a half-day workshop on doing cognitive behavioral therapy (CBT) with children to a large, diverse group of community mental health professionals. As a CBT practitioner, researcher, and leader of a child anxiety disorders program that focused on CBT, I was considered an expert in this field. Despite the size of the audience (about 500 people), the organizers were clear that they wanted an interactive presentation rather than a lecture. They suggested that the morning session focus on cases. I agreed. I was asked to bring two or three CBT cases from my practice and describe my work with them, and they would provide descriptions of two or three children on their caseload for me to comment on.

I began by presenting a case on Tom, a nine-year-old boy with a lifelong history of shyness whose mother was concerned about his lack of friends. Tom protested that the boy he sat next to in class was his friend, but admitted he never saw this boy outside of school and hated recess because he usually spent it alone and was sometimes the target of bullies. Tom did not participate in after-school activities, he avoided answering the telephone at home, and his father complained that he "lacked initiative" because he would spend most of his weekend on the computer rather than engaging in outdoor activities. Despite his problems, Tom was polite and well liked by teachers and other adults, he responded appropriately when other children approached him, and he had no history of medical or developmental difficulties. According to his report cards, Tom was a very good student, but "low class participation" had been noted as a concern each year.

In the interview, Tom said he wanted more friends and hated feeling different from his peers, but was not sure what to do about this. He was cooperative, made good eye contact, and readily answered specific questions but shrugged his shoulders in response to open-ended ones. He had never before seen a therapist. He described an attempt by a teacher to engage him in a game with his peers, but felt he had been "pushed" to do so and was then excluded and ridiculed by his peers because he was not familiar with the rules of the game. He said his shyness became worse after that incident.

After providing this description, I discussed diagnosis (most likely social anxiety disorder), invited suggestions from the audience regarding intervention, and then elaborated on Tom's successful treatment with CBT. Tom was seen individually, with considerable concurrent work with his parents to help them to better understand his difficulty and to appropriately support his attempts to change. Despite his father's initial disparaging remarks about Tom, he became much more supportive once told there were specific things he could do to facilitate social contact for his son. For example, practicing soccer skills with his father made it easier for Tom to play on a team of same-aged peers without risking humiliation. Tom's mother recognized that she had inadvertently encouraged some of his social avoidance because she often worried about him being hurt. After several months of work with Tom and his family, he was still socially reticent, but regularly participated in activities with his peers and was able to initiate contact with them with his parents' encouragement. With support from his teacher, he had also practiced answering questions in class and even entered the school public speaking contest.

The morning seemed to be off to a good start. Next, a member of the audience was invited to present her case to me. Her question was: Is this child a suitable candidate for CBT, and do you have any other recommendations? She presented the case of Vicky.

Vicky was a 14-year-old girl who had not attended school for two years, after being embarrassed by a teacher about a poor mark on a test. There had been two previous attempts at therapy with Vicky, but she had "fired" both therapists, and her parents believed that this occurred because neither "really understood" their daughter. After an episode of self-harm behavior (superficial cutting of her forearm), Vicky was hospitalized and diagnosed with "multiple anxiety disorders and possible mood disorder." Medication had been recommended, but Vicky refused to take it. Since then, Vicky reported that her mood was better, but she "panicked" if her parents tried to escort her to school. Nevertheless, she still went to the mall with her friends several times a week, sometimes during the school day. Her mother did not want to curtail this activity, as she feared her daughter becoming more depressed if she was isolated from her peer group. When the presenter had encouraged Vicky's parents to become more firm in their approach to her school avoidance, they reported that Vicky had threatened suicide. The parents had stopped their efforts to return her to school at that point. They were now considering home schooling for Vicky.

Having heard this story, I made recommendations, but they had nothing to do with CBT! Difficulties in the family system, behavioral issues, and the possibility of an underlying learning problem all needed to be explored and addressed. Then came the inevitable (and legitimate) question from the audience: "Dr. Manassis, isn't CBT the best evidence-based treatment for anxiety disorders in children and youth? Why are you not recommending it in this case?" I answered the question by going over all the factors that made Vicky a poor candidate for CBT (lack of motivation, family's inability to set limits, poor engagement in previous therapy, uncontrolled acting out behavior, long duration of avoidance of school, and so forth). This response resulted in a second question, though: "If CBT is not the evidence-based treatment of choice in this case, what is?"

My attempt to answer that second question became the inspiration for this book. In the next few years, as I taught and supervised community practitioners trying to apply CBT under less-than-ideal conditions with challenging cases, I gradually found some answers. This book is an attempt to share those answers—to help decide when CBT can be helpful to children, when it can be helpful with some modifications, and when it has little hope of succeeding.

## IS THIS BOOK FOR ME?

When I shared the title of this book with colleagues, I was often asked, "What do you mean when you say community practitioner?" My answer is: anyone who has not had expert training in CBT and hopes to practice it outside an academic center. The disciplines of the people in this position I have met and trained have included social work, child and youth counseling, family practice, pediatrics, pediatric nursing, child life, and trainees in all of these areas. Psychiatry residents or psychiatrists who were trained at a time when CBT was not part of the curriculum have also participated, as have psychology interns and students. Many of my trainees have worked on multidisciplinary teams where CBT was their assigned "piece" of the treatment plan. Some have been independent practitioners. Some have been quite knowledgeable about CBT but lacking in experience. For others, CBT concepts were new and outside their usual scope of practice. All were dedicated to providing the best care possible to their young clients.

This book focuses on children with anxiety and depression, as these are the diagnoses where CBT is currently considered the initial treatment of choice (Compton et al., 2004), where the effect sizes (average degree of improvement in study participants) are largest (Butler, Chapman, Forman, & Beck, 2006), and also where most of my own practice has focused. While CBT has been used in other childhood disorders (for example, externalizing disorders), it is usually preceded by or combined with other treatments in these disorders (medical treatment or behavior management without a cognitive component), and child impulsivity can be problematic in implementing CBT strategies with children who have these disorders. References to manuals for these disorders are included in Chapter 5.

## WHAT IS COGNITIVE BEHAVIORAL THERAPY (CBT)?

To begin, a brief definition of CBT is in order to ensure a common, basic understanding of this form of therapy and challenges associated with it in community practice. Cognitive behavioral therapy is a form of brief, structured psychotherapy based on the premise that thoughts, feelings, and behaviors affect each other in reciprocal ways (Kendall, 1993). For example, negative thoughts often engender negative feelings and vice versa. Fearful thoughts, on the other hand, often increase anxious feelings and anxiety-related avoidant behaviors. Angry thoughts can contribute to angry feelings and aggressive behavior. Because changing unpleasant feelings directly can be difficult, CBT aims to do so indirectly by having the client change the associated thoughts and behaviors. Numerous randomized controlled trials in children and adults attest to the ability of CBT to reduce emotional symptoms and their associated diagnoses, especially for anxious and depressive symptoms, relative to nonintervention or (in some studies) alternative intervention (reviewed in Compton et al., 2004).

As cognitive theory has continued to develop, some authors have written about integration between CBT and other therapies (Alford & Beck, 1997). They point out common therapeutic elements among therapies, for example, the ability of psychodynamic therapy to aid desensitization to certain social anxieties. Conceptual similarities also exist in, for example, the similarity between cognitive schemas or beliefs about relationships (in CBT) and core conflictual relationship themes (in short-term dynamic therapy). What distinguishes CBT from other therapies, however, is (1) the highly structured nature of sessions and (2) the discussion of therapeutic elements as explicit strategies with the client (Alford & Beck, 1997). Thus, although the therapist is in charge of preserving the session structure, the therapeutic encounter between therapist and client is highly collaborative and transparent. These distinct elements are often the most challenging to learn when starting CBT, so they are emphasized in this book and in most CBT manuals.

## WHAT IS THE PROBLEM WITH CBT IN
## COMMUNITY PRACTICE?

As illustrated in the two very different cases at the start of this chapter, CBT is not beneficial for everyone. In community practice, there are many children and families for whom it is not ideal or for whom it is no better than other interventions (Southam-Gerow et al., 2010; Weisz et al., 2009). Trying CBT in these cases can result in discouragement for the child, the family, and the practitioner. Why is this dilemma so common?

Too often, CBT is either touted as a panacea for every mental health problem, or cynically considered an "ivory tower" treatment that only works in research centers. Neither of these extreme positions is accurate, but it is easy to see how they can develop. Pressure to make psychotherapy more "scientific," the quest for more time-efficient treatments, and the myth that "one size fits all" (that all children in a given diagnostic category can be treated the same way) have all contributed to broad, sometimes indiscriminate use of CBT in children's mental health settings. Often with inadequate training and support, community practitioners are told to "do CBT." They find themselves struggling to make their clients fit CBT manuals that were designed for research populations, and that were never intended to be used as "cookbooks" or to replace clinician judgment (McNeill, 2006). When CBT fails under these circumstances, the cynical "ivory tower" position emerges.

## ADDRESSING THE PROBLEM: THE FOCUS OF THIS BOOK

CBT can be used effectively in community settings, but doing so requires more information than what is found in most child CBT manuals. That is where this book comes in. In fact, the content of this book can be thought of as "child CBT: what is not in the manuals." There are new approaches to CBT that may address some obstacles to treatment success in the community (see Chapter 10), but most of this work has been done with adults, and typical child CBT manuals do not describe it in detail.

Understanding the differences between children seen in research centers and community clinics, differences between academic and community environments, and the challenges of applying CBT manuals to different children and families are useful starting points. In this book, adaptations that address these differences will be described for each stage of assessment and therapy. Combining CBT with other modalities, working with challenging families, and dealing with obstacles to therapeutic progress are other important aspects of community practice that will be discussed.

The book can be used in more than one way. Practitioners who are starting to use CBT with their clients may wish to read it from cover to cover to gain an overview of the joys and challenges of what lies ahead. It can also be used as a guide for supervisors of new practitioners or as a guide for peer supervision groups, because much of it was written initially to address issues arising in my own supervision of others. In this case, reading about a chapter a week and completing the worksheets and clinical challenges at the end of each chapter will promote active learning and bring the material to life. The first few chapters emphasize assessment, contracting, and starting therapy; the next few the middle stages of therapy; and the last few the issues around termination, therapeutic obstacles, and training others in child CBT. Finally, if there is an issue that comes up frequently in your clientele (for example, most have cognitive limitations or most have family problems), you may wish to skim the entire book but then come back and read thoroughly those chapters that are most relevant to your clients.

Sample modules (units focused on a particular CBT concept or skill), which focus on imagery, are included later in the book for anxious children with cognitive limitations. These modules were written because such children commonly present for treatment in community settings, and existing manuals are often particularly difficult to use with this population (see Chapter 7). They have been pilot tested with several children, but not empirically evaluated yet. There are also some children who have no cognitive limitations, but respond preferentially to imagery rather than words, probably because there are different learning styles and imagery tends to be more appealing to visual learners (Slater, Lujan, & DiCarlo, 2007). Most existing manuals, however, rely more on words than imagery. References are included for existing manuals that are readily available for other populations.

## CHAPTER ORGANIZATION

Each chapter integrates information from empirical studies with my own clinical experiences and those of my supervisees to illustrate an aspect of adapting CBT to community practice. CBT is an empirically validated treatment, but many research questions remain unanswered. To clarify the empirical basis of the information in this book, each chapter contains a section near the beginning titled "What Is Known" and another near the end titled "What We Yet Need to Learn."

The largest section of each chapter is titled "Putting What We Know to Work" and focuses on applying these ideas to your practice. Case examples from my practice and those of my supervisees are used to illustrate key points.

Near the end of each chapter is a worksheet with exercises that allow you to think about the principles described in relation to your clientele. For those who are not yet working with a client in CBT, a hypothetical

"Clinical Challenge" is provided to stimulate your thinking. One possible set of answers to these clinical challenges is provided later in the book, but try to think them through without looking at the answers first.

References to publications about the topics addressed in each chapter are included throughout, to allow you to study a given topic in more detail if you wish.

## THE VALUE OF SHARING IDEAS WITH PEERS

Having worked with groups of community practitioners from diverse settings, it has become clear to me that "more heads are better than one." In other words, discussing with colleagues the topics of this book and how they relate to your work may be very useful. Colleagues may have a fresh perspective on your work, provide useful feedback, and help you apply the principles outlined in this book to your unique clientele and setting. It is also advisable to obtain supervision from a colleague with CBT experience for the first few cases if this modality is new to your practice.

Much of the practical content of this book is the direct result of my attempts to supervise community practitioners and adapt child CBT to their clients. Some of these practitioners also participated in outcome evaluation studies of a CBT teaching program. The results and suggestions that emerged from these studies further influenced the book's content and organization. Clearly, I am indebted to those who participated, and thank them for the opportunity to work together and to share ideas.

To begin the book, ways to address the difference between success in academic settings (called "efficacy") and success in the community (called "effectiveness") are described, including some lessons learned from the outcome studies mentioned. We then examine the importance of assessment in successful cognitive-behavioral treatment of children in the community.

## REFERENCES

Alford, B.A., & Beck, A.T. (1997). *The integrative power of cognitive therapy*. New York: Guilford Press.

Butler, A.C., Chapman, J.E., Forman, E.M., & Beck, A.T. (2006). The empirical status of cognitive-behavioral therapy: A review of meta-analyses. *Clinical Psychology Review*, 26, 17–31.

Compton, S.N., March, J.S., Brent, D., Albano, A.M., Weersing, R., & Curry, J. (2004). Cognitive-behavioral psychotherapy for anxiety and depressive disorders in children and adolescents: An evidence-based medicine review. *Journal of the American Academy of Child and Adolescent Psychiatry*, 43, 930–959.

Kendall, P. (1993). Guiding theory for therapy with children and adolescents. In P. Kendall (Ed.), *Child and adolescent therapy: Cognitive behavioral procedures, Fourth edition*. New York: Guilford Press, pp. 3–26.

McNeill, T. (2006). Evidence-based practice in an age of relativism: Toward a model for practice. *Social Work,* 51, 147–156.

Slater, J.A., Lujan, H.L., & DiCarlo, S.E. (2007). Does gender influence learning style preferences of first-year medical students? *Advanced Physiological Education,* 31, 336–342.

Southam-Gerow, M.A., Weisz, J.R., Chu, B.C., McLeod, B.D., Gordis, E.B., & Connor-Smith, J.K. (2010). Does cognitive behavioral therapy for youth anxiety outperform usual care in community clinics? An initial effectiveness test. *Journal of the American Academy of Child & Adolescent Psychiatry,* 49, 1043–1052.

Weisz, J.R., Southam-Gerow, M.A., Gordis, E.B., Connor-Smith, J.K., Chu, B.C., Langer, D.A., et al. (2009). Cognitive behavioral therapy versus usual clinical care for youth depression: An initial test of transportability to community clinics and clinicians. *Journal of Consulting and Clinical Psychology,* 77, 383–396.

# Acknowledgments

I wish to thank and acknowledge the following organizations (listed alpha-betically) who have financially supported my research: Canadian Imperial Bank of Commerce Children's Miracle Fund, Canadian Institutes of Health Research, Centre for Addiction and Mental Health Foundation, Hospital for Sick Children, Ontario Mental Health Foundation, and Provincial Centre of Excellence in Children's Mental Health at the Children's Hospital of Eastern Ontario (CHEO), Social Sciences and Humanities Research Council. My heartfelt thanks to the Department of Psychiatry at the Hospital for Sick Children and the Anxiety Disorders Team for "holding down the fort" while I took the sabbatical leave that allowed me to write the first edition of this book, and a special thanks to Lisa Fiksenbaum and Phyllis Earley for assisting with the completion of the initial manuscript.

# Author

**Katharina Manassis, MD,** graduated from the Faculty of Medicine, University of Toronto, in 1986. She obtained her diploma in child psychiatry in 1990 and her diploma in psychiatry in 1991. She then became a staff psychiatrist at the Hospital for Sick Children, Toronto, where she founded the Anxiety Disorders Program. The program's main focus is the development and scientific evaluation of cognitive-behavioral treatments for children with anxiety disorders and related conditions.

Dr. Manassis has taught trainees in various mental health disciplines as a professor in the Department of Psychiatry at the University of Toronto and in the Human Development and Applied Psychology Department at the Ontario Institute for Studies in Education. She has led several funded research studies to better understand and treat childhood anxiety disorders and has published more than 80 papers in professional journals in this field. She is the author of widely read books for parents of anxious or depressed children and for child mental health professionals seeking to hone their skills in CBT, problem-solving, and case formulation.

# CHAPTER ONE

# Narrowing the Gap between Efficacy and Effectiveness

Efficacy refers to how well a treatment works under ideal conditions, usually in a research setting. Effectiveness, by contrast, refers to how well a treatment works under "real-world" conditions, usually outside academic centers. Another way of thinking about these ideas is in terms of advantages and disadvantages faced by clients seen in different settings. Thus, your CBT clients may be at a relative disadvantage compared to those seen in academic centers, *even if you are just as skilled as the therapists there are.* Understanding this disadvantage can improve the chances of success with your clients.

## WHAT IS KNOWN

Recent meta-analyses attest to the efficacy of CBT for children and adolescents with anxiety or depression (James, James, Cowdrey, Soler, & Choke, 2013; Klein, Jacobs, & Reinecke, 2007), although results are generally more impressive when CBT is compared with waitlist or other inactive control conditions than when it is compared with other psychological treatments. Large multi-site trials have found enhanced benefits when serotonin-specific medications are added to CBT in both anxious and depressed youth (Domino et al., 2008; Ginsburg et al., 2011).

Studies of effectiveness of CBT in non-academic settings have largely focused on sub-clinical populations in schools (Miller et al., 2011), who show symptomatic improvement relative to waitlist controls. Some studies have examined clinical populations in community treatment, but most are open trials. Among comparative trials, Weersing and Weisz (2002) found worse outcomes for community-treated depressed youth than those treated in academic settings. Weisz and others (2009) found that CBT did not outperform usual care for depressed youth in community settings, and Southam-Gerow and colleagues (2010) reported the same finding for anxious youth.

Relative to clients in academic settings, CBT clients in the community typically have higher rates of ethnic minority status, attend fewer sessions, and have higher rates of comorbid diagnoses. All of these factors have been linked to poor treatment outcome (Crawley, Beidas, Benjamin, Martin, & Kendall, 2008; Weersing & Weisz, 2002). Client differences between academic and community settings underscore the need for thorough assessment, which is detailed in the next chapter. However, therapist and organizational differences may also contribute to outcome differences, and addressing these is discussed further in this chapter. Possible client, therapist, and organizational differences are summarized in Table 1.1.

TABLE 1.1
Child CBT in Community Settings Relative to Academic Settings

| | |
|---|---|
| Typical Clients in Community Settings | More comorbid psychiatric illness |
| | More comorbid medical illness |
| | More suicidal thoughts or other critical issues |
| | More needing psychotropic medication |
| | More intellectual delay or learning disability |
| | More with first language other than English |
| | More family instability |
| | Lower family treatment motivation |
| | Lower child awareness of symptoms |
| Typical Therapists in Community Settings | Less intensive training |
| | Less ongoing supervision |
| | Fewer adherence checks used |
| | Face more competing demands |
| | Lower client/therapist optimism |
| Community Mental Health Organizations | Different mandates |
| | Different organizational structure |
| | Different funding mechanisms |
| | More community perceptions/stigma |

In view of these apparent discrepancies between academic and community practice, my research group developed a group supervision program for community practitioners. We wanted to evaluate our ability to train them in CBT, and to better understand the problems community practitioners encounter when they try to do CBT in their settings. We had previously offered workshops in child CBT, but found that most community practitioners were no longer using CBT techniques six months later because they lacked the confidence to do so independently (Barankin & Manassis, 2003).

The response to our program was overwhelmingly positive, with 85% of participants indicating that they planned to do further child CBT in their settings, even at six-month follow-up (Manassis et al., 2009). Participants' knowledge of child CBT improved on a short test given before and after the program, confidence using CBT increased, and participants were very satisfied with the supervision. Older participants and participants working in settings that used a diagnostic screen at client intake showed the greatest benefit. This finding was consistent with the adult CBT literature, where prior therapy experience and careful case selection have been linked to training success (James, Blackburn, Milne, & Reichfelt, 2001). We subsequently replicated this study with ten rural mental health agencies using tele-health. This program was positively evaluated by training therapists and, more importantly, was associated with significant symptom reduction in participating children (Jones et al., 2015).

In these studies, concerns were raised about difficulty finding suitable cases for supervision, the need for more background information about CBT and its evidence base, and a desire for more observational opportunities of "expert" clinicians. Therapists also identified difficulty adapting CBT to their clientele, their role in their organizations, the time commitment needed to do CBT, and low organizational support of CBT as potential barriers to doing further child CBT. These concerns were very helpful to improve our understanding of obstacles to CBT in the community, and provided some of the ideas for this book.

## PUTTING WHAT WE KNOW TO WORK

To begin narrowing the gap between efficacy and effectiveness, each of the differences between academic and community settings listed in Table 1.1 must be addressed. Many client-related differences can be addressed when a thorough assessment is done, as detailed in Chapter 2. Specific client- and family-related challenges are discussed further in Chapters 7 and 8. In this chapter, therapist and organizational differences are considered.

**Therapist Factors**

In research settings, most therapy is provided by psychology graduate students who receive intensive training and are under close supervision by experienced practitioners. Many must audiotape or videotape their sessions for subsequent review to ensure their work is consistent with the CBT model being studied. Checklists to ensure treatment adherence are part of most protocols (Compton et al., 2004). Supervisors provide guidance not only about specific CBT techniques but also about engaging clients in treatment, when to deviate from treatment manuals, dealing with impasses in treatment, and other important aspects of the therapeutic process. Therapists often have few competing demands, allowing them to focus almost exclusively on their CBT cases. Collegial support and the reputation of the research center often create optimism in both therapist and client, further increasing the chances of treatment success.

These ideal therapeutic conditions may be reproducible, to some degree, in the community. Doing so is one step towards narrowing the efficacy/effectiveness gap. For example, doing one's first few CBT cases with regular meetings or supervision with a more experienced CBT therapist or with a peer supervision group may be helpful. By using first names only, one can avoid compromising client confidentiality in these meetings. Honestly sharing one's difficulties in therapy is also important, as we all learn more when we discuss our therapeutic problems and mistakes as well as our successes. Adherence checklists are not time-consuming, and often very helpful in ensuring that one doesn't deviate from the CBT model. Audiotaping sessions for review in supervision (with client consent, of course) can also provide a valuable learning opportunity. Starting with an easy case (i.e., one that is close to ideal) is advisable. Advocating for some screening for CBT-suitability at intake is also worthwhile, though not all settings are receptive to this practice. In centers where CBT is a new treatment modality, be honest with clients and families about this fact. Then, emphasize CBT's considerable evidence base and the benefits of ongoing supervision to allay any concerns about therapist inexperience and to support therapeutic optimism. Try to limit competing demands by, for example, not scheduling meetings to conflict with supervision times and having an 'on call' roster for unforeseen emergencies so these do not repeatedly disrupt therapy. Ensure that at least one person in a leadership position considers CBT important. Having a local 'CBT champion' is one of the best ways of ensuring optimal therapeutic conditions.

**Organizational Factors**

Community mental health settings vary widely in their mandates, organizational structures, funding mechanisms, and perception by the community. All of these factors can influence the success of CBT in such settings, particularly when it is newly introduced. For example, if the mandate of the organization is to "take all comers" and offer treatment strictly in order of arrival at the clinic, it may be impossible to collect enough suitable children for a CBT group for many months or even a year. Oppositionality, family conflicts, and ADHD are common primary presenting problems in the community, and although CBT may be a useful treatment component at some point in these cases, it is rarely the initial or "first line" treatment of choice. By the time six to eight CBT-suitable children are collected (about the number needed for a group), families referred at the beginning of the waiting period would probably have lost interest. When forming CBT groups, it is desirable to be able to pull at least some children ahead on the waitlist in order to get the group started, but of course this is perceived as unfair in settings where the mandate dictates "first come first serve."

Similarly, organizational structures may be more or less conducive to CBT. The ideal structure, in my opinion, is one that includes a helpful, diagnostically oriented intake screen to improve the odds of finding CBT-suitable cases (Manassis et al., 2009) and conveys the message that therapists are valued professionals, not just service-providers. The latter does not mean that therapists necessarily need to be at the top of the pecking order, but they do need to have some input as to whom they treat, for how long, and how their treatment fits with the client's overall management plan. For example, mental health assessment does not always include assessment for CBT-suitability (see next chapter), so therapists usually need the opportunity to do this piece in the first session or two. In settings where therapists are not allowed to decline cases or offer alternative forms of therapy, this can be problematic.

Organizations that promote regular communication between case managers, physicians, therapists, and other members of the treatment team are also more likely to successfully adopt CBT. In complex cases (and most community cases are complex), CBT may need to be carefully timed in relation to other treatments, and this requires teamwork. For example, a child who is frequently suspended from school for aggressive behavior that is attributed to "underlying anxiety" is unlikely to learn coping skills through CBT until the behavior is contained. A child who is engaged in individual psychodynamic therapy and participating in a CBT group may be overburdened with therapies, and therefore not benefit optimally from either. Family work may need to precede CBT or vice versa, depending on the case. Concurrent medication may help or hinder CBT. There is a subsequent chapter on treatment combinations, but all require teamwork.

Funding for psychotherapy varies by setting, by agency, and by jurisdiction. Lack of funding can reduce the therapist's flexibility in relation to the number of sessions provided, the length of sessions, and (especially relevant to CBT) the location of sessions. Exposure to feared stimuli in anxious children, for example, often works best when the therapist accompanies the child into the anxiety-provoking setting initially, and then gradually encourages independent coping (Bouchard, Mendlowitz, Coles, & Franklin, 2004). When therapists are only paid for work done in the office, however, this may not be possible without significant financial penalties to the therapist. One way to address this dilemma is for parents to become more involved in exposure exercises with their child, but they may have more difficulty doing so than a trained therapist. Funding for work on the telephone, so essential to coordination and teamwork, is also often scarce.

Intake workers, clerical workers, and other support staff are often considered "nonessential" when funds are tight. It is precisely these people, however, who can ensure the smooth transition of the child and family from referral to assessment to treatment and on to further resources if needed. Without them, potentially successful CBT cases may be lost as families struggle to navigate the mental health system without guidance. Therefore, one should certainly advocate for the hiring and retention of such personnel in children's mental health settings.

Community perceptions can affect CBT in certain organizations as well. Some organizations, for example, are known for "family work" or "psychiatric assessments and medication," and people may be less amenable to trying CBT there, because it is not what they expect to receive. Patiently continuing to offer CBT and publicizing the results will often change these expectations over time. Mental health organizations generally may suffer from a certain stigma (Pescosolido et al., 2008), particularly if clients with psychotic or other major mental illnesses are treated there. In this case, making the child mental health area especially child-friendly and separate from the rest of the organization may help to a degree. A preferable option is sometimes to take the treatment to the child, rather than bringing the child to the treatment center. For example, school-based CBT is becoming increasingly popular, and an evidence base is building that supports its effectiveness and acceptability to a wider demographic group than office-based CBT (Shortt, Barrett, & Fox, 2001; Smallwood, Christner, & Brill, 2007).

## WHAT WE YET NEED TO LEARN

The optimal ways to address the factors in Table 1.1 all deserve further study. More specifically, we need more study of how to adapt CBT to different populations and how to best combine it with other treatments. For example, we need further evaluation of CBT protocols specific to anxious children with Autism Spectrum Disorder, selective mutism, medically related anxiety, and other anxious populations. Combination with serotonin-specific medication seems advisable (Ginsburg et al., 2011), but it is not clear whether it is best to introduce one treatment before the other or start both together.

CBT for children who are severely impaired or have multiple concurrent disorders also merits further study. Breaking CBT into modules that focus on specific skills has been proposed as one solution for these children (Chorpita, 2007), but considerable expertise may be needed to combine such modules in an effective, individualized treatment plan and most modules still require considerable verbal reasoning (sometimes problematic in these populations). Transdiagnostic protocols that aim to address depression and various anxiety disorders in a single treatment have been developed, but evaluation in children is limited largely to open trials (Ollendick, Fraire, & Spence, 2014).

Studies of the active ingredients of CBT, termed mediators of change, are also needed. Emphasizing these mediators may make CBT more potent or shorter in duration. Understanding these mediators may also help explain therapeutic benefits that occur with non-CBT psychotherapies. For example, nonspecific therapeutic factors such as positive reinforcement may reduce anxiety with many different types of intervention (Manassis et al., 2010).

Finally, community clients may not always be at a disadvantage relative to clients in academic settings. For example, providing CBT in the context of a long-term therapeutic relationship with the family, which occurs more often in the community, may improve client engagement, increase trust, and ultimately increase CBT effectiveness. Therapists' familiarity with their clients' culture and background may also be greater in community than academic settings. Some children are also remarkably resilient despite disadvantaged backgrounds (Gillham et al., 2007) and may therefore respond better than expected to CBT. Thus, while practicing CBT with children in community settings may seem like an uphill battle, there is much that we do not know about how CBT works that may yet contribute to your clients' success.

## GETTING STARTED WORKSHEET

Near the end of each chapter, you will find a worksheet outlining applications of the material to your practice. In this chapter, we focus on getting started with CBT in your practice environment and ensuring peer support and consultation in doing so.

Review Table 1.1.
Now, ask yourself:

- Which client factors are common in my practice setting?
  1.
  2.
  3.

  To address these, I will: _____

  _____

  _____

- Which therapist factors apply to my practice setting?
  1.
  2.
  3.

  To address these, I will: _____

  _____

  _____

- Which organizational factors apply to my practice setting?
  1.
  2.
  3.

  To address these, I will: _____

  _____

  _____

- Whom will I approach for consultation and/or peer support in doing CBT?
  Consider someone with previous CBT training or experience for regular consultation, and/or a small group of peers who are willing to meet regularly, preferably weekly, and are all committed to learning together using this book and one or more CBT cases each. Having a case ensures active learning and builds confidence using CBT.

  I will approach: _____

  _____

  _____

## CLINICAL CHALLENGE

Review the story of Vicky.

1. Given that Vicky is currently a poor candidate for CBT, what intervention(s) would you pursue first?
2. What would you do next?
3. What changes in Vicky or her family would convince you that Vicky was ready for CBT?

## REFERENCES

Barankin, T., & Manassis, K. (2003). Multimodal evaluations in development of a child CBT course for community professionals (Poster), Canadian Association for Continuing Health Education, Halifax, September, 2003.

Bouchard, S., Mendlowitz, S.L., Coles, M.E., & Franklin, M. (2004). Considerations in the use of exposure with children. *Cognitive Behavioral Practice*, 11, 56–65.

Chorpita, B.F. (2007). *Modular cognitive behavioral therapy for childhood anxiety disorders*. New York: Guilford Press.

Compton, S.N., March, J.S., Brent, D., Albano, A.M., Weersing, R., & Curry, J. (2004). Cognitive-behavioral psychotherapy for anxiety and depressive disorders in children and adolescents: An evidence-based medicine review. *Journal of the American Academy of Child and Adolescent Psychiatry*, 43, 930–959.

Crawley, S.A., Beidas, R.S., Benjamin, C.L., Martin, E., & Kendall, P.C. (2008). Treating socially phobic youth with CBT: Differential outcomes and treatment considerations. *Behavioral and Cognitive Psychotherapy*, 36, 379–389.

Domino, M.E., Burns, B.J., Silva, S.G., Kratochvil, C.J., Vitiello, B., Reinecke, M.A., et al. (2008). Cost-effectiveness of treatments for adolescent depression: Results from TADS. *American Journal of Psychiatry*, 165, 588–596.

Gillham, J.E., Reivich, K.J., Freres, D.R., Chaplin, T.M., Shatta, A.J., Elkon, A.G., et al. (2007). School-based prevention of depressive symptoms: A randomized controlled study of the effectiveness and specificity of the Penn Resiliency Program. *Journal of Consulting and Clinical Psychology*, 75, 9–19.

Ginsburg, G.S., Kendall, P.C., Sakolsky, D., Compton, S.N., Piacentini, J., Albano, A.M., et al. (2011). Remission after acute treatment in children and adolescents with anxiety disorders: Findings from the CAMS. *Journal of Consulting and Clinical Psychology*, 79, 806–813.

James, A.C., James, G., Cowdrey, F.A., Soler, A., & Choke, A. (2013). Cognitive behavioural therapy for anxiety disorders in children and adolescents. *Cochrane Database Systematic Reviews*, Jun 3;6:CD004690, doi: 10.1002/14651858. CD004690.pub3.

James, I.A., Blackburn, I.M., Milne, D.L., & Reichfelt, F.K. (2001). Moderators of trainee therapists' competence in cognitive therapy. *British Journal of Clinical Psychology*, 40(2), 131–141.

Jones, E., Manassis, K. Arnold, P., Ickowicz, A., Mendlowitz, S., Nowrouzi, B., et al. (2015). Translating cognitive behavioral therapy for anxious youth to rural-community settings via tele-psychiatry. *Community Mental Health Journal*, 51, 852–856.

Klein, J.B., Jacobs, R.H., & Reinecke, M.A. (2007). Cognitive-behavioral therapy for adolescent depression: A meta-analytic investigation of changes in effect-size estimates. *Journal of the American Academy of Child & Adolescent Psychiatry*, 46, 1403–1413.

Manassis, K., Ickowicz, A., Picard, E., Antle, B., Mcneill, T., Chahauver, A., et al. (2009). An innovative child CBT training model for community mental health practitioners in Ontario. *Academic Psychiatry*, 33, 394–399.

Manassis, K., Wilansky-Traynor, P., Farzan, N., Kleiman, V., Parker, K., & Sanford, M. (2010). The feelings club: Randomized controlled evaluation of school-based CBT for anxious or depressive symptoms. *Depression & Anxiety*, 27, 945–952.

Miller, L.D., Laye-Gindhu, A., Liu, Y., March, J.S., Thordarson, D.S., & Garland, E.J. (2011). Evaluation of a preventive intervention for child anxiety in two randomized attention-control school trials. *Behavioral Research and Therapy*, 49, 315–323.

Ollendick, T.H., Fraire, M.G., & Spence, S.H. (2014). Transdiagnostic treatments: Issues and commentary. In Ehrenreich-May, J. & Chu, B.C. (Eds.), *Transdiagnostic treatments for children and adolescents: Principles and practice*. New York: Guildford Press, pp. 405–419.

Pescosolido, B.A., Jensen, P.S., Martin, J.K., Perry, B.L., Olafsdottir, S., & Fettes, D. (2008). Public knowledge and assessment in child mental health problems: Findings from the National Stigma Study–Children. *Journal of the American Academy of Child and Adolescent Psychiatry*, 47, 339–349.

Shortt, A.L., Barrett, P.M., & Fox, T.L. (2001). Evaluating the FRIENDS program: A cognitive behavioral group treatment for anxious children and their parents. *Journal of Clinical Child Psychology*, 30, 525–535.

Smallwood, D.L., Christner, R.W., & Brill, L. (2007). Applying cognitive behavior therapy groups in school settings. In Christner, R.W., Stewart, J.L., & Freeman, A. (Eds.), *Handbook of cognitive-behavior group therapy with children and adolescents: Specific settings and presenting problems*. New York: Routledge.

Southam-Gerow, M.A., Weisz, J.R., Chu, B.C., McLeod, B.D., Gordis, E.B., & Connor-Smith, J.K. (2010). Does cognitive behavioral therapy for youth anxiety outperform usual care in community clinics? An initial effectiveness test. *Journal of the American Academy of Child & Adolescent Psychiatry*, 49, 1043–1052.

Weersing, V.R., & Weisz, J.R. (2002). Community clinic treatment of depressed youth: Benchmarking usual care against CBT clinical trials. *Journal of Consulting and Clinical Psychology*, 70, 299–310.

Weisz, J.R., Southam-Gerow, M.A., Gordis, E.B., Connor-Smith, J.K., Chu, B.C., Langer, D.A., et al. (2009). Cognitive behavioral therapy versus usual clinical care for youth depression: An initial test of transportability to community clinics and clinicians. *Journal of Consulting and Clinical Psychology*, 77, 383–396.

# CHAPTER TWO

# Assessing Children for CBT

Adequate assessment is probably the most crucial factor in narrowing the gap between efficacy and effectiveness. Not every child can benefit from CBT, and not every family is prepared to commit to this form of therapy. This chapter helps therapists discern when CBT is the ideal treatment, when it needs to be part of a broader treatment plan, and when it is not helpful. Special considerations for group CBT are also discussed.

## WHAT IS KNOWN

The importance of careful assessment is highlighted in most child mental health practice parameters, but the nature of the assessment recommended varies. Most authors emphasize the need to examine the child's environment in addition to determining the diagnosis, because children are so much more dependent on their environment than adults. Attention to developmental issues has also been advocated (Morris, Hirshfeld-Becker, Henin, & Storch, 2004). Temperamental precursors of some disorders are evident in preschoolers (for example, behavioral inhibition as a precursor of social anxiety). The importance of evaluating baseline somatic symptoms, severity, impairment ratings, and ratings from several sources has been highlighted in recent reviews (Connolly, Suarez, & Sylvester, 2011). Report cards, teacher observations, and schoolyard behavior are often very informative in school-aged children. Environmental and developmental factors can then be integrated into a case formulation that provides a detailed set of hypotheses about the child's difficulties (see Manassis, 2014).

Diagnostic interviews often used for anxious and depressed youth are, respectively, the Anxiety Disorders Interview Schedule for Children (ADIS-IV, Silverman & Albano, 2004) and the Schedule for Affective Disorders and Schizophrenia for School-Aged Children (K-SADS) (Chambers et al., 1985). The inclusion of a clinician's severity rating that can be monitored in relation to intervention is a particular strength of the ADIS.

Assessment for child CBT includes additional components besides a general child mental health assessment. One component has been termed "functional analysis" (Haynes & O'Brien, 1990) or "operationalizing the problem" (Friedberg & McClure, 2001). Both terms refer to a detailed examination of the main behaviors targeted in the child's treatment, including attention to situational/interpersonal, cognitive, behavioral, emotional, or physiological factors that might be contributing to the behavior. This is described in more detail in the section below, "Situational Factors Relevant to CBT Suitability."

Assessing the skills needed to benefit from CBT is another important component. Lickel, MacLean, Blakeley-Smith, and Hepburn (2012) recently defined these as emotion recognition; discrimination among thoughts, feelings and behaviors; and cognitive mediation. They found that emotion recognition skills may require additional attention in autistic children if they are to benefit from CBT. Evaluating cognitive readiness for CBT is discussed further in the section below, "Testing the Waters: Cognitive Readiness for CBT."

## PUTTING WHAT WE KNOW TO WORK

Children are often referred to CBT therapists merely because they meet diagnostic criteria for a disorder shown to be amenable to CBT in research studies, with little thought to the individual child and family's treatment suitability. On the other hand, extremely detailed child and family assessments that include all aspects of the case relevant to treatment suitability may not be feasible in a busy community practice. Therefore, I will now highlight key aspects of assessment that can differentiate children who are likely to benefit from CBT, as described in most treatment manuals, from children who are likely to require a modified approach, and from children who are unlikely to benefit from any form of CBT. Diagnostic, contextual, and situational aspects of assessment that can help identify each type of child are presented first, followed by illustrative case examples. The worksheet at the end of the chapter will help you apply the key ideas to your cases.

## Assessing the Main Problem

*Role of Diagnostic Interviews and Impairment*—In some settings, children are referred to CBT therapists with diagnostic labels attached, while in other settings the therapist is expected to diagnose or formulate the case. In either situation, it is helpful to have access to standardized instruments that can confirm or deny your suspicions about the child's main problem.

As mentioned above, several structured and semistructured interviews exist for determining diagnoses in children. In the community, however, training in such interviews may be difficult to obtain, and the time required to complete them may be excessive for the busy practitioner. Nevertheless, it is important to obtain clear and complete diagnostic information, so it is important to at least screen for each major child psychiatric disorder as described in diagnostic manuals (American Psychiatric Association, 2013).

A rough four-question screen for anxiety disorder or obsessive compulsive disorder (OCD), for example, might include the following: What does the child avoid due to fear or anxiety? Does the child worry on a daily or almost daily basis? Does the child have sudden attacks of anxiety or panic? Does the child perform repetitive rituals? Any affirmative answer is then followed by an invitation to further describe the problem, and reference to relevant diagnostic criteria. For depression, the following screening questions might be used: Has the child appeared consistently sad or irritable (often a depressive equivalent in children) for more than two weeks? Has the child recently withdrawn from previously enjoyed activities? Have the child's sleep or activity levels changed recently? Has the child recently made negative or hopeless comments about himself or herself or life in general?

Using paper and pencil screens (see below) can also be useful. Children do not always recognize or acknowledge their negative feelings, however, so a negative screen on these instruments does not rule out the possibility of a significant clinical problem (Barbosa, Manassis, & Tannock, 2002). Most children with elevated scores do have significant problems though, so the screens can still be worthwhile. Whenever parent versions of these instruments are available, these should also be administered, because parent and child reports do not always correspond when assessing anxiety disorders and depression (see below).

In the case of anxiety, preadolescent children often meet criteria for multiple anxiety disorders, but this is likely a reflection of the undifferentiated nature of childhood anxiety rather than indicating severity. Impairment of functioning is a key indicator of severity, and also of the need for treatment regardless of disorder(s) present (Connolly, Bernstein, & AACAP Work Group on Quality Issues, 2007). The Clinician's Global Assessment

Scale (CGAS) (Shaffer et al., 1983) and the ADIS Clinician's Impairment Rating (Silverman & Albano, 2004) are two standardized tools for assessing impairment. Treatment for depression is also guided by severity of impairment, with severely impaired children often needing medication as well as psychotherapy. One cautionary note: Young children's mood problems are often highly dependent on the environment (Belden & Luby, 2006; Birmaher, Brent, & AACAP Work Group on Quality Issues, 2007), and environmental factors may need to be addressed first.

For example, I once saw a seven-year-old boy, Ralph, who had previously been raised solely by his mother, who met diagnostic criteria for depression after moving with her into a new home with her new partner. The new partner had two young twins who commanded most of the couple's attention. Losing his familiar home, familiar school, and the regular attention of his mother was overwhelming for Ralph. He improved dramatically when his mother and her partner were able to show empathy for his plight and adjust their schedules to better support him.

Most children who benefit from CBT have mild to moderate impairment. Very mild impairment may be amenable to parenting advice as described in books for anxious and depressed children (Manassis, 2008; Manassis & Levac, 2004) or to reduction of stressful circumstances in the child's life. These children are often not motivated to participate in therapy, because it would interfere with enjoyable after-school activities, and their level of distress is minimal. Severe impairment, by contrast, may require medication or other interventions before considering CBT. Children who are selectively mute, for example, may have difficulty engaging with the therapist unless they are receiving some medication for anxiety (Manassis & Tannock, 2008). Children who have not attended school for extended periods may need medication in order for behavioral measures have a better chance of working (Bernstein et al., 2000).

Remembering to screen for additional diagnoses once the main one is established is essential. Concurrent behavioral problems such as *conduct disorder* or *oppositional defiant disorder* can undermine CBT. Prioritizing which diagnosis needs attention first is important in children with more than one. Anxious parents often attribute behavioral problems to anxiety, perhaps because it is more socially acceptable to have a child that is fearful than one that is defiant. If so, gently explain the need to contain behavior before anxiety can be successfully addressed. Similarly, parents of depressed children or teens may need gentle persuasion to consider medication as a way of facilitating therapeutic progress, given that these children are sometimes too withdrawn or unmotivated to work successfully in therapy otherwise and may benefit more from the combination of CBT and medication than either alone (TADS Team, 2004). Traumatic events or medical conditions should be suspected and probed for in children with sudden onset of symptoms. Children described as "easygoing" and "happy" are unlikely to suddenly become anxious or depressed without a substantial physiological change or traumatic event (Manassis, 2004).

*Role of Standardized Questionnaires*—Several well-validated measures of anxiety and depression exist for children that are at least age eight and of average academic ability. The Multidimensional Anxiety Scale for Children (MASC) (March, 1998; March & Sullivan, 1999), the Screen for Child Anxiety-Related Emotional Disorders (SCARED) (Birmaher et al., 1997; Monga et al., 2000), and the Spence Anxiety Inventory (Spence, Barrett, & Turner, 2003) all use three- or four-point scales to rate symptoms. An older, true–false measure, the Revised Children's Manifest Anxiety Scale (RCMAS) (see Seligman, Ollendick, Langley, & Baldacci, 2004), is also widely used. There are some scales specific to social anxiety (for example, LaGreca & Stone, 1993) and obsessive compulsive disorder (for example, the children's Yale Brown Obsessive Compulsive Scale [Y-BOCS]) (Storch et al., 2006). The Children's Depression Inventory (CDI) (Kovacs, 1985) is the most widely used and studied in childhood depression. Detailed psychometric properties can be found in journal articles describing the measures that allow a comparison of relevant strengths and weaknesses of each. Copies of most can be obtained from catalogues of psychological measures or local suppliers of these measures. A few are available by writing to the authors. I would suggest investigating several measures, finding one child anxiety measure and one child depression measure that you have confidence in, and then using those consistently.

None of these measures, however, can be considered diagnostic. Interviews of children and parents are needed to establish diagnosis. What, then, are some questions these measures can answer?

First, a standardized measure can tell us whether or not the child acknowledges his or her anxiety, because many children anxious by parent-report do not acknowledge anxiety themselves. This is important information, since children who appear anxious but deny it may need particular help recognizing anxious feelings. This topic is typically included in CBT programs for child anxiety, but may need additional emphasis in children with this profile.

Second, a standardized measure often serves as a useful baseline of symptom severity in children who do acknowledge anxiety or depression. Monitoring changes in the measure every month or two can be a useful indicator of therapeutic benefits, or lack of these. Because therapeutic change is often imperceptibly slow, families and children may become discouraged without evidence of progress. Standardized measures are sensitive to even minor changes and can thus offer evidence that change is occurring and, consequently, that it is worth persevering with treatment. Conversely, lack of change in the measure over several months may suggest a change in therapeutic strategy is needed.

Finally, children's attempts to complete these measures can provide additional, relevant information at assessment. For example, inability to complete a measure can sometimes provide evidence of an undiagnosed reading or fine motor problem. Children who repeatedly ask for clarification of questions may have comprehension problems or, alternatively, lack confidence in their academic abilities due to anxiety. Paralyzing inability to choose among several responses may be a clue to obsessive or perfectionistic thinking.

Information about children's emotional symptoms often differs from one informant to the next (Barbosa et al., 2002). This fact highlights the need to obtain such information from multiple sources and across multiple environments. For example, a child who looks very anxious at school may appear quite relaxed or even oppositional at home. Other children show symptoms only in the home environment, or only in social situations. In general, emotional symptoms can be assumed to be present when reported by any informant. One possible exception is a highly anxious informant who claims that the child has every symptom you ask about, even if one symptom is the opposite of another (for example, insomnia versus excessive sleep). This occasionally occurs in families where several members are clinically anxious. In this case, a more objective informant (for example, another relative or a teacher) could be asked to report which symptoms have actually been observed to affect the child's functioning on a frequent basis, to ensure a more accurate diagnostic picture. The very young child (below school age) may also have difficulty accurately reporting about his or her emotions. As a rule, children can report more detail about internal symptoms (for example, obsessions or worries), while parents and teachers can report more detail on specific behaviors (for example, avoidance of certain situations or tantrums when asked to face certain feared stimuli) (Edelbrock, Costello, Duncan, Conover, & Kala, 1986).

### Assessing the Child in Context

*Contextual and Developmental Factors Relevant to CBT Suitability*—Besides establishing a diagnosis, assessment should include a review of factors potentially contributing to the problem and those potentially ameliorating it. Addressing contributing factors or placing more emphasis on ameliorating factors can sometimes reduce anxiety or depression to a level where CBT is no longer needed. For example, being bullied at school is likely to exacerbate a child's anxiety and can be readily addressed within the school.

A particular aptitude (for example, musical ability) may strengthen self-confidence and thus ameliorate anxiety, or serve as a vehicle for overcoming certain fears in CBT (for example, performance anxiety). For Ralph, the seven-year-old boy described above, parental empathy and support were powerful ameliorating factors for depression. For other children, regulating their sleep and exercise routines can dramatically improve their ability to manage their moods and anxieties. Even if addressing these factors results in only a modest reduction of symptoms, it is still helpful to the child and provides useful background information for the therapist. Most children are easier to engage in treatment when we take an interest in their world, not just their symptoms.

Common contributing factors to probe for in anxious or depressed children include:

- Medical problems (thyroid problems, anemia) can affect mood or anxiety level, so work with a family doctor to investigate these
- Consuming caffeine products (colas, energy drinks) increases anxiety
- Poor exercise and sleep routines (excessive television or computer, lack of regular aerobic activity, irregular sleep or very late sleep onset) can all contribute to anxiety and depression, as well as being symptomatic of these disorders
- Starting or changing dose of a medication (several can affect mood or anxiety, so discuss with prescribing doctor)
- Anxious, depressed, or ill family member
- Family history of anxiety, depression, or alcohol abuse
- Family conflict or instability
- Developmental disabilities or delays (speech, motor, fine or gross motor coordination, social communication)
- Learning difficulties
- Difficult temperament (behavioral inhibition, sensory sensitivities, rigidity, emotional intensity, irregularity of sleep/eating routines)
- Cognitive changes with development (recognition of death as permanent around age 8; increased hypothetical/abstract reasoning around age 11; increased self-consciousness in adolescence)
- Recent stressful events or significant changes (serious illness in self or family, move of house, new school, academic problems, loss of friend, conflict with peers, peer pressure, family separation, loss or death of family member)
- Onset of puberty, especially in girls
- Previous negative experiences with mental health providers

Common ameliorating factors to probe for in anxious or depressed children include:

- Ability to confide in one or both parents
- Family cohesion
- Supportive friend, relative, or mentor
- Being well liked by teachers
- Being well liked by peers
- Being athletic
- Being intelligent
- Being attractive
- Being successful at school
- After-school activity or hobby that is a source of enjoyment or pride
- Feeling close to a pet
- Being verbal and aware of feelings
- Previous positive experiences with mental health providers

*Situational Factors Relevant to CBT Suitability*—Situations where anxiety, depressive symptoms, or family conflict most typically "flare up" are usually worth exploring in detail with children and families. It is helpful to get a description of what happens step by step, as though you were watching a videotape of the interactions between the child and those around him or her. In textbooks, this is typically referred to as "functional analysis" (Haynes & O'Brien, 1990) or "operationalizing the problem" (Friedberg & McClure, 2001). Ask the child and family, "What do you notice first?" (for example, thought, feeling, physiological reaction, behavior, other person's behavior), "What do you do?" or "What do you say?" Then ask, "What does he or she do?" or "What does he or she say?" until you have a clear picture of the sequence of events.

This picture will tell you the antecedents of depressive or anxiety-related behaviors, improving the chances of reducing them in therapy. For example, children whose anxiety is triggered by sudden or unexpected transitions may improve significantly when they are warned of such events ahead of time and given a chance to prepare. By contrast, adolescents who experience panic attacks as they attend to minor physical symptoms may do better with a gentle reminder: "It's the anxiety acting up again. You'll be OK. Just breathe." Alternatively, a depressed teen who notices a dip in mood when ignored by others at school may need to tell himself, "They're focused on their own problems. Don't take it personally."

Family interactions around depressive or anxiety-related behaviors also become obvious when one obtains detailed descriptions of situations. For example, a child who is not attending school may get "stuck" at any number of points in the morning routine. The child may refuse to get out of bed, get dressed, eat, gather school books, go out the door, get into the bus or car, get out of the bus or car, enter the school building, or enter the classroom. Families often either fight or give up on encouraging school attendance at one of these points. Their willingness to seriously consider alternative behaviors is often a good clue to the likelihood of success with CBT.

Quantifying symptoms in these situations (how often, how intense on a 10-point scale, how many situations, how much interference in daily activities, how much effort does the child make to cope, what makes it worse, what helps, and so on.) can serve as a useful baseline to measure improvement, particularly in children who cannot do standardized questionnaires or do not acknowledge symptoms on them. Baselines are further discussed in Chapter 4.

The situations will also tell you who needs to be involved in the child's therapy; if symptoms flare at school, teachers and other school personnel may need to work collaboratively with the therapist to ensure progress. If symptoms only occur at home, parental involvement will be important, and the school need not know about the child's diagnosis unless he or she chooses to tell them. Involve only who needs to be involved, and respect the child's desire for privacy in other situations.

If no such situations are volunteered, they can usually be elicited by going through a typical day or typical week in the child's life. Conflict at home often flares up in the morning before school, after school, when asked to do homework, or at bedtime. School-related symptoms may be heightened during certain classes, during recess or lunch breaks (especially in socially anxious children), or around tests or performance situations. Weekend anxiety or depressive withdrawal may be observed in relation to social events, scheduled activities, family outings, or making telephone calls.

**The Ideal Candidates for CBT**

The characteristics listed in Table 2.1 describe children and families ideally suited to CBT. They are deliberately presented as a wish list, recognizing that these types of cases are uncommon in many community settings. However, the more of these characteristics the child and parents show, the more likely they are to benefit from CBT. Most of these characteristics can be determined through interviews. The ability to stay on task and to be able to work on symptoms using a cognitive-behavioral model may require, in addition, some brief testing.

TABLE 2.1
Characteristics of Ideal Candidates for Child CBT

| | |
|---|---|
| Child Characteristics | • Suffering from an internalizing disorder, where this is the most urgent and impairing mental health problem |
| | • Showing few or no externalizing symptoms |
| | • Stabilized on psychotropic medication, if it is needed |
| | • Of at least average intelligence |
| | • 8 years or older |
| | • Able to stay on task for a 45-minute session |
| | • Aware of their anxious or depressive feelings |
| | • Willing and able to work on their anxious or depressive symptoms |
| Parent/Family Characteristics | • A stable home |
| | • Stable custody arrangements if divorced |
| | • Limited interpersonal conflict |
| | • Limited parental psychopathology |
| | • Good parental organizational skills (to ensure regular attendance at appointments) |
| | • Parental commitment to his or her child's treatment |
| | • No current major life crises in family (for example, recent separation, life-threatening illness) |
| | • Parent has an appreciation of his or her important role in the child's therapeutic progress |

**When CBT Is Part of the Solution**

Many children with less-than-ideal presentations can benefit from CBT if it is part of a thoughtful treatment plan and the goals of therapy are realistic. For example, children with serious medical illnesses can often use CBT techniques, but may need considerable information about their illness and how they can participate in managing it before feeling better. Parents in these circumstances may need additional help addressing their own anxieties about the child, or grief about loss of the ideal child, and allowing the child an age-appropriate level of independence.

Children with continuing severe symptoms despite medication can sometimes use CBT to improve functioning. In this case, the goals of therapy should be to get the child able to do certain key age-appropriate activities (for example, basic self-care, increased school attendance) regardless of his or her symptoms. Emphasizing symptom reduction as a goal may not be realistic and may prove discouraging in this case.

I have often been surprised at the creativity of my colleagues in community settings, when hearing of situations where CBT succeeded "against the odds." For example, Mike was an anxious boy of eight from a highly conflicted family whose parents refused to participate in therapy. Nevertheless, he was treated with CBT. There was only periodic telephone contact with the parents. Reassured by the fact that something therapeutic was being done for their son, the parents gradually became more relaxed, more trusting of the therapist, and eventually amenable to family therapy. After CBT and family therapy concluded, Mike's anxiety was minimal.

Combining different treatment modalities must be done carefully, however, as shown in the next example. CBT can be a helpful component of a therapeutic plan for anxious children with complex presentations, provided it is not seen as the solution to *all* of the child and family's problems.

For example, Jill was an eleventh-grade student who suffered from depression and ongoing school avoidance for the past year and a half. She was amenable to CBT and always did the cognitive exercises assigned between sessions. When it came to working on school return, however, it was a different story. "My mother needed me to pick up some groceries" was her excuse for not trying to get near the school building one day. Another day, her mother called to say that Jill was not feeling well. Another day, the dog needed to be taken to the veterinarian, and her mother said, "She finds the dog so comforting. Being around him really lifts her spirits. It was important for her to be there, don't you agree?" Eventually, it became clear that Jill's mother suffered from significant anxiety and depression and relied on Jill for emotional support. Unfortunately, she did not perceive this and became quite angry when referred for treatment; as she stated, "It's your job to help Jill, not to psychoanalyze me!" Jill learned many mood and anxiety management strategies, but was not able to apply them outside the home and eventually obtained her high school diploma by correspondence.

Other times, CBT can be part of the solution but its timing in relation to other treatments is a matter of debate. For example, when a child has symptoms that seem to relate to a recent loss or bereavement, some would argue that this loss must be discussed in supportive therapy first, before addressing the anxiety symptoms with CBT. If the anxiety is debilitating, however (for example, if the child is too anxious to sleep), it may be helpful to address this disability by providing CBT-based coping strategies sooner rather than later. There is no easy answer to this debate. A sensitive therapist with experience in both CBT and supportive interventions may be needed to help the child mourn his or her loss, while maintaining as much age-appropriate functioning as possible. Combining CBT with medical interventions and with other psychotherapies will be discussed further in the next chapter.

### Testing the Waters: Cognitive Readiness for CBT

In community settings, not all children come to the clinic after getting a full intellectual and academic assessment. This leaves the clinician uncertain as to what cognitive interventions the child can understand or find helpful. If other, contextual factors have been assessed, and the child is clearly a candidate for CBT in some form, it may be useful to test out the child's ability to work with verbal and nonverbal materials before proceeding. A rough rule of thumb for what is needed in order to do verbally based CBT is that the child can do third-grade academic work. School expectations may vary, however, so it is helpful to obtain a more precise idea by testing certain abilities.

For verbally based approaches, the child should at least be able to grasp the connection between thoughts and feelings, and the idea that different types of thoughts can be associated with different types of feelings. For example, the therapist could ask, "Which would be most comforting if your mother was late picking you up: thinking about car accidents, thinking about the hockey game, or thinking about your mom being stuck at the office or in traffic and getting to you soon?" The child who grasps the thought–feeling connection will usually pick the final response and should be able to articulate why it is comforting to think this way. Some children do favor distraction (thinking about the hockey game), but when asked "Wouldn't you still wonder what had happened to your mom?" can acknowledge that the worry persists. If they deny any worries, but have behavioral symptoms of separation anxiety, they may not be ideal candidates for verbally based CBT. Similarly, if they cannot see that thinking about car accidents would make them feel worse, or cannot explain why the final response is most comforting, they may struggle with verbally based CBT.

I often also have children do a short memory test: the digit span backward. This crude test of verbal working memory asks the child to repeat back a series of digits you say out loud, but in the reverse order you presented them (Needelman, Schnoes, & Ellis, 2006). If children cannot do at least five or six digits backward, they may struggle with cognitive restructuring (a key strategy in verbally based CBT approaches). For example, Philip Kendall's F.E.A.R. plan in *Coping Cat* (a common child CBT program for anxiety disorders) (Kendall, 2006) includes six items: feeling frightened, expecting bad things to happen, attitudes that help, actions that help, results, and rewards. Thus, the child must be able to retain and manipulate six items to use this approach with ease.

Nonverbal cognitive interventions, by contrast, require little working memory and less psychological sophistication. They do require the child to have some capacity for externalization, however. To test this, a therapist might ask: "What have you tried to do to fight (or handle, or cope with) your anxiety?" In the ensuing discussion, most children can see that they have already fought/handled/coped with anxiety in certain situations. If they cannot see that they have ever done anything to overcome anxiety because they cannot see anxiety as a problem to be tackled (rather than an intrinsic aspect of themselves), they may struggle with externalization.

As many nonverbal strategies rely on imagery, it is also helpful for the child to be able to work with mental images. Most children can do this quite readily and may, in fact, do it more easily than adults. The therapist might ask the child, "Imagine yourself in your favorite place in the world. Describe it to me. What do you see there, hear there, etc.?" The child who can provide at least a few specific descriptors is usually able to use imagery. A useful follow-up question is "How do you feel, now that you're in that place?" Most children who can use imagery therapeutically will describe happy, nice, or calm feelings in their "favorite place."

For example, Carmen was a young adolescent with a learning disability who struggled with generalized anxiety disorder. She had found a relaxation tape that included some imagery helpful in reducing her worries. After using it for a couple of weeks, she reported, "I'm not using the whole tape any more. I always come back to the same part: picturing my worries like actors crossing a stage and then exiting my mind." For her, focusing on a concrete image was more useful than focusing on breathing or muscle relaxation, although these were also included on the tape.

Tony had mild developmental delay and severe separation anxiety. When asked what he had tried to do to handle his anxiety, he drew a blank. When the therapist pointed out that he already used his teddy bear to cope with separation from his mother occasionally, he agreed that this helped but was "not enough." He was not willing to consider any other actions his therapist suggested to reduce his anxiety in such situations because, "It wouldn't help get my mom there faster." He could see no other solution to his problem than obtaining faster access to his mother and became quite angry when these were suggested. Eventually, the therapist worked on a behavioral approach with Tony's parents to gradually desensitize him to situations involving separation because he was unwilling to learn anxiety management strategies for coping with them.

## When Individual Treatment Is Preferable to Group Treatment

In community settings, large volumes of referrals often necessitate CBT group treatment. Ideally however, this should not be the only treatment format offered, because some combinations of children cannot work well together in groups, and some children have needs that are better addressed in individual treatment. It is also sometimes difficult to form certain groups in a timely manner. For example, if one is planning a group for obsessive compulsive disorder within a three-year age range and there are few referrals with this diagnosis for several months, it may not be possible to offer group treatment quickly, and individual work may need to be considered for children waiting for this group. Families in settings where group treatment is offered should always be cautioned about this possibility to avoid disappointment or seeking treatment elsewhere.

Limiting the number of disruptive children in a group to no more than one or two is essential to maintain an organized, focused group therapy. Even so, a second group therapist is usually needed to manage periodic behavior problems if such children are included. Ages of group members should be within a three- or at most four-year range, to ensure a similar level of cognitive maturity. Exceptions can be made if a child is older but cognitively immature for age, as long as the child does not stand out from the rest of the group in another important way. For example, a group of 8- to 11-year-old children can include a 12-year-old who is cognitively "young," as long as the child has not yet developed the physique or interests of a teenager. CBT can work in single-gender or mixed-gender groups, but groups with only one member of a particular gender can be awkward. In these circumstances, the "lone boy" or "lone girl" often drops out of treatment because of discomfort in the group or a lack of common interests with other group members.

Individual treatment may be preferable to group treatment to address some children's needs. Children who are extremely shy may feel overwhelmed in a group situation with other, less shy children (Manassis et al., 2002). They often contribute little to the group, are easily neglected, and may be unable to learn strategies in the group because this is a highly anxious situation for them. As with disruptive children, a skillful cotherapist may be able to focus on engaging such a child and helping him or her learn, if group is the only treatment format available. Similarly, highly distractible children may benefit more from individual than group therapy. Their need for frequent redirection to the task at hand can be difficult to meet in a group environment. Children with learning or language difficulties can also be problematic in groups, depending on how far behind their academic or linguistic skills are relative to other group members. Minor problems can often be addressed with extra help by a cotherapist (for example, scribing for the child, helping with reading, offering repeated explanations of concepts), but more significant delays may result in stigmatization for "slowing down" the pace of the rest of the group.

In deciding whether or not to include a child in a group, the above considerations must be balanced against the unique benefits children can obtain from groups (Scapillato & Manassis, 2002). Universality, the sense of not being the only one affected by a certain problem, is a group benefit that is not obtained with individual treatment. Peer support and encouragement, mutual support among parents when these are in a group, and the fact that "many heads are often better than one" in generating solutions to problems are also group-specific benefits.

**When CBT Is Not Helpful**

Helping children acquire skills to better manage anxious feelings may seem like a universally helpful intervention, so it is difficult to imagine situations where CBT would be harmful. A few I have encountered include:

- A boy with conduct disorder, whose anxiety prevented him from engaging in serious criminal activity. Anxiety was protective in this case.
- Vicky's case in the preface: a two-year history of school avoidance initially related to anxiety, but with many behavioral and family problems since then. Regardless of initial diagnosis, Vicky's oppositional behavior and the family's inability to limit it is now the main issue, and CBT is very unlikely to result in school return unless this is addressed.
- A girl who was referred for treatment of anxiety about her father's untreated alcoholism, which sometimes resulted in abusive behavior toward her and her mother. To treat her would have tacitly condoned the father's problem and allowed a dangerous situation to continue.
- A girl whose mother wanted her treated with CBT for school avoidance "until she feels ready to go back," but was unwilling to work on a plan for school return. In this case, CBT would have provided an excuse for professionals not to address the enmeshed mother–daughter relationship that was preventing school return.
- A teenage boy who was depressed and suicidal to the point of trying to jump in front of a subway train (a friend stopped him). This boy's parents felt he "just needs the right therapist" and did not see the need for urgent hospitalization. Respecting their wishes by offering CBT outside hospital would have endangered the boy's life.

More often, we encounter situations where the likelihood of success is so slim that the time and energy required for CBT is not considered worthwhile. Working with a child who has severe mental handicaps, a family that has just separated, or parents who are too disorganized to bring the child to appointments regularly are common examples of such situations.

One may still be able to provide some helpful techniques based on CBT in these circumstances. For example, the mentally handicapped child may be able to learn diaphragmatic breathing or another relaxation technique. Similarly, the disorganized parents may be referred to a particular chapter of a CBT-based self-help book to address their child's main fear. However, these techniques do not constitute a course of therapy, and should not be described as such in clinical notes.

## WHAT WE YET NEED TO LEARN

Several aspects of assessment for child CBT merit further study. When ascertaining the diagnosis, it may be difficult to select the optimal diagnostic interview in community settings, as youth there often have both anxiety and depression as well as additional diagnoses. Given the high service demands in community settings, brief screens for CBT suitability are also sorely needed.

Combining discrepant information from parents and children is a further challenge, regardless of treatment setting. Parent-child agreement is low for internalizing problems like anxiety and depression, probably because they are less easily observed than behavioral problems (Barbosa et al., 2002; Manassis, Mendlowitz, & Menna, 1997). They are lower still for children with several diagnoses (Barbosa et al., 2002), commonly seen in community practice. Most researchers suggest "counting" a symptom or diagnosis if it is reported by either the child or the parent (Morris et al., 2004) because some children minimize their symptoms and some parents are not aware of how their child is feeling. This can be misleading, however, because parents' own anxiety may make the child appear worse than he or she is, and reports from very young children may be affected by their lack of a good vocabulary for feelings. Therefore, combining information clinically requires some judgment regarding the reliability of the informant. One should also consider whether or not reported symptoms are impacting the child's functioning as, by definition, diagnosis requires the presence of significant impairment in the child's daily activities (American Psychiatric Association, 2013). Nevertheless, the best way to address informant differences has yet to be determined.

# ASSESSMENT WORKSHEET

Assessment of a child for CBT must include thorough diagnostic evaluation of the child and family and should allow one to answer certain questions. Ask yourself:

- Are you certain that the main, most impairing problem is an anxiety disorder or depressive disorder (circle)?
  Yes      No

- Have contextual factors not amenable to CBT been addressed?

  Factors: _____
  
  _____
  
  _____

  How addressed: _____
  
  _____
  
  _____

- Have key situations to be targeted by CBT been identified?

  Situation 1: _____
  
  _____
  
  _____

  Situation 2: _____
  
  _____
  
  _____

  Situation 3: _____
  
  _____
  
  _____

- Are there any standardized measures that could help you quantify the child's symptoms and monitor progress? If not, is there another aspect of the child's symptoms or functioning you could quantify and monitor with treatment?

  Will monitor: _____
  
  _____
  
  _____

- Review Table 2.1. Is this child suitable for CBT as described in most manuals (that is, an "ideal candidate" or close to it)?
  "Ideal" characteristics: _____
  
  _____
  
  _____

- Is this family suitable for supporting their child's progress in CBT as described in most manuals?

  "Ideal" characteristics: _____

  _____

  _____

- Will this child require additional interventions besides CBT, and when should these occur in relation to CBT (further described in next chapter)?

  Additional interventions needed: _____

  _____

  _____

  1.
  2.
  3.

- Will this child require a modified CBT approach, and why (further described in subsequent chapters)?

  Modification(s): _____

  _____

  _____

- Will this child require nonverbal as well as verbal strategies (circle)?

  Yes, because: _____

  _____

  _____

  No _____

  _____

  _____

- Will this child benefit more from group or individual CBT (circle)?

  Group, because: _____

  _____

  _____

  Individual, because: _____

  _____

  _____

- Does this child or family have any contraindications to CBT?

  Yes, because: _____
  _____
  _____

  No _____
  _____
  _____

## CLINICAL CHALLENGE

Answer the questions above in relation to Tom, the nine-year-old boy described at the beginning of the book.

## REFERENCES

American Psychiatric Association. (2013). *Diagnostic and statistical manual of mental disorders, Fifth edition (DSM-5)*. Washington, DC: American Psychiatric Association.

Barbosa, J., Manassis, K., & Tannock, R. (2002). Measuring anxiety: Parent–child reporting differences in clinical samples. *Depression and Anxiety*, 15, 61–65.

Belden, A.C., & Luby, J.L. (2006). Preschoolers' depression severity and behaviors during dyadic interactions: The mediating role of parental support. *Journal of the American Academy of Child and Adolescent Psychiatry*, 45, 213–222.

Bernstein, G.A., Borchardt, C.M., Perwien, A.R., Crosby, R.D., Kushner, M.G., Thuras, P.D., et al. (2000). Imipramine plus cognitive behavioral therapy in the treatment of school refusal. *Journal of the American Academy of Child and Adolescent Psychiatry*, 39, 276–283.

Birmaher, B., Brent, D.A., & AACAP Work Group on Quality Issues. (2007). Practice parameter for the assessment and treatment of children and adolescents with depressive disorders. *Journal of the American Academy of Child and Adolescent Psychiatry*, 46, 1503–1526.

Birmaher, B., Khetarpal, S., Brent, D., Cully, M., Balach, L., Kaufman, J., et al. (1997). The Screen for Child Anxiety Related Emotional Disorders (SCARED): Scale construction and psychometric characteristics. *Journal of the American Academy of Child and Adolescent Psychiatry*, 36, 545–553.

Chambers, W.J., Puig-Antich, J., Hirsch, M., Paez, P., Ambrosini, P.J., Tabrizi, M.A., et al. (1985). The assessment of affective disorders in children and adolescents by semi-structured interview. *Archives of General Psychiatry*, 42, 696–702.

Connolly, S.D., Bernstein, G.A., & AACAP Work Group on Quality Issues. (2007). Practice parameter for the assessment and treatment of children and adolescents with anxiety disorders. *Journal of the American Academy of Child & Adolescent Psychiatry*, 46, 267–283.

Connolly, S.D., Suarez, L., & Sylvester, C. (2011). Assessment and treatment of anxiety disorders in children and adolescents. *Current Psychiatry Reports*, 13, 99–110.

Edelbrock, C., Costello, A.J., Duncan, M.K., Conover, N.C., & Kala, R. (1986). Parent-child agreement on child psychiatric symptoms assessed via structured interview. *Journal of Child Psychology and Psychiatry*, 32, 666–673.

Friedberg, R.D., & McClure, J.M. (2001). *Clinical practice of cognitive therapy with children and adolescents: The nuts and bolts*. New York: Guilford Press.

Haynes, S.N., & O'Brien, W.H. (1990). Functional analysis in behavior therapy. *Clinical Psychology Review*, 10, 649–668.

Kendall, P.C. (2006). *Coping Cat workbook* (2nd ed.). http://www.workbook publishing.com.

Kovacs, M. (1985). The Children's Depression Inventory (CDI). *Psychopharmacology Bulletin*, 21, 995–998.

LaGreca, A.M., & Stone, W.L. (1993). Social Anxiety Scale for children—Revised: Factor structure and concurrent validity. *Journal of Clinical Child Psychology*, 22, 17–27.

Lickel, A., MacLean, W.E., Blakeley-Smith, A., & Hepburn, S. (2012). Assessment of the prerequisite skills for cognitive behavioral therapy in children with and without autism spectrum disorders. *Journal of Autism and Developmental Disorders*, 42, 992–1000.

Manassis, K. (2004). An approach to intervention with childhood anxiety disorders. *Canadian Family Physician, 50*, 379–384.

Manassis, K. (2008). *Keys to parenting your anxious child* (2nd ed.). Hauppauge, NY: Barron's Educational Series, Inc.

Manassis, K. (2014). *Case formulation with children and adolescents*. New York, NY: Guilford Press.

Manassis, K., & Levac, A.M. (2004). *Helping your teenager beat depression*. New York: Woodbine House.

Manassis, K., Mendlowitz, S., & Menna, R. (1997). Child and parent reports of childhood anxiety: differences in coping styles. *Depression & Anxiety, 6*, 62–69.

Manassis, K., Mendlowitz, S., Scapillato, D., Avery, D., Fiksenbaum, L., Freire, M., et al. (2002). Group and individual cognitive behavior therapy for childhood anxiety disorders: A randomized trial. *Journal of the American Academy of Child and Adolescent Psychiatry, 41*, 1423–1430.

Manassis, K., & Tannock, R. (2008). Comparing interventions for selective mutism: A pilot study. *Canadian Journal of Psychiatry, 53*, 700–703.

March, J. (1998). *Manual for the Multidemensional Anxiety Scale for children*. Toronto, ON: Multihealth Systems.

March, J.S., & Sullivan, K. (1999). Test-retest reliability of the Multidimensional Anxiety Scale for children. *Journal of Anxiety Disorders, 13*, 349–358.

Monga, S., Birmaher, B., Chiappetta, L., Brent, D., Kaufman, J., Bridge, J., et al. (2000). Screen for Child Anxiety-Related Emotional Disorders (SCARED): Convergent and divergent validity. *Depression and Anxiety, 12*, 85–91.

Morris, T.L., Hirshfeld-Becker, D.R., Henin, A., & Storch, E.A. (2004). Developmentally sensitive assessment of social anxiety. *Cognitive and Behavioral Practice, 11*, 13–28.

Needelman, H., Schnoes, C.J., & Ellis, C.R. (2006). The new WISC-IV. *Journal of Developmental and Behavioral Pediatrics, 27*, 127–128.

Scapillato, D., & Manassis, K. (2002). Cognitive-behavioral/interpersonal group treatment for anxious adolescents. *Journal of the American Academy of Child and Adolescent Psychiatry, 41*, 739–741.

Seligman, L.D., Ollendick, T.H., Langley, A.K., & Baldacci, H.B. (2004). The utility of measures of child and adolescent anxiety: A meta-analytic review of the Revised Children's Manifest Anxiety Scale, the State-Trait Anxiety Inventory for Children and the Child Behavior Checklist. *Journal of Clinical Child and Adolescent Psychology, 33*, 557–565.

Shaffer, D., Gould, M.S., Brasic, J., Ambrosini, P., Fisher, P., Bird, H., et al. (1983). A Children's Global Assessment Scale (CGAS). *Archives of General Psychiatry, 40*, 1228–1231.

Silverman, W.K., & Albano, A.M. (2004). *The Anxiety Disorders Interview Schedule for Children IV (ADIS-IV)*. San Antonio, TX: Graywind Publications.

Spence, S.H., Barrett, P.M., & Turner, C.M. (2003). Psychometric properties of the Spence Children's Anxiety Scale with young adolescents. *Journal of Anxiety Disorders, 17*, 605–625.

Storch, E.A., Murphy, T.K., Adkins, J.W., Lewin, A.B., Geffkin, G.R., Johns, N.B., et al. (2006). The children's Yale-Brown obsessive compulsive scale: Psychometric properties of child- and parent-report formats. *Journal of Anxiety Disorders, 20*, 1055–1070.

TADS Team. (2004). Fluoxetine, cognitive-behavioral therapy, and their combination for adolescents with depression: Treatment for Adolescents with Depression Study (TADS) randomized controlled trial. *Journal of the American Medical Association, 292*, 807–820.

# CHAPTER THREE

# Priorities and Timing
of Therapy

The previous chapter answered the question "Can this child and family benefit from CBT?" This one addresses two further questions: "Can this child and family benefit from CBT *now?*" and "What else is needed?" Answers to these questions are particularly important in community settings, where complex presentations are the rule rather than the exception. The focus of the chapter is formulating treatment plans that include multiple interventions, so evidence for combining CBT with other interventions is reviewed first.

## WHAT IS KNOWN

Several studies have examined combining child CBT with psychotropic medications (see below) or therapeutic work with families. Several protocols include parental or family participation, and there is evidence of benefit particularly when focused on contingency management in anxiety disorders (Manassis et al., 2014). The evidence is less consistent for family involvement in CBT for depressed youth (reviewed in Manassis, 2005). The role of the family in child CBT is discussed further in Chapter 8.

Large randomized controlled trials have examined CBT in combination with medication for obsessive compulsive disorder (OCD) (POTS Study: POTS Team, 2004), depression (TADS Study: TADS Team, 2004; ADAPT Study: Goodyer et al., 2008; TORDIA Study: Brent et al., 2008), and non-OCD anxiety disorders (CAMS Study: Walkup et al., 2008). The POTS and CAMS studies found that combining CBT with sertraline, a serotonin-specific medication, resulted in greater improvement than providing either intervention alone. All three active treatments (sertraline, CBT, sertraline + CBT) were superior to placebo, and medication was generally well tolerated by participants. By contrast, the TADS study found that combining CBT with fluoxetine, a serotonin-specific medication, or providing fluoxetine alone was superior to CBT alone or placebo, and ADAPT found that adding CBT to fluoxetine treatment did not improve outcomes for depressed youth. However, TORDIA found that adding CBT to a medication switch for treatment refractory adolescents was helpful, and there is preliminary evidence that adding CBT may also reduce depressive relapse (Kennard et al., 2008). Another commonly cited large trial, the MTA study (March et al., 2000), examined use of a stimulant medication with or without intensive behavioral intervention in children with attention deficit hyperactivity disorder (ADHD), some of whom also had anxiety disorders. Stimulants resulted in significant improvements in children with ADHD with or without anxiety disorders. In children with ADHD and anxiety disorders, however, the behavioral intervention conferred additional benefit.

Small trials have examined other specific diagnostic groups. A randomized controlled trial examining trauma-focused CBT with or without concurrent use of sertraline in children with posttraumatic stress disorder (Cohen, Mannarino, Perel, & Staron, 2007) found minimal benefit from adding sertraline to the trauma-focused CBT. In a small, non-randomized follow-up of children with selective mutism who had all received some behaviorally focused school consultation, my research group found that those who were treated with a serotonin-specific medication showed greater improvements in speech six months after initial assessment than those who were not (Manassis & Tannock, 2008).

The overall message from these findings appears to be that combining CBT and medical treatment can be helpful, but the benefits vary from one disorder to another, so it is worth reading literature specific to the main diagnosis of the child you are seeing. Selecting and prioritizing treatments for anxious children with or without concurrent disorders is further described in two clinical papers I wrote several years ago (Manassis, 2004; Manassis & Monga, 2001). Emslie, Mayes, Laptook, and Batt (2003) have provided a concise summary of treatment considerations in depressed youth.

## PUTTING WHAT WE KNOW TO WORK

### The Case of Carrie

Carrie was a seven-year-old girl from a single-parent family who had been avoiding school for a month. She lived with her mother, who was unemployed and had been involved in a serious car accident four months earlier.

Carrie was also in the car and had been separated from her mother as they traveled to hospital. She still had nightmares about the event. Carrie was also overweight and had been teased by several of her peers recently. She had sustained a head injury in the accident that had affected her ability to concentrate at school. She did not have friends and spent her days at home with her mother, her gerbil, and her pet cat. She met diagnostic criteria for a mood disorder. An aunt, who was on antidepressants, had urged Carrie's mother to get similar medication for her daughter. The school social worker had advocated "urgent CBT" to facilitate school return, and a group for girls with low self-esteem. The family doctor had recommended psychiatric assessment for Carrie's mother, but she had missed her appointment with the psychiatrist because she had slept in that day.

You are referred this child to provide "urgent CBT." She looks sad and is reluctant to talk to you, providing one-word answers to all specific questions and a shoulder shrug in response to open-ended ones. Carrie's mother attends the appointment with her. She is tearful and says she is confused as to how to help her child.

Needless to say, this is not a case where one grabs the nearest CBT manual for childhood depression and gets started. There are several problems in this child and family that need to be addressed, and it is not entirely clear where to begin. Listing the problems is often a useful starting point. In this case, problems would include:

- School avoidance
- Possible depression in the child
- Possible posttraumatic stress disorder (PTSD) in the child
- Low self-esteem and weight concerns in the child
- Peer teasing and social isolation in the child
- Possible depression in the mother
- Possible posttraumatic stress disorder in the mother
- Parent–child interaction that may be fostering school avoidance
- Financial stresses in the family
- Probable ambivalence about therapy in both parent and child

Because not all of these problems are amenable to CBT, one needs to think about which problem should be addressed first, or if several problems can be addressed concurrently. One may also need to address the school social worker's misconception that CBT is an urgent or emergency treatment that will allow rapid school return, perhaps in days. CBT is a skill-building therapy, and skills are rarely built and applied consistently by children in a very short period of time.

To begin prioritizing these problems, one might ask:

1. Which problem is causing the most impairment? Impairment is the degree of interference the problem causes with age-appropriate daily activities the child is expected to do at home, at school, or socially.
2. Which problem can be addressed most easily or most quickly? Sometimes therapy can be paired with brief interventions that address some of the contributing factors to the child's symptoms, as mentioned in Chapter 2.
3. Which problems can be addressed at the same time? If several problems can be addressed concurrently with no ill effect, it is certainly worth doing.
4. Where are people motivated to start working? If there are several problems amenable to CBT, it is usually best to start with the one the child and family are most eager to address.

Carrie's school avoidance is clearly causing the most impairment, because it prevents her from engaging in an age-appropriate, expected daily activity. Given her age, there is also a relatively simple solution: She can be escorted to school on a regular basis by an adult other than her mother, who may not be able to do so because of her own problems. Of course, simple solutions are not always easy to implement. Carrie's mother might object to the plan, fearful of harming her child. Alternatively, she might agree but not ensure that Carrie is dressed and ready to go by the time the adult arrives at her home. Carrie might attempt to run away from the adult on the way to school, or run away from school after she is dropped off there. However, because Carrie is a child with no past history of behavior problems, a fairly short duration of school absence, and a mother who expresses at least some willingness to help her daughter, it is certainly worth trying.

Carrie and her mother may be more amenable to this intervention if supportive counseling is offered to both concurrently. Such counseling may also help to clarify diagnostic issues around depression versus post-traumatic stress (and thus which one should receive greater emphasis in therapy) in both Carrie and her mother, and to elucidate factors in the parent–child interaction that may be hindering school return. It should not be considered CBT, however, because the focus is on supporting the dyad around the difficult task of returning Carrie to school, rather than any specific set of skills. Skill-building can be done later, once the "hot" issue of school avoidance is better managed and the diagnoses are clear. Some people would, of course, consider escorting the child to school a form of behavior management and therefore part of CBT. In the absence of the cognitive component, however, it is really an exclusively behavioral intervention. This is not bad; exclusively behavioral interventions are sometimes highly effective in the initial stages of work with school avoiders (King, Tonge, Heyne, & Ollendick, 2000).

Few interventions would be considered "easy" in this case. Nevertheless, it would be worth checking if Carrie's mother is obtaining as much financial support as she is entitled to, to reduce this source of family stress, and to talk to the school about ways to reduce bullying and teasing among all their students. Carrie may also benefit from a thorough psychoeducational assessment, because the effects of her head injury on academic performance may be a significant contributing factor to her depressed mood, and her poor concentration may affect her ability to participate in CBT.

I have already mentioned using a behavioral intervention concurrently with supportive counseling for both parties in this case. Should one also offer a self-esteem group or antidepressant medication to Carrie, as some people suggested to Carrie's mother? My answer is "probably not." The self-esteem group is premature, given the degree of Carrie's social withdrawal and low mood. It may also be overly stressful for her to begin this new activity when she is still finding school attendance challenging. Children may also find participation in more than one therapy at the same time stressful (in this case, individual supportive counseling and self-esteem group). The group may be helpful to Carrie once her mood and overall level of functioning is consistently better. The medication is not indicated in the absence of a clear diagnosis. Also, depression in young children can be highly dependent on environmental stresses, and Carrie's mood may improve dramatically once her circumstances improve. In addition, both depression and posttraumatic stress are often closely linked to parental depression and parental posttraumatic stress in this age group (Schreier, Ladakakos, Morabito, Chapman, & Knudson, 2005). Thus, addressing her mother's problems may reduce or eliminate Carrie's need for medication or therapy. If it is established that Carrie really is depressed even when her difficult circumstances and her mother's problems have been addressed, this issue could be revisited in the future.

Once Carrie is back in school, contributing factors have been addressed, and she appears ready for CBT, what should be the focus? The answer is: It depends. Ideally, one should start with the most impairing problem, but that may not be where the child wants to start. For example, it may be clear that Carrie is struggling most with the posttraumatic effects of her accident (suggesting this be the focus for therapy), but she may want to begin by talking about how to handle teasing from the other children. Usually, it is best to start with problems the child feels comfortable discussing, and move toward the more difficult issues later, even if this means seeing him or her for a bit longer than anticipated. Children who do not feel understood may terminate prematurely, but with patience several problems can often be addressed sequentially. Therefore, Carrie's therapist should ask the fourth question listed above: Where are people motivated to start working?

**The Case of Roger**

Unlike Carrie, many children seen in the community suffer from both internalizing and externalizing problems. That is, they may have anxiety or depression that is readily amenable to CBT, but also behavioral or attention problems that require other interventions. Roger is an example of a boy with this profile.

Roger was a 10-year-old boy who had been seen by a service specializing in ADHD. They concluded he had generalized anxiety disorder (a tendency to worry excessively accompanied by physical symptoms of anxiety) in addition to ADHD. He was then referred back to a community mental health center to obtain stimulant medication for his ADHD and CBT for his anxiety. They recommended a group, as the mental health center was known for providing CBT groups. Unfortunately, the doctor prescribing the stimulants did not realize he had to make an additional referral to obtain the CBT, so Roger did not see a therapist for several months.

His mother was furious. She demanded "immediate CBT group" for her son. She also complained that the stimulants were ineffective, that the mental health system had failed her son, that Roger had already been suspended twice from school since being assessed, and that she was planning legal action against the mental health center unless her son received "immediate CBT group." There was no such group available for at least three months, and it was not clear that Roger was a good candidate for it, given his ongoing inattention despite large doses of stimulant medication.

As the therapist responsible for providing the CBT group, what do you do? First, you meet with Roger and his mother. While you are talking with his mother, Roger rearranges the toys in your office, accesses several questionable websites on your computer, and repeatedly bounces a rubber ball against a wall, leaving numerous marks. He answers questions briefly and then tells you about incidents in his life that are unrelated to the question. His mother wants to know how soon you will help her son "become normal" by providing CBT.

One of the first things to do here, clearly, is to clarify reasonable expectations of CBT. These are outlined in the next chapter. Next, it is important to consult with the prescribing physician to determine if there is any way of better controlling Roger's ADHD symptoms. In some cases, for example, an extra dose of stimulant medication prior to therapy sessions is helpful to improve the child's ability to focus on CBT.

Assuming that Roger's ADHD symptoms will persist to some degree, further conversation with his mother is indicated about the merits of group versus individual therapy. Children who are highly distractible almost always need individual treatment, and their treatment-related gains are often modest. Work on parental behavior management and consultation with schools is almost always needed. Parents like Roger's mother may need to be told that CBT cannot be effective without such additional interventions, and that addressing anxiety through CBT will not necessarily address all of the child's other problems (for example, Roger's behavioral problems that led to school suspensions). On the other hand, there is good evidence from the MTA study that adding behavioral measures to medication in the child with ADHD and anxiety is worthwhile (March et al., 2000), so she has every right to ask for additional, nonmedical intervention for her son. A calm, thoughtful approach is needed to explain to parents like Roger's mother that their children are not being denied care, but offered a type of care that is more likely to succeed than what was originally promised.

Again, it may be useful to go back to the four questions listed above:

1. Which problem is causing the most impairment?
2. Which problem can be addressed most easily or quickly?
3. Which problems can be addressed at the same time?
4. Where are people motivated to start working?

In this case, school suspensions are clearly causing the most impairment, and behavioral measures are therefore the initial intervention of choice. Medication adjustments can be done relatively quickly with stimulants, so should definitely be prioritized. Concurrent measures should include parent counseling and school consultation, in addition to the stimulants and behavioral measures, to allow the adults around Roger to work more effectively together for his benefit. Only after these initial measures have been taken to stabilize the situation, and the upset emotions related to it, can CBT have a chance to succeed. Although the child and family may be motivated to pursue CBT first, it is not really feasible until later in the treatment plan. As mentioned, it should probably be individual rather than group CBT, with a focus on anxiety.

## Additional Considerations

So far, prioritization in complex cases has been summarized as listing the therapeutic problems, and answering the questions:

1. Which problem is causing the most impairment?
2. Which problem can be addressed most easily or quickly?
3. Which problems can be addressed at the same time?
4. Where are people motivated to start working?

There are some additional considerations, however. First, parenting and teaching children with complex problems requires more patience, calmness, and perseverance than parenting and teaching children with only one major mental health concern. Progress often goes "two steps forward, one step back" in these cases, and it is easy for everyone to get discouraged. Empathy is crucial for teachers and parents if they are to avoid giving up on the child and discontinuing therapy. Second, expectations of progress in these children must be more modest than those for children with only one mental health problem. CBT can only address one problem at a time, and resolving one issue does not always improve the others. For example, teens with both anxiety and externalizing problems may become less anxious as a result of CBT, but then show additional behavior problems because they are less fearful of the consequences. Coordination with schools and other professionals is also more essential in these cases than in those with a single problem. The mistake Roger's physician made above is not unusual, and similar lack of coordination often results in children and teens "falling between the cracks" and missing opportunities for potentially helpful interventions. Finally, treatment combinations must be planned carefully to ensure a sequence of treatments that makes sense and to avoid one treatment interfering with another.

One "combination" that is sometimes overlooked is the need to teach children basic life skills while CBT or other therapies are going on. Anxious children who have been avoiding peer situations for a long time, for example, may lack basic athletic skills or knowledge of common games. Conversation starters and assertiveness skills may also need to be rehearsed with such children. Similarly, depressed teens may have fallen behind in developing independent life skills such as using public transit, school avoiders may require academic remediation, and so on.

Having examined two specific cases, let us look at some general rules for combining CBT with other interventions. These are summarized in Table 3.1.

## CBT and Other Psychotherapies

All forms of psychotherapy have certain attendant risks as well as benefits. Children treated with CBT, for example, may become more symptomatic before they become better because of the initial emphasis on recognizing one's feelings in most child CBT programs. Other therapies, too, can temporarily heighten symptoms for various reasons. Psychotherapy is also perceived as stigmatizing by some children. After all, it is more acceptable in most peer groups to be going to soccer practice weekly than to a psychiatrist weekly. Psychotherapy can also be time consuming, potentially interfering with school attendance or important social activities. Each of

TABLE 3.1
Combining CBT with Other Interventions

| CBT and Other Psychotherapy | Consider risks of more therapy time, stigma, child resistance |
| --- | --- |
| | Combinations that avoid multiple weekly appointments for child are easier to manage |
| | Make sure therapies do not work at cross-purposes |
| | Consider sequencing of therapies, or "therapy breaks" |
| | When sequencing, periodically reevaluate symptoms, because one therapy is sometimes enough |
| | Communicate regularly with other therapist |
| CBT and Psychotropic Medication | Use for severely impaired children |
| | May make children more amenable to CBT |
| | Consider short trial of CBT if parents want medication "as a last resort" |
| | Dosage reduction may help CBT motivation if symptoms have been eliminated by medication |
| | Consider stabilizing medication before CBT to avoid erroneous attributions |
| | Communicate regularly with prescribing physician around dosage adjustments and tapering |

these risks is increased when more than one therapy is provided at the same time. When total therapy time increases, children can also become more resistant to participating in therapy as they feel it encroaching on other aspects of their lives. Multiple therapies usually also imply multiple therapists. There is an attendant risk of miscommunication or lack of communication between the therapists, with potentially adverse consequences for the child. Each of these potential problems must be borne in mind and addressed when therapies are combined.

Nevertheless, it is sometimes necessary to combine therapies in complex cases such as those described above, and some therapeutic combinations are easier to manage than others. In general, combinations that involve different family members are easier than those that require the same family member to attend multiple weekly appointments. Thus, it is often desirable to have an anxious or depressed parent participating in their own psychotherapy while the child participates in CBT. The child only attends one weekly appointment, and the parent usually understands the reasons why both therapies are needed. For young children, the parent will usually bring the child and participate in at least part of the appointment. Similarly, marital counseling for the parents may be recommended, if needed, and can usually be done concurrently with child CBT.

Combining family therapy with child CBT may be desirable if family conflict makes it difficult to apply CBT strategies in the home. In this case, the child does have to attend more than one weekly appointment, but having at least one parent doing the same makes it seem "fair," and most children can understand the reasons for both of these therapies.

Multiple child-focused therapies tend to be the most challenging to combine. The child may feel overburdened, unduly stigmatized, increasingly resistant, or all three. Group and individual therapy combinations are sometimes acceptable to children, especially if the group is seen as being fun or as a social opportunity in addition to being a therapy. Nevertheless, the readiness of the child to participate in both must be considered carefully, as shown in the example of Carrie above.

Having two concurrent individual child therapies is usually not advisable. This situation is most likely to occur in a child engaged in ongoing long-term play therapy or psychodynamic psychotherapy who is referred for a course of CBT. My usual approach in this case is to negotiate with the long-term therapist a temporary "break" from their work for the three- or four-month duration of CBT, or at least a decrease in the frequency of sessions. This reduces undue stigma and burden to the child, while still preserving the potential benefits of both therapies. One additional concern with concurrent psychodynamic and cognitive behavioral therapy is that they sometimes work at cross-purposes. For example, a coping skill learned in CBT may be considered a "defense mechanism" by a psychodynamic therapist, and some CBT therapists consider the unstructured approach of psychodynamic sessions unduly anxiety provoking for highly anxious children.

To avoid the attendant risks of concurrent therapies, it is often worth considering "sequencing" of therapies. For example, in Carrie's case we considered doing individual work first and deferring group therapy until Carrie's functioning improved. In Roger's case, we considered working on behavioral interventions with his mother and teachers before providing anxiety-focused CBT.

Communication with other professionals involved in the child's care is essential, regardless of whether the therapies are sequential or concurrent. In concurrent work, it ensures a coordinated effort that benefits the child. In sequential work, it ensures that there is a smooth transition from one therapy to the next, and that the work of one therapy builds on that of the other and repetition is avoided.

Periodically reevaluating the child's symptomatic changes from baseline is often helpful, because some children benefit so much from their initial therapy that a second therapy is no longer needed once they conclude the first. For example, coping better with school as a result of CBT may improve self-esteem to the point where an intervention targeting self-esteem is no longer needed. In other cases, therapy addressing a traumatic event or bereavement may reduce depressive symptoms to the point where depression-focused CBT is no longer needed.

## CBT and Psychotropic Medications

Like psychotherapy, psychotropic medications have attendant risks as well as benefits, so the decision to use them is not taken lightly by families and physicians. In cases where a child is severely impaired, however, the use of medication can alleviate suffering and allow the resumption of usual activities more quickly than psychotherapy alone. In the absence of medication, these children may fall further behind their peers in important developmental tasks, often with adverse effects on self-esteem. Recall that depressed teens also show limited benefits from CBT without medication treatment (TADS Team, 2004). Therefore, the potential benefits of medication often outweigh the risks in severely impaired children and in depressed teens.

Another potential benefit of psychotropic medications is that they sometimes improve the child's ability to participate in CBT. In Roger's case, for example, adjusting his ADHD medications might improve his ability to focus in therapy sessions and therefore improve his ability to learn CBT strategies. In severely anxious or severely depressed children, medications that reduce anxiety or depression may also increase the benefits of CBT. Children learn best when their anxiety level is mild and learn poorly when they feel highly anxious and overwhelmed. By reducing anxiety to a milder level, medication can sometimes improve a child's ability to learn CBT strategies. Reducing depressive symptoms with medication may be helpful in very withdrawn children, who would otherwise have difficulty engaging in therapy.

It is sometimes challenging to convince parents of severely impaired children to combine CBT and psychotropic medication. Families will often want CBT first and medication "only as a last resort." Explaining the potential benefits of combining the two, and the evidence for these benefits, is reassuring to some families. In other cases, however, one may want to contract for a small number of sessions (perhaps three or four) to test the child's ability to participate in CBT and learn CBT strategies without medication. Then, if the child is struggling with CBT, the issue of medication may be revisited to improve the chances of success with CBT. Needless to say, this approach requires regular communication between the therapist and the prescribing physician.

There are some potential disadvantages to combining CBT and psychotropic medication. One possibility is that the medication works "too well" in reducing symptoms, leaving the child minimally symptomatic and thus minimally motivated to learn CBT strategies. This difficulty can often be addressed with a slight reduction in dosage, in consultation with the prescribing physician. Families are often agreeable to this measure, as the coping strategies learned in CBT can be used in perpetuity, whereas most would like to see their child eventually discontinue or reduce the use of medication.

Another potential disadvantage relates to attributions regarding improvement. If a medication is started at the same time as CBT or partway through a course of CBT, children and families often attribute subsequent improvements to medication and discount the effects of CBT. This reduces motivation to use CBT strategies and leaves the child vulnerable to relapse once medication is reduced or discontinued. One way to address this problem is to stabilize medication dosage before starting CBT. This allows the child, family, and therapist to disentangle the benefits of each intervention. In longer-acting medications (for example, antidepressants) it may be worth making the last dosage adjustment a full month before starting CBT, because the benefits of these medications often take several weeks to manifest.

As mentioned, communication between therapist and prescribing physician is essential. Not only does this allow the child to optimally benefit from both interventions, but it also avoids premature discontinuation of one or the other. For example, the physician may assume that, once the child has completed a course of CBT, medication is no longer needed and can be tapered. Some children, however, need time to consolidate the gains made in CBT and apply them consistently in their day-to-day lives. Being on medication during this time allows them to build confidence without much risk of setbacks, until they are ready to face the challenge of a gradual dosage reduction. Conversely, a CBT therapist may assume that the child does not need further sessions because symptoms are minimal. With a reduction in medication, however, the symptoms may reemerge, and the child may need additional CBT sessions to cope with them. Both CBT and medication need to be tapered in a coordinated fashion that does not leave the child vulnerable to overwhelming symptoms. This can only occur when therapist and physician work together.

## When a Full Course of CBT Is Not Possible

There are situations where a child may benefit from some intervention based on CBT principles, even when a full course of CBT is not possible. For example, a child with cognitive limitations that preclude learning certain cognitive strategies may still benefit from behavioral or environmental interventions. Increasing structure and routine, increasing positive health habits (nutrition, exercise, sleep), increasing consistency of parenting practices, reducing the expression of negative emotion toward or in front of the child, and reducing situations that repeatedly trigger symptoms (for example, sudden environmental changes that are introduced with no warning) are almost universally helpful environmental interventions for anxious or depressed children (reviewed in Manassis, 2008; Manassis & Levac, 2004).

Positive reinforcement for coping with stressful situations even occasionally can also decrease symptoms in some children. Similarly, allowing natural consequences to occur for certain symptomatic behaviors may decrease them. Examples might include allowing a child anxious about schoolwork to deal with teacher criticism if homework is avoided, or allowing a child with tactile sensitivity to wear the same clothes for several days even if peers start to comment on this. Natural consequences and intermittent positive reinforcement can be particularly helpful when families are stressed or disorganized and thus have difficulty maintaining more structured, consistent reinforcement systems.

Some children can learn simple cognitive strategies, even if they cannot do a full course of CBT as described in most manuals because of difficulties with cognition, attention, ability to attend sessions consistently, or the need to prioritize other problems besides those amenable to CBT. They may be able to use a single strategy that is simple, can be learned in one session, and can be used across multiple situations. Learning to breathe from the diaphragm when stressed is an example of one such strategy. For managing anger, learning to "count to 10" or to use a simple reminder like "stop and walk" may be helpful. Other children can learn to label a feeling state and then do something consistent in response. For example, "It's one of those nervous times again" or "I'm feeling sad again" are phrases that can be used by children to remind themselves to talk to an adult or engage in a distracting activity.

Learning one of these strategies makes minimal demands on the child and family, but can dramatically enhance the child's sense of confidence and of being able to master upsetting situations. Because children have more limited control over their lives than adults and often lack the sophistication to reassure themselves with perspective taking or probabilistic thinking, a sense of mastery is crucial to symptom reduction. Basic life skills, mentioned above, can also make a substantial difference in children's sense of self-confidence and mastery.

## WHAT WE YET NEED TO LEARN

There has been minimal study of combining CBT with other psychotherapies or psychosocial interventions, and little comparison of CBT with other psychotherapies (Compton et al., 2004). The optimal sequencing of CBT and medication (whether one should begin or even complete one intervention before the other) also awaits further study. Finally, there are several diagnostic groups (e.g., children with selective mutism or Autism Spectrum) for whom CBT protocols are either still in development or require further evaluation in relation to medication or other interventions.

# TIMING WORKSHEET

- In the child I am currently considering for CBT:

    1. Which problem is causing the most impairment?

    _____
    _____
    _____

    2. Which problem can be addressed most easily or quickly?

    _____
    _____

    3. Which problems can be addressed at the same time (see Table 3.1)?

    _____
    _____

    4. Where are people motivated to start working?

    _____
    _____

- Based on these responses, the order of interventions should be:
    1.
    2.
    3.
    4.

    Reasons: _____
    _____
    _____

- Interventions that I would consider combining with CBT include:
    1.
    2.

    Reasons: _____
    _____
    _____

- Contact any other professionals who would need to be in agreement with this plan, and determine how you will work together.

    Professional 1 (Plan): _____
    Professional 2 (Plan): _____

## CLINICAL CHALLENGE

Answer the four questions listed earlier in this chapter with respect to the following case.

Jerry is a 13-year-old boy with a history of tics and rituals. His mother reports that he currently washes his hands until they are raw because of an intense fear of germs and stays up late at night praying repeatedly, fearful that if he does not get the prayer exactly right something awful will happen to him. His hands indeed appear raw. Jerry is currently receiving an anti-psychotic medication to control his tics and a serotonin-specific medication to control his rituals. He has recently had a growth spurt, and his mother thinks he has "outgrown his dose" for the serotonin-specific medication, so the rituals have resurfaced. He has never had CBT or any other psychological intervention.

Jerry's parents have recently separated. They are involved in a custody dispute, and Jerry's father claims his son has no psychiatric problems apart from "Munchausen-by-proxy." He reports that his wife has a history of obsessive compulsive disorder, and believes that she has convinced his son that he has the symptoms as well. He thinks his son needs to stop his medications and get counseling "to deal with his mother's influence."

Jerry reports that he does some hand-washing and praying but does not think it is excessive. His bigger concern is that he is being teased at school regarding some effeminate behaviors. He protests, "I'm not gay. How can I make them stop saying it?"

He is willing to take whatever medications his parents agree on.

## REFERENCES

Brent, D., Emslie, G., Clarke, G., Wagner, K.D., Asarnow, J.R., Keller, M., et al. (2008). Switching to another SSRI or to venlafaxine with or without cognitive behavioral therapy for adolescents with SSRI-resistant depression. *Journal of the American Medical Association*, 299, 901–913.

Cohen, J.A., Mannarino, A.P., Perel, J.M., & Staron, V. (2007). A pilot randomized controlled trial of combined trauma-focused CBT and sertraline for childhood PTSD symptoms. *Journal of the American Academy of Child and Adolescent Psychiatry*, 46, 811–819.

Compton, S.N., March, J.S., Brent, D., Albano, A.M., Weersing, R., & Curry, J. (2004). Cognitive-behavioral psychotherapy for anxiety and depressive disorders in children and adolescents: An evidence-based medicine review. *Journal of the American Academy of Child and Adolescent Psychiatry*, 43, 930–959.

Emslie, G.J., Mayes, T.L., Laptook, R.S., & Batt, M. (2003). Predictors of response to treatment in children and adolescents with mood disorders. *Psychiatric Clinics of North America*, 26, 435–456.

Goodyer, I.M., Dubicka, B., Wilkinson, P., Kelvin, R., Roberts, C., Byford, S., et al. (2008). A randomized controlled trial of cognitive behavior therapy in adolescents with major depression treated by selective serotonin reuptake inhibitors. *Health Technology and Assessment,* 12, iii–iv, ix–60.

Kennard, B.D., Emslie, G.J., Mayes, T.L., Nightingale-Teresi, J., Nakonezny, P.A., Hughes, J.L., et al. (2008). Cognitive-behavioral therapy to prevent relapse in pediatric responders to pharmacotherapy for major depressive disorder. *Journal of the American Academy of Child & Adolescent Psychiatry,* 47, 1395–1404.

King, N., Tonge, B.J., Heyne, D., & Ollendick, T.H. (2000). Research on cognitive-behavioral treatment of school refusal: A review and recommendations. *Clinical Psychology Review,* 20, 495–507.

Manassis, K. (2004). An approach to intervention with childhood anxiety disorders. *Canadian Family Physician,* 50, 379–384.

Manassis, K. (2005). Empirical data regarding the role of the family in treatment. In R. Rapee & J. Hudson (Eds.), *Psychopathology and the family.* New York: Elsevier Press, pp. 283–300.

Manassis, K. (2008). *Keys to parenting your anxious child* (2nd ed.). Hauppauge, NY: Barron's Educational Series, Inc.

Manassis, K., Lee, T.C., Bennett, K., Zhao, X.Y., Mendlowitz, S., Duda, S., et al. (2014). Types of parental involvement in CBT with anxious youth: A preliminary meta-analysis. *Journal of Consulting & Clinical Psychology,* 82, 1163–1172.

Manassis, K., & Levac, A.M. (2004). *Helping your teenager beat depression.* New York: Woodbine House.

Manassis, K., & Monga, S. (2001). A therapeutic approach to children and adolescents with anxiety disorders and associated comorbid conditions. *Journal of the American Academy of Child and Adolescent Psychiatry,* 40, 115–17.

Manassis, K., & Tannock, R. (2008). Comparing interventions for selective mutism: A pilot study. *Canadian Journal of Psychiatry,* 53, 700–703.

March, J.S., Swanson, J.M., Arnold, L.E., Hoza, B., Conners, C.K., Hinshaw, S.P., et al. (2000). Anxiety as a predictor and outcome variable in the multimodal treatment study of children with ADHD (MTA). *Journal of Abnormal Child Psychology,* 28, 527–541.

POTS Team. (2004). Cognitive behavior therapy, sertraline, and their combination for children and adolescents with obsessive-compulsive disorder: The Pediatric OCD Treatment Study (POTS) randomized controlled trial. *Journal of the American Medical Association,* 292, 1969–1976.

Schreier, H., Ladakakos, C., Morabito, D., Chapman, L., & Knudson, M.M. (2005). Posttraumatic stress symptoms in children after mild to moderate pediatric trauma: A longitudinal examination of symptom prevalence, correlates, and parent-child symptom reporting. *Journal of Trauma,* 58, 353–363.

TADS Team. (2004). Fluoxetine, cognitive-behavioral therapy, and their combination for adolescents with depression: Treatment for Adolescents with Depression Study (TADS) randomized controlled trial. *Journal of the American Medical Association,* 292, 807–820.

Walkup, J.T., Albano, A.M., Piacentini, J., Birmaher, B., Compton, S.N., Sherrill, J., et al. (2008). Cognitive-behavioral therapy, sertraline and their combination for children and adolescents with anxiety disorders: Acute phase efficacy and safety. *New England Journal of Medicine,* 359, 2753–2766.

# CHAPTER FOUR

# Treatment Expectations

Having found what appears to be a good candidate for CBT, it is tempting to begin quickly in the hope of seeing quick results. Unfortunately, this may prevent adequate discussion with families about what they can expect from treatment, sometimes resulting in disappointment later. Sharing treatment expectations with children and families at the outset can reduce the chances of premature termination or treatment failure and enhance the therapeutic alliance.

## WHAT IS KNOWN

Studies have examined the role of the therapeutic alliance, and treatment expectations can affect the quality of that alliance. A good therapeutic alliance is more likely to develop when expectations are realistic and can be met for the most part.

The facts that children rarely refer themselves for treatment, may not recognize or acknowledge their problems, and often have different goals for therapy than their parents do have been cited as challenges to the therapeutic alliance when working with children (Kazdin & Weisz, 1998). The latter point raises an interesting question: Is the therapeutic alliance an alliance with the child, with the parents, or both? In younger children, the answer is almost invariably both, since the parents are usually responsible for bringing the child to sessions. Adolescents have greater autonomy than young children, so additional emphasis may need to be placed on the alliance with the young people themselves in this age group.

In cognitive behavioral therapy with anxious children, no significant relationship between the quality of the therapeutic alliance and outcome has been found (Kendall, 1994; Liber et al., 2010), although child involvement in therapy has been found to relate to outcome (Chu & Kendall, 2004). The fact that all therapists in these studies rated quite highly, however, may account for this result. Therapist behaviors involving collaboration were positively correlated with the quality of the alliance (Creed & Kendall, 2005). A more complete discussion of the therapeutic alliance in CBT with anxious children is provided by Chu and colleagues (2004).

With OCD, on the other hand, stronger therapeutic alliance was predictive of better CBT outcome (Keeley, Geffken, Ricketts, McNamara, & Storch, 2011). Similarly, Ormhaug, Jensen, Wentzel-Larsen, and Shirk (2014) found the therapeutic alliance predicted outcomes in trauma-focused CBT but not in treatment as usual with traumatized youth. They suggest that the requirement for clients to complete specific therapy tasks may make the therapeutic alliance particularly important in CBT.

In CBT with depressed youth, one study suggested that the quality of the therapeutic alliance was not predictive of symptom reduction, but changes in automatic thoughts were predictive of symptom reduction (Kaufman, Rohde, Seeley, Clarke, & Stice, 2005). Outcome studies in this population are marked by high attrition rates, however (reviewed in Wilansky-Traynor et al., 2010), suggesting that a strong therapeutic alliance may be important for treatment completion. Parental involvement predicted treatment participation in a recent CBT study (Wilansky-Traynor et al., 2010), suggesting that a good therapeutic alliance with parents may be important in youth depression despite the adolescent age of most clients.

Overall, the above results suggest that clients are more likely to complete therapy if a good therapeutic alliance is present, and in some disorders the alliance predicts symptomatic change. Another possible interpretation of these results is that a "good enough" therapeutic alliance is necessary for CBT to be completed successfully, but having a superb therapeutic alliance may produce no better results than having an alliance that is merely good. If so, we should strive to establish and maintain an alliance that keeps our clients motivated and engaged in therapy, without worrying unduly about not having a "perfect fit" with every client.

## PUTTING WHAT WE KNOW TO WORK

Expectations of CBT that should be discussed at the outset include: goals of therapy, the time frame, roles of each participant (child, parents, and therapist), the nature of therapeutic progress, and how therapy will conclude.

Common misconceptions about CBT that may need to be addressed are also described in this chapter.

## Goals and Changes from Baseline

Agreeing on one or more specific, symptom-based treatment goals is important in CBT. Too often, children and families engage in CBT with a vague goal of having the child "get better." Problems arise when the child, parents, and therapist have different ideas as to what constitutes improvement. For example, an anxious child may think she is doing better when she can get through a mathematics test without panicking, while her parents do not consider her better until she can sleep in her own room alone. Alternatively, a therapist may think a depressed teen has improved significantly when he can attend school consistently, has regular social contact with his friends, and starts making plans for the future, but the teen's mother may feel he is no better because he still tells her "life sucks" on a daily basis. In the case of a perfectionistic child, a parent may report substantial gains, but the child may be dissatisfied, feeling she must be completely asymptomatic before therapy is successful.

Young children often begin therapy with no clear goal in mind, and this lack of clarity can increase their anxiety. It is reassuring for them to have the goals spelled out by the therapist, especially if their parents are present and agree with the goals. Adolescents may want to participate in defining the goals, rather than being told what to do in therapy by the adults in their lives. Extra time may be needed to help the teen link symptom reduction with benefits in other areas of life. For example, overcoming anxiety about using the telephone may reduce boredom on the weekend; leaving one's room to eat with the family (often difficult for depressed teens) may reduce parents' worries and annoying questions.

Parents sometimes superficially agree with the symptom-based goals spelled out by the therapist but have "hidden agendas" that are worth exploring. For example, many parents of anxious or depressed children secretly hope the therapy will make their child better behaved, more agreeable, or more willing to "open up" about their feelings at home. None of these will necessarily occur with CBT that targets anxious or depressive symptoms. Other parents have difficulty focusing exclusively on symptoms, and hope (unrealistically) that a short course of CBT will help their child fully realize his or her potential as a human being. To get away from these overly lofty goals, it may help to talk about the child in relation to average children of the same age. A goal of reducing symptoms to the point where the child is closer to the developmental average may not sound grand enough to these parents at first, but it is definitely more realistic and attainable.

Spelling out clearly the symptoms that will be targeted in therapy can not only avoid differences in expectations, but also help to monitor progress. Recall from Chapter 2 that it is often useful to record a baseline of symptoms that occur in specific situations, or that are endorsed on standardized questionnaires. The questionnaires elicit ratings of severity and frequency of common symptoms, and a sum total of those ratings. Specific ratings or the total (in the case of a child with many symptoms) can be monitored over time to measure change. For children who cannot validly complete questionnaires (for example, young children, children lacking insight into their difficulties), the baseline should be recorded in relation to specific situations where symptoms flare. One could record for each symptom how often it occurs, how intense it is on a 10-point scale, in how many situations it occurs, how much it interferes in daily activities, how much effort the child makes to cope, what makes it worse, or what helps.

Pick something that is easy for the child or parents to observe. If the symptom occurs mainly at school, pick something that is easy for the teacher to observe, and communicate with the teacher about this. Avoid tracking symptoms that occur infrequently (for example, panicking the morning of a school field trip), are very subjective (such as feeling sad when the weekend is over), or are difficult for the child to control (for example, vomiting in anticipation of an athletic competition).

When symptoms are targeted with specific CBT strategies, there is a good chance that they will improve. At the very least, the child will learn to manage them better and gain confidence. They may not, however, completely disappear, and this should be clarified when discussing treatment goals. It is also possible that the child has so many symptoms that not all can be targeted in therapy, or that new symptoms emerge during the course of therapy. Neither of these situations is disastrous because many coping skills can be used for several symptoms, and by learning an approach to coping better the child builds confidence that can facilitate further gains beyond the end of the therapy sessions. Reviewing these facts is often reassuring for families and allows them to see how relatively modest treatment goals can make a significant difference in the child's life. It is usually only feasible to monitor a couple of symptoms consistently, but the child often makes gains beyond these.

### Time Frame

Planning the length of therapy ahead of time is helpful in CBT for several reasons. Knowing how many sessions are left is often motivating to the child and family. It also allows the therapist to address issues related to ending therapy when there is still adequate time to do so. Having a prescribed number of sessions reduces the tendency of some children and families to become overly dependent on the therapist, neglecting the development of their own coping abilities. Alternatively, the child who claims to be "fine" after a few sessions can be reminded of the original plan, and of the need for further practice and repetition to consolidate gains if, in fact, these have been made.

The time frame is sometimes dictated by the particular manual or program used, although there may need to be some flexibility, depending on the pace the child and family can manage. The next chapter addresses this issue further. Alternatively, the therapist may have certain time constraints. For example, psychotherapy trainees often rotate from one setting to another every few months. This, too, should be spelled out at the beginning of therapy. Financial constraints may also limit the number of sessions.

Time limits can also be used to periodically reevaluate children and families who are less-than-ideal candidates for CBT. An example was mentioned in the last chapter in relation to medication. In this example, a severely impaired child whose family will not consider medication is given a "trial of CBT" for a few sessions to determine the feasibility of this form of treatment alone. Similar "trials" can be used in other situations where the therapist has doubts about the child or family's suitability for CBT. Sometimes the child does better than expected in the "trial," and a full course of CBT is then planned. Sometimes the "trial" reveals what other intervention is needed. Sometimes it is simply reassuring to families that CBT was attempted, and they can rule it out as a treatment option for the time being. In any case, little time is wasted, and disappointment is minimized.

## Roles

When discussing realistic expectations of treatment, it is important to review not only what the treatment can do for the child and family, but also what the child and family can do to increase the chances of treatment success. The child, the parents, and the therapist each play a role in determining treatment outcome. The parent who expects the therapist to magically "fix" the child's problem is usually disappointed, as is the child who thinks that his or her feelings will change without doing some work.

An athletic metaphor is often useful in explaining this concept. CBT for children is a skill-building therapy. CBT will help the child become more proficient at coping with upsetting thoughts or situations, and the process is very similar to developing proficiency in a sport. The child, like an athlete, will learn new skills and practice them regularly in order to improve. Practice between sessions is crucial to the child's success, just like an athlete must hone skills between games. The therapist, like a coach, will guide the child in developing the skills and will encourage practice, but cannot transfer those skills directly. The parents' role initially is that of adoring fans, cheering the child's every small success. Because the therapist regularly meets with the parents, however, they too learn new skills and eventually become as proficient as the "coach" in guiding and supporting their child in building his or her coping abilities. Thus, by the end of therapy, the child has acquired a set of skills that will continue to be practiced, and the parents have, similarly, acquired a set of skills for coaching the child. The therapist is, essentially, unnecessary at this point, but (much like a more experienced coach or manager) remains available if needed to "refresh" forgotten skills or manage new challenges that the family cannot deal with on their own.

One additional point to emphasize is that, as in a competitive sport, everyone involved needs to feel comfortable calling a "time-out" for reassessment if the situation is deteriorating or there is no appreciable progress. Anxious children and their parents are sometimes unassertive, resulting in "voting with their feet" when they are disappointed with therapy rather than confronting the therapist. Encouraging them to express dissatisfaction openly reduces the chances of premature termination.

**Progress in Therapy**

Discussing the nature of therapeutic change is helpful. Without such a discussion, families may become discouraged after a few sessions. As mentioned, we track change using a baseline recorded at the beginning of therapy. The baseline measure should be repeated every month or so. This will allow detection of subtle changes that children and families often miss. Alternatively, the baseline measure may show no difference, but a sign of progress may be evident in another area not previously considered. For example, a child with separation anxiety who cannot sleep alone may still be struggling in this area, but no longer insist on following his or her mother into the bathroom or asking for reassurance as to her whereabouts as frequently as before.

Even if no change is evident outside the sessions, the therapist can often take this opportunity to review what has been learned and determine if there are additional ways to facilitate its use outside the office. Skills do not automatically generalize from one setting to another, so problem-solving with families around how to transfer them to the child's home, school, and social environments is often very fruitful. If there has been some inconsistency in attending sessions or completing homework, return to the athletic metaphor and encourage more practice. For families who often miss sessions, I sometimes add a mathematical twist: learning coping skills is like learning algebra. You cannot solve equations if you have not mastered the four basic operations. Analogously, long gaps in therapy undermine the child's ability to master basic skills, and then the more sophisticated skills needed to deal with "real life" situations never develop. In this case, attending enough sessions to master the basics may yet allow progress to occur.

Finally, because it takes children several sessions to understand the cognitive strategies used in CBT, it may not be realistic to expect any changes in the first month or so of therapy. If the child and family are participating actively in therapy and willing to persevere, this is not necessarily problematic. In our own clinic, we often see children who are clearly engaged in treatment but appear to show little progress until the very end of a three-month therapy. As long as their families are able to remain hopeful and encouraging, these children typically make further gains after therapy ends.

Common patterns of progress include early improvement, early deterioration or stagnation followed by improvement, and "two steps forward, one step back." It is also possible to have a sudden crisis in the child's life (for example, a parental separation) that derails therapeutic progress, but this is, fortunately, less common. Early improvement, before the child has learned substantial CBT skills, does not appear to make sense. The knowledge that the child is being treated and the relief from tension it brings to families, however, can often be very beneficial to the child. The child may feel more hopeful, knowing that help is imminent, reducing symptoms. The act of labeling the child's specific problem at assessment can allow families and schools to blame the problem rather than blaming the child, often improving the child's experience in those environments dramatically. Any of these mechanisms can result in apparent early improvement in CBT.

Early deterioration or stagnation followed by improvement can be understood if one understands when certain skills are taught in most CBT programs. Feeling recognition is often emphasized early in therapy, and managing feelings is discussed later. Thus, the child who has tried to deal with upsetting feelings through distraction or other defenses may find those defenses dismantled early in therapy, resulting in feeling worse. In subsequent sessions, as feeling management is learned, the child's symptoms begin to improve. Another possibility to explore with early deterioration, however, is an adverse effect of therapy on other aspects of life. As mentioned in Chapter 3, the burden and potential stigma associated with therapy appointments can be very upsetting to some children.

"Two steps forward, one step back" is probably the most common pattern. In this case, the child makes gradual progress, but it is not consistent. Skills are learned but can only be applied in certain situations, so the child appears to falter from time to time. An optimistic, supportive attitude by parents and therapists can go a long way toward helping these children persevere.

At the same time, it is important not to categorize children according to these patterns too quickly. Every child is different from every other child, and CBT is, in principle, an empirical approach. Thus, the approach of the CBT therapist should be to test out what works for a given child. If something is not working, it may need to be modified. Parents can often be very helpful in predicting what is likely to work or not work based on their years of previous experiences with their child. Involving parents in problem-solving and testing out what works is also empowering for families. Parents who are able to do this become more confident and are more likely to continue supporting their child's progress after the therapy concludes.

### What Happens When the Therapy Is Over?

This question often reflects anxiety in the child or the family about coping in the future without the therapist's help. It is not always raised by clients at the beginning of therapy, but should probably be addressed by the therapist in discussing treatment expectations, because it will inevitably become a concern if it is not. The therapist cannot promise that the child will be fine and need no further intervention when CBT ends and should be honest about this fact. What can be promised is a reevaluation of the child's symptoms when therapy ends and the opportunity to discuss further treatment options at that point. Successful conclusion of therapy is also discussed further in Chapter 11 of this book.

No two children respond to CBT in exactly the same way, so there are a variety of such options. Some children truly do not need more intervention when CBT ends. In this case, it is still worth telling the child and family that "the door is open" in the event of future problems. Knowing they can access care readily if needed is reassuring to most children and families and, paradoxically, sometimes gives them the confidence to deal with minor ups and downs and avoid calling unless there is a major crisis.

Other children learn CBT strategies but have difficulty applying them consistently without some additional support. For these children, a few booster sessions are often helpful. These sessions are usually spaced further apart than therapy sessions (for example, monthly rather than weekly) and do not cover new material. Instead, they allow for a review of progress, a review of helpful strategies, and further problem-solving around consistent application of those strategies outside the office. Another way of thinking about these sessions is as a way of gradually weaning the child and family from dependence on the therapist by reinforcing their independent management of symptoms. In fact, some anxious children do not need to review strategies at all during booster sessions, but do better if they are encouraged to "come back and brag," to increase their confidence. The therapist is there simply to positively reinforce what the child is already doing, but should also talk to the parents about how they can assume this role at home.

For other children, CBT is only a part of the overall treatment plan. In this case, the child and family should be told that all aspects of the plan will be reviewed when CBT concludes, and if additional treatment referrals are needed, they will be made at that time. Parents are often reassured if told that the therapist will facilitate such referrals, rather than leaving them to navigate the mental health system alone.

## Common Misconceptions about CBT

Common misconceptions about CBT may need to be addressed at the beginning of therapy as well. The examples in the previous chapter illustrated one such misconception: that CBT is an urgent or emergency treatment. Another common misconception is that CBT makes the child feel better, and that this new feeling of well-being will change the child's behavior. As discussed, progress usually occurs the other way around: Children's upset feelings change as a result of changing their behaviors and cognitions. The distinction is an important one, because the first idea implies an almost magical "feel-good" therapy, while the second implies a coordinated effort involving the child and parents as well as the therapist.

There are a number of other misconceptions. Many are illustrated in the following fictional case example, a composite of several discussions I have had with parents whose children were starting therapy.

## Mrs. Smith's Treatment Expectations

Mrs. Smith has a 10-year-old daughter, Jenny, with generalized anxiety disorder that is interfering with her ability to write tests and complete school work. The daughter has been referred to you for CBT and seems a soft-spoken, compliant girl. It is August 15, and you are contracting for a series of treatment sessions with Mrs. Smith. She makes the following statements during the discussion:

1. "Doctor, my Jenny has seen two therapists already, and she just didn't open up to them. I know it will be different with you, though. You have such a wonderful reputation for working with children."
2. "I know you can find the root cause of Jenny's anxiety and get rid of it once and for all."
3. "Jenny wouldn't have these problems if she had better self-esteem. I'm really hoping you can give her that."

4. "I'm hoping we can start soon. I really want her better by the time she starts school."

5. "My sitter will drop her off for most sessions. Maybe we can touch base every month or two, so I can let you know how Jenny's doing, and you can fill me in on everything she's told you."

6. "Just make her feel better. If she felt better, I'm sure she would do her homework."

7. "Jenny has ballet Tuesdays and Thursdays, jazz dancing on Wednesdays, and piano lessons on Mondays. I know she would be embarrassed if she had to miss any school time. How about having her sessions Fridays at 5:30?"

Take a moment to think about how to respond to each of the statements above and why a response is needed.

Some of my thoughts on each statement include:

1. The child's progress is not wholly dependent on the therapist's skill or ability to pry information out of her. Particularly in manualized, evidence-based therapies like CBT, a relatively inexperienced therapist with supervision can often be as helpful to the child as a so-called expert. By the way, if you are just starting to use CBT, it may be helpful to emphasize this fact with families who question your credentials. In Jenny's case, it would be helpful to determine what went wrong with the last two therapies from both her point of view and her mother's point of view in order to avoid similar problems. Reframing the therapist as "coach" rather than magician, as in the athletic metaphor described earlier, would be helpful here too.

2. Apart from posttraumatic anxiety, most childhood anxiety or depression is at least partly related to biological vulnerability. CBT focuses on coping with that vulnerability, not on "root causes." Jenny's mother may be disappointed if she hopes you will enlighten her about such causes. Nevertheless, many children still benefit from this form of therapy. Furthermore, CBT rarely "gets rid of" or eliminates all symptoms, but it usually improves functioning. Thus, Mrs. Smith should be told that therapy may reduce Jenny's anxiety-related impairment, but some anxiety will remain and require continued use of coping skills learned.

3. The therapist cannot infuse the child with "self-esteem," and it is not clear what the parent means by that term. To clarify, it would be helpful to determine exactly what behaviors the parent would like to see change. If it is still unclear, I often cite a simple definition of self-esteem: having a sense of being a competent and loveable person.

In some children, CBT enhances this sense indirectly by building competence and reducing negative feedback from the environment prompted by anxious or depressive behaviors, but it does not "give self-esteem" directly.

4. Two weeks is usually not sufficient to show significant gains with CBT. Thus, Jenny is unlikely to be better by the time school starts.

5. Brief contacts between parent and therapist every month or two are probably not sufficient to support a preadolescent child's progress in CBT. Mrs. Smith needs to know what coping skills her daughter is learning and how she can support the use of those skills outside the therapist's office, and there may be other parenting issues relevant to Jenny's symptoms that need to be addressed as well. This cannot be done in monthly contacts. In addition, you must indicate that you will not tell Mrs. Smith "everything" her daughter has told you, as some things will remain between yourself and her (respecting her right to privacy). You will, however, tell Mrs. Smith anything that might result in serious harm to Jenny or those around her, and you will explain this to Jenny as well.

6. As mentioned, children usually do better before they feel better, not the other way around. Also, even if Jenny feels better, she may not be motivated to complete more homework. In fact, if CBT reduces her anxiety about teacher criticism, she might do less homework.

7. Therapists have a life too. Appointments usually occur during regular business hours, and some school time may have to be missed, but this is generally acceptable as the therapy is time-limited. Children can be assisted in finding acceptable ways of leaving school weekly that do not result in undue attention or embarrassment. I often provide notes for teachers to this effect, and encourage the child to provide a "short and sweet" explanation to curious peers that is not too far from the truth. "I have a doctor's appointment once a week" or "I'm taking a course about handling stress" are common examples.

Even when a thorough pretreatment assessment is done and treatment expectations are clearly defined, be prepared for the unexpected! No clinician can anticipate every possible therapeutic obstacle, children and families do not disclose every relevant detail about themselves in one or two pretreatment visits, and life circumstances occasionally impinge on even the most thoughtfully designed therapy. Children and families also remember the information you provide selectively and sometimes "hear what they want to hear." Our challenge as clinicians is to not get too anxious or frustrated about any of this and to continue to learn from our therapeutic experiences.

## WHAT WE YET NEED TO LEARN

Most research studies follow protocols that routinely advise children and families about what to expect in CBT, so the role of initial treatment expectations has not been studied. It therefore deserves research attention, especially in relation to community practice where families' prior knowledge of CBT may be more limited than in research settings.

Attention to the therapeutic alliance with parents is clearly important in child CBT when treating young children, but may be relevant to the treatment of adolescents as well and merits study in this age group. The role of the therapeutic alliance with parents as well as with youth in boys and girls of different ages, socioeconomic backgrounds, and cultural backgrounds also requires further study.

# EXPECTATIONS WORKSHEET

Review with the child you are seeing and with his or her parents the treatment expectations just outlined. Have the child and parents summarize what they have heard, to check for accuracy, record their words below, and listen for any evidence of the common misconceptions outlined above. Then, provide clarification and check for accuracy again. In the client's/parent's words:

- The symptom-based treatment goals are:
  1.
  2.
  3.

  Possible misconceptions: _____

  _____

  _____

  Clarification: _____

  _____

  _____

- The time frame for CBT is: _____

  _____

  _____

  Possible misconceptions: _____

  _____

  _____

  Clarification: _____

  _____

  _____

- The role of the child, parents, and therapist in CBT is:

  Child: _____

  _____

  _____

  Parents: _____

  _____

  _____

  Therapist: _____

  _____

  _____

Possible misconceptions: _____

_____

Clarification: _____

_____

The nature of progress to expect in child CBT is:

_____

Possible misconceptions: _____

_____

Clarification: _____

_____

- What happens when child CBT concludes?

_____

Possible misconceptions: _____

_____

Clarification: _____

_____

## CLINICAL CHALLENGE

Think about how you would engage Josh, a 15-year-old depressed teen, in a discussion of treatment expectations. Josh was referred to you by his family doctor for CBT, and his parents have ensured he attends by threatening to remove his computer from his room if he does not. He protests that there is nothing wrong with his brain and blames his teacher for a "lousy year at school." Josh says the only thing he still enjoys in life is playing "Dungeons of Doom," an online video game. He reports that his mother took him to a therapist previously, and he has no interest in talking about "feelings and junk" because it changes nothing. He says, "No offense, but therapists are pretty useless."

1. What would you say to Josh?
2. What (if anything) would you say to Josh's parents?

## REFERENCES

Chu, B.C., Choudhury, M.S., Shortt, A.L., Pincus, D.B., Creed, T.A., & Kendall, P.C. (2004). Alliance, technology, and outcome in the treatment of anxious youth. *Cognitive and Behavioral Practice*, 11, 44–55.

Chu, B.C., & Kendall, P.C. (2004). Positive association of child involvement and treatment outcome within a manual-based cognitive-behavioral treatment for children with anxiety. *Journal of Consulting and Clinical Psychology*, 72, 821–829.

Creed, T.A., & Kendall, P.C. (2005). Therapist alliance-building behavior within a cognitive-behavioral treatment for anxiety in youth. *Journal of Consulting and Clinical Psychology*, 73, 498–505.

Kaufman, N.K., Rohde, P., Seeley, J.R., Clarke, G.N., & Stice, E. (2005). Potential mediators of cognitive-behavioral therapy for adolescents with comorbid major depression and conduct disorder. *Journal of Consulting and Clinical Psychology*, 73, 38–46.

Kazdin, A.E., & Weisz, J.R. (1998). Identifying and developing empirically supported child and adolescent treatments. *Journal of Consulting and Clinical Psychology*, 66, 19–36.

Keeley, M.L., Geffken, G.R., Ricketts, E., McNamara, J.P., & Storch, E.A. (2011). The therapeutic alliance in cognitive behavioral treatment of pediatric obsessive-compulsive disorder. *Journal of Anxiety Disorders*, 25, 855–863.

Kendall, P.C. (1994). Treating anxiety disorders in children: Results of a randomized clinical trial. *Journal of Consulting and Clinical Psychology*, 62, 100–110.

Liber, J.M., McLeod, B.D., Van Widenfelt, B.M., Geodhart, A.W., van der Leeden, A.J., Utens, E.M., et al. (2010). Examining the relation between the therapeutic alliance, treatment adherence, and outcome of cognitive behavioral therapy for children with anxiety disorders. *Behavioral Therapy*, 41, 172–186.

Ormhaug, S.M., Jensen, T.K., Wentzel-Larsen, T., & Shirk, S.R. (2014). The therapeutic alliance in treatment of traumatized youths: Relation to outcome in a randomized clinical trial. *Journal of Consulting and Clinical Psychology*, 82, 52–64.

Wilansky-Traynor, P., Manassis, K., Monga, S., Shaw, M., Merka, P., Levac, A.M., et al. (2010). Cognitive behavioral therapy for depressed youth: Predictors of attendance. *Journal of the Canadian Academy of Child & Adolescent Psychiatry*, 19, 81–87.

# CHAPTER FIVE

# Using Manuals Appropriately

## WHAT IS KNOWN

Perhaps because CBT was developed as a structured, evidence-based treatment from the outset, comparisons of CBT with and without the use of manuals are generally not done. Studies directly comparing child CBT to nonmanualized child therapies are also lacking, although some disorder-specific reviews have done informal comparisons based on studies of each type of therapy. For example, Cohan, Chavira, and Stein (2006) reviewed psycho-social interventions for children with selective mutism and concluded that behavioral and cognitive-behavioral interventions have the most empirical support. Also, the intensity required in many nonmanualized therapies is sometimes contrasted with CBT to bolster the argument that CBT is more cost effective. Research support for child CBT is more substantial than for nonmanualized child therapies, but it is unclear whether it is the use of manuals that accounts for the difference or some other element of the therapy.

Manualizing a therapy has a number of potential benefits. The manual provides a framework for the therapy, so there is less variability in how the therapy is done from one practitioner to the next (Wilson, 1996). Standardization can also facilitate communication between professionals. Thus, when someone says "I did *Coping Cat* with this child" (a common anxiety-focused program by Philip Kendall, 2006), the listener has some idea of the concepts that the practitioner taught or tried to teach the child. Manuals may have the further benefit of focusing therapy on key techniques, to ensure these are learned and practiced frequently. Repetition in a variety of contexts both within sessions and between sessions is likely to result in the child's long-term use of new coping strategies (Kendall & Southam-Gerow, 1996), and this repetition is more likely to occur when a manual is followed.

Clinician judgment and skill are required in the implementation of manualized, evidence-based treatments (McNeill, 2006; Wilson, 1996). Interestingly, neither adherence to a manual nor therapeutic flexibility in the use of manuals has been found to relate to treatment outcome (Kendall & Chu, 2000; Liber et al., 2010). These studies, however, focused on well-trained therapists in academic centers who had regular supervision, and results might have differed in a community practice. Without further studies of the processes of change in CBT with children and adolescents, it is difficult to empirically define what elements of a manual must be adhered to and which ones can be omitted or modified.

Below is a list of some common, disorder-specific CBT manuals for children. The list is by no means exhaustive, but it highlights some manuals that have undergone empirical evaluation, are in the public domain, and are often used in child CBT. Child manuals are constantly being updated, so it is worth checking http://www.workbookpublishing.com or other online resources to ensure you get the most current and complete version. For disorders not in this list, look up a recent CBT outcome study on the topic and then contact the authors regarding the manual they used. Many authors are willing to share their insights and/or materials as long as you respect their authorship and do not distribute the materials further.

### Anxiety-Focused Manuals

- Flannery-Schroeder, E., & Kendall, P.C. (1996). *Cognitive behavioral therapy for anxious children: Therapist manual for group treatment.* Philadelphia, PA: Workbook Publishing.
- Kendall, P.C. (2006). *Coping Cat workbook* (3rd ed.). Philadelphia, PA: Workbook Publishing.
- Kendall, P.C., Choudhury, M., Hudson, J., & Webb, A. (2002). *"The C.A.T. Project" workbook for the cognitive-behavioral treatment of anxious adolescents.* Philadelphia, PA: Workbook Publishing.
- March, J., & Mulle, K. (1998). *OCD in children and adolescents: A cognitive-behavioral treatment manual.* New York: Guilford Press.
- Rapee, R. et al. *Cool kids.* http://centreforemotionalhealth.com.au/pages/products-coolkids.aspx.

### Depression-Focused Manuals

- Clarke, G., DeBar, L., Ludman, E., Asarnow, J., & Jaycox, L. (2002). *Steady project intervention manual.* Available free of charge at http:www.

kpchr.org/public/acwd/acwd.html; ideal for older adolescents who are on concurrent antidepressant medication.

- Langelier, C. (2001). *Mood management: A cognitive behavioral skills-building program for adolescents; skills workbook.* New York: Sage.
- Stark, K.D., & Kendall, P.C. (1996). *Taking action: A workbook for overcoming depression.* Philadelphia, PA: Workbook Publishing.
- Stark, K.D., Simpson, J., Schnoebelen, S., Hargrave, J., Molnar, J., & Glen, R. (2007). *"ACTION" workbook: Cognitive-behavioral therapy for treating depressed girls.* Philadelphia, PA: Workbook Publishing.
- Stallard, P. (2002). *Think good—feel good: A cognitive behaviour therapy workbook for children and young people.* London, UK: John Wiley.

### Manuals Focused on Externalizing Problems

- Child Development Institute. (2002). *S.N.A.P.: Stop now and plan program.* Toronto, ON: Child Development Institute.
- Kendall, P.C. (1996). *Stop and think: Workbook for impulsive children* (2nd ed.). Philadelphia, PA: Workbook Publishing.
- Nelson, W.M. (1996). *Keeping your cool: The anger management workbook.* Philadelphia, PA: Workbook Publishing.

## PUTTING WHAT WE KNOW TO WORK

Manuals sometimes provide a false sense of security, particularly for the inexperienced CBT practitioner. It is tempting to believe that doing what is in the manual is all that is required for therapeutic success. This assumes, however, that the practitioner is using the best manual for the child in question, that modifications are made when the child or family is not ideally suited to the treatment program, and that basic therapeutic skills that are needed to keep the child and family engaged and motivated throughout the program are not sacrificed for the sake of "following the manual." Those assumptions are not always met.

A common analogy has been used to describe this problem: A manual is not a cookbook. Let us suppose, for a moment, however, that it is. As any cook with even limited experience will tell you, following recipes does not ensure a delicious result. If you are baking a cake, for example, your oven may be a bit hotter than average on the top rack. Putting your cake there may burn it. The eggs you buy may be slightly larger than average, resulting in too much liquid in the mix if you do not make adjustments. Familiarity with these factors allows you to make minor modifications that are needed, but that familiarity only comes with experience. It also helps if you do not start with the most complicated, multistep recipe. A simple one is more likely to turn out well for the novice baker. If you have never baked before, it may help to get advice from a more experienced neighbor, or even bake the first cake together. Adding ingredients to the recipe or substituting one ingredient for another is probably not advisable until you have developed some confidence with the basics. You will also not find certain things in the recipe, because it is assumed you are aware of them. For example, it will be assumed that you know you need a large mixing bowl and a pan in the shape of the cake you are making, that you know to preheat the oven, and that you have obtained the recipe from a trusted source with expertise in baking cakes (as opposed to cookies, casseroles, or other products).

Let us take each sentence in the "bake a cake" analogy above, and think about how this might translate into using "recipes" (manuals) in child CBT.

One translation might be:

- Know the environment you work in and how it differs from "research conditions" (see Chapter 1). Make adjustments accordingly.
- Know the children you typically see, and how they differ from typical research subjects (see Chapter 2). Make adjustments accordingly.
- Start with a case that is relatively uncomplicated and close to an "ideal candidate" for CBT (see Chapter 2).
- Do not hesitate to get supervision or peer support, especially on the first few cases.
- Addition or substitution of ideas in the manual should not be done until you are confident with that particular model. Even so, it is not always advisable (see below).
- Do not neglect therapeutic common sense for the sake of following a manual. For example, take some time to build rapport with the child, even if the manual does not tell you to do so.
- Find a manual that is as specific to the child in question as possible (good match in terms of diagnosis, age, cognitive level, etc.) from a source specializing in child CBT (as opposed to adult CBT or child therapy of another sort).

Attempts have been made to describe the best use of manuals more systematically. A number of authors have proposed checklists of "treatment adherence" that allow therapists to review for themselves whether they are adhering (literally, sticking) to the treatment described in the manual closely enough (for example, DeRubeis & Feeley, 1990). Before getting to those, however, some discussion about how to select the right manual for your client is in order.

**Manual Selection**

Some people may wonder, "Why use a manual at all?" After all, shouldn't an experienced therapist know how to provide CBT without referring to a text? The answer is "yes and no." While it is true that one may do what is in the manual more easily or automatically with experience, it is still worth checking consistency with the manual on a regular basis. It is simply human nature to gravitate toward the familiar, and if one is familiar with therapeutic approaches other than CBT (as most therapists are), one tends to drift into those approaches unless there is at least periodic checking of the manual.

In selecting a manual, go with a reputable source. Manuals that have been evaluated in randomized studies and that come from centers specializing in child CBT are preferred. One excellent source of CBT manuals for many childhood disorders and age groups is http://www.workbookpublishing.com. This site features manuals by Philip Kendall and colleagues at Temple University in Philadelphia, one of the foremost research groups in this field. A number of adaptations of this work have also been done. For example, *Coping Cat* (Kendall's classic child anxiety manual) has been adapted in Australia as *Coping Koala*, in Canada as *Coping Bear*, and so on. Usually, these adaptations are done in university-based clinics or research centers, so check these resources in your area if you want a manual that is reputable and culturally specific.

Select a manual that is as specific as possible to the client(s) you are seeing. Look for a good match in terms of diagnosis, age, and cognitive level. For example, do not assume that a manual developed for grade school children is suitable for teens or vice versa. If there is a discrepancy between age and cognitive level (for example, in a child with intellectual delay or significant learning disabilities), this can pose particular challenges, because the language and examples in the child manual may seem "babyish," but the teen manual is too cognitively complex for the youth to master. In this case, my preference is usually to work with the child manual, but edit it ahead of time to make the examples and language sound "older." It is easy to replace references to "children" with "people," for example. Similarly, cute cartoon characters can be used as mascots for the program, without expecting the youth to take them too seriously.

If the child or youth has several diagnoses, decide which one is best to address first (as described in Chapter 3) and look for a manual for that one. It may not address all of the problems, and this should be discussed with the client and family, but it will provide a good start. It is usually better to build confidence by focusing on one problem and dealing with it successfully, rather than trying to address several problems at once and not taking the time to really solve any one of them. There are also a number of common elements across manuals (for example, improving the client's problem-solving skills) that may have positive effects on the diagnoses that are not targeted directly.

If you are planning to do a CBT group, look for a group-specific manual. Individually focused manuals may cover the same content, but that content is not always presented in a way that is engaging for groups and takes advantage of group processes. For example, recognizing physical sensations associated with anxiety can be done individually by having the child look at a drawing of a human body and identify the body parts where he or she has experienced discomfort when anxious. In a group, this exercise is much more effective when one group member's body outline is traced and hung on the wall. The other group members then take turns marking where in the body they experience anxiety using different colored markers. Thus, the group works together to produce an impressive anxiety-ridden figure, and everybody discovers (from their peers) at least one new way to recognize anxiety.

## Adherence

A colleague of mine coined a wonderful term several years ago: "pseudo-CBT." I knew immediately what he meant. All too often, we see children whose families claim they have had CBT, but on closer inquiry it turns out they have not. What they have usually received is some form of eclectic therapy that includes a few CBT principles, but without the structural elements of true CBT. For example, they will describe relaxation strategies or positive thinking strategies, but cannot name specific situations that these were applied to. Alternatively, they will describe learning strategies for certain situations, but never being assigned tasks between sessions to practice them. Sessions with no formal structure, where the client talked about his or her feelings about various things, and suggestions were made as to how to handle those feelings also do not constitute CBT.

What are the key elements needed for a therapy to be considered CBT? First, there must be a defined session structure. Once past the first session (where rapport-building is often prioritized), this structure looks something like the following:

1. Review homework the child has done since the last session, and positively reinforce either doing it or attempting to do it.
2. Set agenda for the current session (including therapist and client elements), and ensure the child is in agreement with this.
3. Teach a new CBT skill (usually one spelled out in a manual or book specific to the client's disorder), including questions to ensure the child understands it.

4. Practice the new skill in the session with positive reinforcement for doing so.
5. Assign homework based on the new skill.
6. Check that the child understands the homework assigned.
7. Allow a few minutes for the child's part of the agenda (most children choose to either play a game or talk about something that interests them).

Some authors also advocate creating a "bridge" to the previous session before introducing new material, for example by asking the client to recall what was helpful (or not) about that session (Beck, 1995). Personally, I find keeping notes about what was discussed in the session in addition to the exercises in the manual facilitates session-to-session continuity for the therapist. "Bridging" questions may improve continuity for the child.

The homework is sometimes given a more pleasant name (for example, a "Show That I Can" task in *Coping Cat*), or just called "real-world practice" (a term often more acceptable to teens). It includes one or, at the most, two specific tasks that incorporate the skill(s) learned in the session. It does not include anything that has not been tried at least once with the therapist in a session. It need not be a written task, as long as it allows practice of the skill(s) learned in the session. Some children and teens actually find homework based on implementing a new skill more relevant and acceptable than writing about thoughts and feelings.

Lack of homework completion by clients is common, and therapists address the issue in different ways. One can explore reasons why it was not done and address these, give incentives to increase motivation to do homework, or allow a natural consequence. A natural consequence involves doing the homework at the beginning of the session, with the result that the time for unstructured discussion or play (element 7 of the structure described above) is reduced. This approach also ensures that the child understands the homework material, and offers a helpful review if he or she does not. Some authors also advocate exploring automatic thoughts that might interfere with homework completion (Beck, 1995) (for example, "What thoughts went through your mind when you remembered you had homework to do?"). If anxious or depressive thoughts interfered, this could be a nice *in vivo* cognitive exercise to address these thoughts, but only in an adolescent or older child who is able to access automatic thoughts in this way.

Beyond the session structure described above, the only other common element on most adherence checklists is a reminder to check for consistency between the content in the manual and the content that has been covered with the child. As described below, some modification of content is possible while still maintaining good consistency.

Personally, I would advocate one additional item on the checklist when working with children: a reminder to spend time with parents reviewing what the child has learned and how they can support the child's practice of the new strategy or strategies in the home. Use questions to ensure that the parents have understood this information and that they believe that what you have proposed is feasible in their home.

If some practice at school is planned, determine who will contact the teacher to explain this and involve him or her if needed. Depending on the child's age and circumstances, this could be the child, the parent, or the therapist. I usually encourage the child or parent to speak to the teacher directly and offer to be available to answer any questions, rather than taking the lead on teacher communication. This practice reduces dependency on the therapist and often increases children's and families' ability to problem-solve school issues independently, as they will have to once the therapy ends.

As you can see, most elements that are essential to ensuring adherence are structural, rather than content based. This makes sense, because the mechanisms of change in CBT are thought to relate to repetition and practice of new skills. Adequate repetition and practice of new skills are far less likely to occur in therapies that are unstructured than in those that follow the structure described above. The same elements apply whether CBT is offered in a group or individual format.

What about adherence to parent-focused manuals? If possible, one should follow the same structure as outlined for children above. Doing so may be difficult, however, especially if one is working with a lively group of parents who may not follow the agenda as prescribed. Having a "one problem at a time" rule is often helpful here. In other words, the therapist can insist that the group generates one or more solutions to a given problem and decides how to implement these between sessions, before moving on to the next problem. This usually slows down the interactions and helps keep the group focused on learning and practicing new parenting skills.

**Modifications That May Help**

Some modification of the content of CBT manuals can be helpful in certain children. In fact, following the manual word for word may come across as stilted or culturally insensitive in some cases. Simplify manuals for younger children or for learning impaired adolescents, and modify examples to make them culturally relevant if the child is from an ethnic minority. Other modifications that are sometimes helpful include:

- Adding concrete reminders to help children remember or generalize certain concepts from the manual beyond the office. Particularly in younger children, the use of pictures, cue cards, mnemonics, audiotapes, or transitional objects (reassuring reminders of home) can be very helpful, even if these are not spelled out in the manual.

- Reducing the number of exercises focused on the same concept. Some manuals contain three or four exercises to teach a single concept, and a child who has a short attention span or who writes or thinks more slowly than the average may find this frustrating. If the child can demonstrate a good grasp of the concept by answering specific questions about it, reducing the number of exercises on that concept is usually not harmful. The concept must still be practiced between sessions, however, because applying it in the "real world" is different from using it in the office.

- Taking extra time or even an extra session to master a concept if the child does not grasp it easily. This is well worth doing, as many programs are designed to build upon concepts learned in the early sessions, and neglecting one of these may undermine the success of the program. An example would be role-playing a situation where the child plans to apply a new CBT skill, even if the role-play is not prescribed by the manual.

- Running a session or two behind in the manual because the child needed more than one session to establish a good rapport with the therapist. This modification is helpful in children who are difficult to engage due to oppositionality, severe shyness, or some other difficulty. Sometimes having a few sessions to warm up to the therapist helps these children work more productively in CBT subsequently. An extra session or two may also be needed if a child lacks a particular skill that is a prerequisite for doing what the manual prescribes. For example, a child who does not know how to start a conversation may need to practice this before doing exposure exercises to reduce social anxiety. Standing silently in the midst of a social situation could make the child appear odd, possibly prompting peer ridicule that would make the anxiety worse. Let the family know early, however, that a couple of sessions extra may be needed at the end of therapy, to avoid disappointment.

- Making the CBT "come alive" in the session if you see the opportunity to do so. For example, the child with separation anxiety may practice coping in the waiting room for a few minutes while you talk to the parents. Then, take a few minutes to review the experience with the child and the coping skills that helped. This exercise may not be prescribed in the manual, but it is a powerful, relevant application of the skills presented there. Of course, this type of exercise should not be done if the child has not yet been taught any coping skills, or if you anticipate the child becoming overwhelmed.

- Using your knowledge of the cognitive basis of the disorder to help the child learn concepts (Alford & Beck, 1997). For example, depressed teens are prone to overgeneralization of negative outcomes. Therefore, they may need extra emphasis on exercises that help them identify partial successes or appreciate the value of their efforts. Anxious children tend to underestimate themselves. Therefore, they may need extra emphasis on anxious situations where they have already demonstrated some ability to cope.

- For parent-focused work, spending more time on concepts that are highly relevant to the child and the parent–child dyad in question, and less time on concepts that are less relevant to these. For example, little discussion of time-outs and other behavior control measures is needed if the child is very compliant and conscientious at home, unless there are disruptive siblings the parents need to manage using these measures. Overprotective parents, on the other hand, may need extra time to learn how to encourage age-appropriate independence, or to engage in joint problem-solving with their children rather than constantly reassuring them or constantly providing them with solutions to problems. By contrast, in working with the child we assume that concepts in the manual are all relevant to children with that diagnosis, unless a modular approach is being used (see below).

**Modifications That Are Inadvisable**

The following are some common mistakes that well-intentioned therapists often make in an attempt to adapt manuals to their clientele and practice environment:

- Abandoning the structure of CBT in order to appear friendlier or less rigid to the child. For all the reasons described in the "Adherence" section above, this is not advisable.

- Talking in generalities rather than applying CBT concepts to specific problem situations that often occur in the child's life. If the child cannot come up with such situations, ask the parents. If neither parent nor child can identify such situations, ask why they are coming to you for therapy (i.e., review treatment expectations). Also check, in consultation with the prescribing physician, if symptoms have been eliminated by medication. Occasionally, you will see children who used to have many problem situations and have improved now, but are still interested in CBT "in case the problems come back." Hypothetical problem situations can sometimes be used in CBT with these children, recognizing that the lack of opportunity to practice skills learned may limit the gains. Nevertheless, knowing what could be done in the future is often reassuring to these children.

- Adding concepts to the manual without increasing the number of sessions. This practice is based on the mistaken belief that, if a few CBT concepts are good, more must be better. In fact, more concepts often confuse the child and almost always interfere with essential repetition and practice of concepts in the manual.

- Reducing the number of sessions or reducing practice of CBT skills between sessions. This is particularly tempting to do in bright children who seem to learn the material quickly. They can fool the therapist into believing that several sessions can be compressed into one, and that homework is not really needed. Unfortunately, these children often learn CBT strategies at an intellectual level, but do not necessarily connect them with their most troubling feelings or use them routinely outside the office. They "talk the talk," but do not necessarily "walk the walk." For CBT strategies to be helpful, they need to become an integral part of the child's life and be used almost automatically. This "gut level" learning usually does not occur in condensed therapies. A very astute trainee once told me "the best thing about working with a manual is it really slows everything down." I could not agree more.

## Manuals and the Therapeutic Relationship

Ideally, a manual should help rather than hinder a good therapeutic relationship. The best way to ensure this happens is to pay attention to how your clients respond to the work you do with them from the manual. If their eyes begin to glaze over or they appear increasingly restless, stop. Take a moment to figure out what is bothering the client about the interaction. Disengaged clients are not going to absorb the material you are working on anyway, so pressing on to complete the session as described in the manual makes no sense in this situation.

Gently confront the issue by, for example, saying, "You look bored (or tense, or whatever the affect seems to be). What's going on?" If the child denies any problem, take an educated guess as to what is going on. There are really only two possibilities: Something about the work you are doing together is bothering the child, or something outside the therapeutic situation is bothering the child. Given the short time perspective of young children, the culprit is often an event that happened the same day. Lack of sleep is another common problem. If you still draw a blank, ask if the child is ready to continue or not, and respect the choice he or she makes. Everyone is entitled to the occasional "off day." Try again in the next session, and consider exploring the issue further with the parent(s) if the pattern repeats.

Demystifying the manual can also help the therapeutic relationship. Personally, I like to sit beside the child and look at the manual together. Sitting across from the child can convey the mistaken impression that I know it all and am keeping that knowledge hidden in the manual until I am ready to share it with the child. Working side by side contributes to a more collaborative interaction, and seeing the manual as the therapist sees it is often experienced by the child as empowering. Some children like to look ahead in the manual or look back, because it reduces uncertainty and can contribute to a sense of mastering the material. As long as this does not heighten the child's anxiety and does not take up too much time, that is fine. In anxious children who look ahead repeatedly, I sometimes point out how hard it is to cope with not knowing what is coming next. If the child recognizes this as a problem, we can then apply coping skills from the manual to improve his or her ability to tolerate uncertainty (another way to make CBT "come alive" in the session).

Another aspect of demystifying therapy is "walking the walk" with the child. Children and adolescents are often suspicious of therapists who instruct them about CBT strategies, but cannot describe how they have used those strategies themselves. Take some time before starting your first case (or at least during the first few sessions) to keep a record of your own anxious or depressive cognitions, situations where they arose, how you felt, and how you responded. If they are rare because you are a calm, optimistic person by nature, pay attention to any negative cognitions about being a novice CBT therapist. "I don't know what I'm doing here. How can I be helpful?" "I feel like a fraud," or "I feel like a mean teacher assigning homework. How can this be therapeutic?" are some common ones. You may even have some negative cognitions about your client or his or her parents. Find some adaptive thoughts and/or actions to address what you have noticed. If that is hard, ask a colleague or supervisor to help. Having used your new coping strategy, what do you notice? Do you feel any better? Is CBT working for you? Most new therapists find this exercise not only lends them credibility with their clients, but also increases their personal enthusiasm for CBT.

Finally, therapeutic skills that are not spelled out in the manual can often be helpful. For example, recognizing family dynamics that are interfering with the use of new coping strategies outside the office can be very helpful. This does not mean, however, that you interrupt CBT and begin family therapy at this point. Instead, keep the information in mind as you work with the child and family in CBT. As you discuss specific situations where coping skills were not successfully applied, encourage parents and children to think about what got in the way. Parents will often recognize the maladaptive patterns themselves, if they appear in several situations, and then either try to change them or recognize the need for additional family work.

Some therapists use humor very effectively. When working with anxious children, for example, I sometimes encourage them to exaggerate their "worst case scenarios" to an implausible, almost ridiculous extreme that begins to seem funny. Self-deprecating humor (for example, a brief anecdote about something foolish one has done that relates to the material being discussed) can sometimes help children feel that they are not alone in their struggles. Be careful, however, to make sure that the humor is not at the child's expense (laugh with the child, never at the child) and that any self-disclosure is limited and not burdensome to the child.

## CULTURAL DIFFERENCE AND MANUALIZED THERAPY

Huey and Polo (2008) have eloquently described the many effects cultural differences can have on evidence-based treatments in children, including CBT, and have reviewed relevant studies of this subject. While minority youth are clearly underrepresented in existing studies, most of the evidence suggests that they benefit from evidence-based treatments, and that ethnicity does not necessarily have adverse effects on outcome. In comparison to typical research subjects, however, ethnic minority youth in the community may face additional disadvantages (low socioeconomic status, unsafe neighborhoods, and so forth), so it is not clear if we can generalize these findings to community practice. Those disadvantages may need to be addressed in order for the child to benefit.

An ethnic match between client and therapist has been found to sometimes predict treatment success, but results are less consistent for tailoring the treatment itself to ethnicity (Huey & Polo, 2008). The latter is thought to be due to the fact that therapists sometimes compromise the core components of treatment for the sake of cultural relevance. For example, one might be tempted to focus one or more sessions on the child taking pride in certain aspects of his or her cultural identity, with the goal of enhancing self-esteem. Doing so, however, may result in less attention to other CBT concepts that are important for that particular manualized therapy, adversely affecting outcome. Changing the ethnic features of cartoon characters in the manual, by contrast, should not adversely affect outcome, because it does not interfere with the child learning core CBT concepts, and may enhance engagement by increasing cultural relevance.

Cultural sensitivity training for therapists and culturally valid outcome measures have also been advocated. If the latter are not available, one can sometimes work with children or families to define specific behavioral goals for therapy. For example, a socially anxious teenage girl in my practice encountered a questionnaire item "able to call up a friend to go to the movies" and laughed. In her culture, she would never be allowed to go out to the movies unaccompanied by a family member. We talked about what social approach behaviors were permissible and discovered that she really wanted to be able to sit with a group of her peers in the cafeteria and contribute to the conversation. She focused on this goal in therapy and was pleasantly surprised by how accepting her peers were when she achieved it.

Apart from being trained in cultural sensitivity, I have found that therapists who work well with children from diverse backgrounds share a common characteristic: a genuine, respectful curiosity about the child and family in relation to their background. They are respectful in that they humbly acknowledge their lack of information about a particular culture. Thus, rather than making assumptions based on what they have heard or read about a particular culture, they ask the child and family about their customs and beliefs. They inquire about how those cultural factors might affect the child and family's view of the therapy or the therapist (Is there some stigma attached to mental health services in their culture? What role do doctors/therapists play in their culture? What child behaviors are considered normative/expected in their culture?) and where therapy would fit in that family's cultural context. They also wonder about where the child and family see themselves within their culture (As progressive or traditional? As sharing more values with the cultural majority or sharing more values with their own ethnic group?). Furthermore, they maintain this respectful, inquisitive attitude throughout therapy, rather than assuming culture was "dealt with" at the beginning, and they keep it in mind when formulating goals, overcoming therapeutic obstacles, and celebrating success. For example, for a Jewish boy getting through his Bar Mitzvah may be far more important than being able to present a project in class.

Within-cultural differences have been further described by Carter, Sbrocco, and Carter (1996) in their work on African Americans in CBT. They described clients on two dimensions: racial identity and level of acculturation to the prevailing culture. Clients high on both dimensions did well in therapy, provided the therapist was able to appreciate their ethnicity. By contrast, clients high on racial identity but low on level of acculturation expressed their symptoms differently (for example, more somatic symptoms and fewer emotional symptoms) and were less trusting of therapists not of the same culture than clients high on level of acculturation. For these low-acculturation clients, taking additional time to learn about cultural differences and expectations was essential to therapeutic engagement and treatment success. Cultural considerations in CBT are discussed further in Chapter 7.

## When There Is No Manual That Fits Exactly (Modular Approaches)

One of the great weaknesses of manualized therapies is their implicit assumption that "one size fits all." In other words, every child with the same diagnosis is provided with the same set of strategies in the same order. Even with judicious manual selection and with the modifications discussed above, this approach does not work for all children who could benefit from CBT. One child, for example, may need to develop increased treatment motivation before learning new strategies. Another child may need to develop certain skills before exposure to feared situations. A parent of a child with oppositional traits may need to learn behavior management strategies before learning how to support the child's new coping skills. The opposite may be true of a parent of a very compliant but inhibited child.

To address this individual variation, several authors have recently described an approach termed "modular CBT." In this approach, the strategies described in a given treatment manual are organized into shorter units, or "modules," each focused on a particular problem and a particular therapeutic goal. For example, in the treatment of anxious children, Bruce Chorpita (2007) has described modules focused on anxiety recognition, gradual exposure, several types of cognitive restructuring, social skills, and several aspects of parenting. Using this approach, the therapist begins by formulating a treatment plan based on a thorough understanding of each child problem that could be addressed with a module. The problems are then put in the order in which they are likely to respond to intervention, and this dictates the order in which the modules are provided in a given case.

While promising, particularly in complex cases, modular approaches need further evaluation. The formulation of the treatment plan can also be rather complicated, especially for therapists with limited CBT experience. Most cognitively focused modules require substantial verbal reasoning and verbal working memory (the ability to hold and manipulate verbal information at the same time), limiting their utility in children with learning deficits in these areas.

In this book, anxiety-focused modules are provided that rely less on verbal skills and more on imagery. They are designed to provide coping skills for anxious children with verbal deficits. These modules can be used in several ways. In anxious children who show limited avoidance behavior, these modules may serve as a stand-alone treatment. In anxious children who show substantial avoidance behavior, these modules can be used in conjunction with exposure-focused modules, such as those described in Chorpita's book, or used to replace cognitively focused sessions in a standardized child anxiety manual (for example, *Coping Cat*). Finally, because of their emphasis on developing a sense of mastery rather than engaging in probabilistic thinking, these modules can be used to foster resilience in children with a variety of anxiety-related conditions (for example, anxiety related to frightening illnesses or life events). Like all modular CBT approaches, this one awaits further evaluation. Similar imagery-based modules could be developed for depressed children or adolescents, but there is an existing CBT approach focused on behavioral activation, attending to positive experience, problem-solving, and simple cognitive techniques (see Stark & Kendall, 1996, listed above) that is evidence based and useful for most young or cognitively limited depressed children.

### How Do You Know Which Modules to Use?

Using modules can be a bit daunting, because it can seem like you are designing your own manual with little guidance. It does not need to be, however, if you remember you are designing a CBT program specifically for the child in front of you and if you base your work on sound CBT principles. If you know the key problems the child presents with and which one everyone has agreed to prioritize and treat first (see Chapter 4), the CBT skills needed for that problem become obvious. The child's age and cognitive level then determine how to best help the child learn those skills. These considerations determine which specific modules are needed in the program.

To decide how to put the modules in order, go back to basic CBT principles. Every therapy needs an initial session or two to build rapport, some further sessions to ensure the child can recognize the problematic feeling(s) that are the focus of treatment, sessions to learn skills to manage those feelings, sessions to ensure practice both within and outside the office, and sessions to consolidate gains and conclude therapy (see Chapter 11). Total length is usually somewhere between eight and fifteen sessions, occasionally up to 20 if the child needs to work at a slow pace. More than this is usually not advisable, because it suggests one is trying to "bite off more than one can chew." Remember, you are trying to reduce a single group of symptoms, not cure the child of every mental health problem that seems to be present.

Before starting to work with the child, read the whole program once yourself to check that there are no modules that assume familiarity with skills that the child has not previously learned. If you find one, add session(s) or module(s) to teach those skills prior to the module in question. Session structure, as described above, should be maintained regardless of the content of the program. A page to record a running tally of points that positively reinforce child participation and practice of CBT skills is a nice addition to any manual. If in doubt about your "designer manual," ask a colleague with CBT experience to take a look at it. There may be no perfect manual for the child you are treating, so focus on the key ideas and skills you are trying to convey, but do not be discouraged if you need to "fine-tune" a few things along the way.

## WHAT WE YET NEED TO LEARN

The optimal use of therapeutic flexibility when working with manuals still requires empirical study. In describing flexibility, Kendall, Chu, Gifford, Hayes, and Nauta (1998) emphasize selecting those strategies or exercises that will aid the therapist in achieving goals with a given child. Thus, some strategies may be excluded and others expanded upon, depending on what the child needs in order to grasp and apply key concepts. Flexibility may also involve taking into account cultural differences between the client and the author of the manual, for example, by modifying examples in the manual to make them more relevant to the client's cultural context and using culturally valid measures of outcome (Huey & Polo, 2008). Webb, Auerbach, and DeRubeis (2012) emphasize the role of theory-specified CBT techniques in ensuring adherence while allowing for flexibility when working with depressed youth. Further studies of processes of change in child and adolescent CBT are needed to empirically define the difference between non-adherence and flexibility in manualized treatment.

## USING MANUALS WORKSHEET

- Select a CBT manual for your case, using the principles described in this chapter.

  Manual chosen: _____
  _____
  _____

  Reasons: _____
  _____
  _____

- What modifications of the manual, if any, would be helpful in this case? List them:

  1.

  Reason: _____
  _____
  _____

  2.

  Reason: _____
  _____
  _____

  3.

  Reason: _____
  _____
  _____

- Once you start treatment, do an "adherence check" after the first three sessions (circle "Yes" or "No").

  Are you still using the session structure outlined in the chapter?
  Yes        No

  Is the child practicing strategies between sessions?
  Yes        No

  Are the parents working with the child to aid practicing strategies between sessions?
  Yes        No

  Has the child learned all the key concepts in the manual for those three sessions?
  Yes        No

If using a manual for parents, have the parents learned all the key concepts in the manual for those three sessions?
Yes          No

Do you have a good therapeutic relationship with the child?
Yes          No

Do you have a good therapeutic relationship with the parents?
Yes          No

For all "No" responses, outline the reasons and a plan for addressing these:

Reasons: _____

_____

_____

Plan: _____

_____

_____

## CLINICAL CHALLENGE

Look back at Jenny Smith in the previous chapter. Suppose you have had a thorough discussion of treatment expectations with her mother (Mrs. Smith), she seems to understand these, and Jenny is willing to participate in CBT.

1. Which CBT manual would you use with Jenny?
2. Would you modify it in any way?
3. Would you add any interventions for Mrs. Smith? Which ones?
4. Six weeks into the therapy, Mrs. Smith tells you Jenny (who has always feared needles) is overdue for an immunization, and the school is about to suspend her unless she gets it. She has heard there is a great manual for needle phobia and suggests you switch to using this manual with her daughter. What do you do? Why?

## REFERENCES

Alford, B.A., & Beck, A.T. (1997). *The integrative power of cognitive therapy*. New York: Guilford Press.

Beck, J.S. (1995). *Cognitive therapy: Basics and beyond*. New York: Guilford Press.

Carter, M.M., Sbrocco, T., & Carter, C. (1996). African-Americans and anxiety disorders research: Development of a testable theoretical framework. *Psychotherapy*, 33, 449–463.

Chorpita, B.F. (2007). *Modular cognitive behavioral therapy for childhood anxiety disorders*. New York: Guilford Press.

Cohan, S.L., Chavira, D.A., & Stein, M.B. (2006). Practitioner review: Psychosocial interventions for children with selective mutism: A critical evaluation of the literature from 1990–2005. *Journal of Child Psychology and Psychiatry*, 47, 1085–1097.

DeRubeis, R.J., & Feeley, M. (1990). Determinants of change in cognitive therapy for depression. *Cognitive Therapy and Research*, 14, 469–482.

Huey Jr., S.J., & Polo, A.J. (2008). Evidence-based psychosocial treatments for ethnic minority youth. *Journal of Clinical Child and Adolescent Psychology*, 37, 262–301.

Kendall, P.C. (2006). *Coping Cat workbook* (3rd ed.). Philadelphia, PA: Workbook Publishing.

Kendall, P.C., & Chu, B.C. (2000). Retrospective self-reports of therapist flexibility in manual-based treatment for youths with anxiety disorders. *Journal of Clinical Child Psychology*, 29, 209–220.

Kendall, P.C., Chu, B.C., Gifford, A., Hayes, C., & Nauta, M. (1998). Breathing life into a manual: Flexibility and creativity with manual-based treatments. *Cognitive Behavioral Practice*, 5, 177–198.

Kendall, P.C., & Southam-Gerow, M.A. (1996). Long-term follow-up of a cognitive-behavioral therapy for anxiety-disordered youth. *Journal of Consulting and Clinical Psychology*, 64, 724–730.

Liber, J.M., McLeod, B.D., Van Widenfelt, B.M., Goedhart, A.W., van der Leeden, A.J., Utens, E.M., et al. (2010). Examining the relation between the therapeutic alliance, treatment adherence, and outcome of cognitive behavioral therapy for children with anxiety disorders. *Behavioral Therapy*, 41, 172–186.

McNeill, T. (2006). Evidence-based practice in an age of relativism: Toward a model for practice. *Social Work*, 51, 147–156.

Webb, C.A., Auerbach, R.P., & DeRubeis, R.J. (2012). Processes of change in CBT of adolescent depression: Review and recommendations. *Journal of Clinical Child & Adolescent Psychology*, 41, 654–665.

Wilson, G.T. (1996). Manual-based treatments: The clinical application of research findings. *Behavioral Research and Therapy*, 34, 295–314.

# CHAPTER SIX

# How Child CBT Differs from Adult CBT

## WHAT IS KNOWN

CBT was originally developed by Aaron Beck, who focused on challenging cognitive distortions in depressed adults (Beck, 1963). Since then, adult CBT programs have been developed and studied for most mental health problems (Butler, Chapman, Forman, & Beck, 2006). Effect sizes (the average degree of improvement in participants) are largest for anxiety disorders and depression in both adults and children (Butler et al., 2006).

Child CBT was originally developed by adapting adult models to child clients (Kendall, 1993), but difficulties in child CBT can occur when we treat our child clients as "little adults" rather than appreciating their unique therapeutic needs. Turner (2006) has described how different cognitive, behavioral, and family factors may be implicated in the etiology and maintenance of the same disorder for children versus adults. Morris, Hirshfeld-Becker, Henin, and Storch (2004) have described the need for developmentally sensitive assessment of disorder because the conclusions drawn and intervention provided could differ depending on whether or not this is done. Finally, intervention itself must be developmentally sensitive. Hirshfeld-Becker, Micco, Mazursky, Bruett, and Henin (2011) have described CBT adaptations for very young children, and Sauter, Heyne, and Michiel Westenberg (2009) have described CBT approaches that address the unique needs of adolescents.

While the principles of child CBT and adult CBT are the same, the manner in which they are communicated to and applied with the client is quite different. There are differences in the therapeutic experience, the role of the family and other environmental factors (see Chapter 8), the client's cognitive level, and motivational factors. Awareness of these differences is fundamental to child CBT and will therefore be the focus of this chapter.

## PUTTING WHAT WE KNOW TO WORK

### The Therapy Experience from a Child's Point of View

To understand differences between child CBT and adult CBT, it may help to contrast the experiences of a child client with those of an adult client. An adult CBT client usually comes to see you voluntarily because he or she is experiencing symptoms that are distressing and hopes that you will provide relief from that distress. The client understands that he or she will spend time talking with you, that new skills will be learned, and that he or she will have to change some old patterns of thinking and behaving outside the sessions in order to get better.

The child CBT client, by contrast, comes to see you because his or her parents have insisted upon it. The child may or may not know why this has happened, and may even assume that it is some sort of punishment for being "bad." Almost always, the child does not know any other children who see a therapist and therefore assumes that seeing a therapist means he or she is different from other children in a negative way. The child has little idea what to expect from you or what you will expect from him or her, causing anxiety about seeing you. The child may or may not report distressing symptoms, and may or may not understand that thoughts, feelings, and behaviors are connected.

When contrasting these experiences, it becomes obvious that children in CBT need extra time to learn to trust the therapist and to understand why they are being seen. The reasons for the therapy and how it is supposed to help need to be spelled out (see Chapter 4), and the role of the parents in therapy needs to be clarified. Also ask about other significant adults that have frequent contact with the child (teachers, relatives that live in the home or often look after the child, sports coaches, and so forth), and spell out their involvement. If they do not want to be involved, ask to talk to them once to provide information about coping skills the child will be learning, address any concerns they have, and ensure that their behavior toward the child generally facilitates (or at least does not impede) the use of new coping skills.

Older children and adolescents may want some say in how much or how little their parents know about what happens in therapy. It is helpful to tell them that you will preserve confidentiality "except if the situation is dangerous." It makes sense to negotiate some contact between parents and therapist, however, as long as the young person is living at home. Their perspective on the young person's difficulties and strengths can be invaluable, and their reactions to new behaviors learned in CBT can either help or hinder progress. In younger children, treatment expectations need to be described very simply, and high parental involvement is usually assumed. These issues are discussed further in the chapter on diverse families (Chapter 8).

Developing the child's trust in the therapist may take time, but can be facilitated in several ways. Examples include sitting beside (rather than opposite) the child, taking an interest in the child's world, starting your work together by focusing on issues relevant to the child, and consistently praising even minimal child participation in the interaction. Sometimes, it can also be helpful to offer limited self-disclosure (for example, by providing an example of how you dealt with a fairly generic anxious situation such as giving a presentation), as long as this is done for the child's benefit (rather than your own), and to normalize certain symptoms by pointing out that you have met other children who experience them as well (without disclosing details about those clients, of course). Probing for possible negative attitudes toward therapy either in the child or in the child's peer group can also foster trust and avert problems later. For example, you can say to the child, "Some kids think it's weird to come to a place like this. Do you think so? Do your friends think so?"

In adolescents, additional time may be needed to discuss treatment goals and their relevance to the young person's life in order to enhance client motivation. Therapists may also tailor their language, materials, activities, and tempo to suit the adolescent in order to enhance engagement in treatment (Sauter et al., 2009). Parents can sometimes enhance motivation through praise or offering an extra privilege for working hard in treatment, but emphasis is placed on the client's personal motivation and on self-reward for a job well done. Motivational interviewing is helpful as a prelude to CBT in some adolescents who are highly ambivalent about treatment (Baer & Peterson, 2002).

Providing clear expectations or "ground rules" for your interaction with the child can be reassuring as well. The child needs to know what the goals of therapy are, how your time together will be structured to achieve those goals, what behaviors will or will not be tolerated in therapy, and consequences for breaking the rules. These rules are experienced as reassuring by most children. In fact, they sometimes express relief at hearing them. "You mean that's all I have to do?" remarked one anxious child.

Furthermore, friendly overtures toward the child without such clear limits usually do not result in the structured, focused, skill-building sessions needed to do CBT. For example, some children or teens enjoy talking about events in their lives and having an attentive listener, but do not realize that this activity does not constitute therapy. When redirected to the task at hand, they may become sullen or withdrawn. Rather than considering the child oppositional, it is often helpful to provide a frank explanation of the nature of therapeutic change. You might say, "I know this exercise is not as much fun as just talking, but it's important work that will help you handle things better in the long run. We'll talk about other things at the end if there's time left over. Let's see if we can get through it!" Then, keep your word about the time to talk about "other things" at the end! It is usually better to err on the side of formality in the first session or two. You can then become less formal as you get to know the child if that is your therapeutic style. Trying to increase formality later is rarely successful.

Ground rules are equally or more important in group CBT. In this case, the group is often asked to participate in making the rules and designing consequences for rule-breaking. "Wait for someone else to finish before you talk," "No putting down other people's ideas," and "No telling people outside the group what someone else in the group said" are common examples of child group rules. Consequences for rule-breaking may need to be modified by the group therapist, because children sometimes design more harsh penalties than an adult would.

## Cognitive Differences between Children and Adults

Developmental texts often spell out different cognitive abilities corresponding to different ages. According to these texts, the ability to "think about one's thinking" that is central to most cognitive strategies does not develop until age 11 or 12, yet children much younger than this can benefit from CBT. How does this happen? One rather radical idea is that cognitive strategies are not a key ingredient for successful CBT in children, and they benefit from some other aspect of therapy (for example, behavior modification or receiving attention from a concerned adult). Alternatively, perhaps cognitive strategies are essential, but not all children follow the textbooks.

One helpful way to reconcile these disparate ideas is shown in Figure 6.1. The figure provides a guide to what strategies should be emphasized in child CBT. The child's age is on the horizontal axis, and level of functioning is on the vertical axis. Children who are young and low functioning (very impaired by their symptoms) are clearly in the "behavioral" triangle, while older adolescents who are high functioning are in the "cognitive" triangle, and other children are in between. "Behavioral intervention" usually implies the use of reinforcement strategies and therefore, of necessity, a high degree of parental involvement. Thus, a preschooler with severe separation anxiety who cannot leave his mother's side for even a

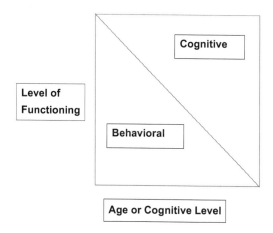

FIGURE 6.1   Treatment emphasis in child CBT.

few moments requires a mainly behavioral, parent-focused intervention. A high school student who is successful and popular but worries excessively about examinations requires a mainly cognitive intervention with limited parental involvement. The proportion of cognitive to behavioral strategies used depends on where your client falls on the graph in Figure 6.1.

Suppose your client is relatively high functioning but young or cognitively delayed. In this case, you will use some cognitive strategies, but they will be far simpler than the ones used in adults. Manuals that are focused on elementary school children versus adolescents are already widely used, but those for very young children (younger than age seven) are still being studied, so they are less widely available. Many child manuals contain simplified cognitive strategies, but the following list highlights some common ones:

- Take extra time to teach the child feeling recognition, especially recognition of his or her own feelings (versus others' feelings).
- Make recognizing and sharing feelings with helpful adults a treatment goal, because it often reduces acting out in response to unrecognized or unacknowledged feelings.
- Label the emotional symptoms, and make them concrete (also called "externalization") by, for example, encouraging the child to defend against "thought bullies," "snowball thoughts" (for catastrophic thinking), or "black cloud thoughts" (for negative thinking). Similarly, not letting the symptoms control one's life can be concretized as "controlling more territory than the problem" (as in March & Mulle, 1998) on childhood obsessive compulsive disorder).

- Rate feelings on a scale of 1 to 10 rather than 1 to 100, or in the very young child, use pictorial or analogue scales to rate feelings (for example, the Koala Fear Questionnaire, Muris et al., 2003; Mood Assessment via Animated Characters, Manassis et al., 2013).

- If the child cannot generate adaptive thoughts, provide some, and ask the child to choose which one(s) ring true to him or her.

- Repeat adaptive thoughts that are meaningful to the child, and use them for several situations. Some children use the same coping thoughts repeatedly almost like a mantra (for example, "I can do it" or "I've done it before so I can do it again"), rather than evaluating the evidence as adults or adolescents do.

- Use "cheat cards" (cards with key coping strategies printed or drawn on them, to be kept in the child's pocket for daytime fears or on the bedside table for nighttime fears) and other concrete reminders to help the child remember and implement the new strategies.

- Use superheroes or other brave characters to stimulate adaptive thinking (for example, "What would [child's favorite superhero] say to himself?" "What would [child's favorite brave character] do?").

- Remember that all adaptive strategies break down into "What can you say to yourself that would help?" and "What can you do that would help?"

- Do not insist on accurate spelling or grammar, and read or scribe for the child if needed. If writing is very aversive (for example, due to negative school experiences or fine motor problems), assign exercises that can be done orally, both in session and between sessions.

- If writing exercises down works, do not use more than four columns (situation, thought, feeling, behavior), and use fewer columns for younger children.

- Emphasize helpful actions rather than thoughts in the very young child. Planning ahead for difficult situations or doing relaxation strategies are common examples. The latter can be as simple as slow "balloon breathing" that uses the diaphragm. "Pretend to squeeze a lemon, then let it go" or "make your arms as limp as cooked spaghetti" are simple prompts for muscle relaxation.

Another alternative for children with cognitive limitations is the use of less verbal, imagery-based modules such as those described later in this book.

The manner of communicating cognitive strategies also varies with age. In very young children, these are often communicated using puppets or play materials. This approach should not be confused with unstructured play therapy, however, as play materials are used in a directive manner to teach specific concepts when used in CBT. In young school-aged children, strategies are communicated verbally but with little emphasis on reading or writing. Adaptive thoughts are usually provided by the therapist, and the child selects those that seem helpful. In older school-aged children, adaptive thoughts are elicited using leading questions and can then be noted by the child or therapist. As mentioned above, concrete materials such as cue cards are often used in this age group to facilitate generalization of strategies across different situations. In adolescents, the ability to 'think about thinking' is more fully developed than in younger children. Therefore, the client can reflect upon his or her thinking errors or cognitive distortions, and use this exercise to generate adaptive thoughts. In older adolescents, certain maladaptive thinking patterns may be habitual, so the therapist may need to challenge these patterns or beliefs in addition to addressing specific thoughts.

What if your client is low-functioning but clever? Vicky, at the beginning of the book, is an example of such a client. Sometimes, these clients can benefit from cognitive work in conjunction with behavior modification. Feeling that someone is listening to their point of view and addressing their concerns makes the behavioral change more palatable. It may also help to involve two therapists (if available): One to encourage the child and work with her on developing coping strategies (the "good cop," from her point of view) and the other to work with the parents and other adults to ensure firm, consistent behavior management (the "bad cop," from her point of view). With good communication between therapists, this approach can sometimes reduce resistance to change in both the child and family. Alternatively, meet separately with parent and child, focusing more on behavioral strategies with the parent and cognitive strategies with the child. If the client's motivation is doubtful, however, then prioritize behavioral work. Some of these youth appear to be cooperating by talking to a therapist, but in the absence of behavioral change the benefits of "talk therapy" are minimal.

### Getting Children to Use What They Learn (Encouragement to Practice)

Regardless of age or type of psychopathology, people are more likely to practice what they learn from someone under certain conditions. These conditions require even more emphasis when working with children than adults, however, because (as mentioned earlier) the therapeutic relationship between child and therapist is often somewhat involuntary. They include therapist characteristics that children like and respect, strategies to facilitate learning, and strategies to improve motivation. I briefly highlight key ones here, recognizing that some (but not all) manuals do include more detailed descriptions of each.

Some positive therapist characteristics are intrinsic to CBT. Being transparent about what one is thinking about the child's difficulties is important, because it facilitates joint problem-solving, makes the therapist seem friendlier and less mysterious, and reassures the child that the therapist is not hiding important information from him or her. Focusing on what works or is based on evidence is important too. Not only is this approach basic to CBT, but it also makes the therapist seem more objective and less judgmental to the child. This is especially important when working with children who have been shamed or criticized by adults. The therapist who models key coping strategies is usually respected for having shared some of the child's difficult experiences and overcome them. Going into some difficult situations with the child before expecting the child to do this alone also increases therapeutic trust, as well as being a helpful aspect of graded exposure. Having clear rules and expectations has already been discussed in Chapter 4.

Other positive therapist characteristics are helpful regardless of one's theoretical orientation. These include following up with the child on anything one commits to, respecting the child's privacy unless it must be breached due to safety concerns, listening to and addressing serious concerns in the child's life (for example, mental illness in another family member) even when this is not the main focus of therapy, and being courteous and respectful when with the child. In addition, being familiar with current cultural trends that affect the child demonstrates the therapist's interest in the child's world and lends credibility to the therapist. For example, know what websites are frequented by children of his or her age, or what musical groups are currently popular in his or her peer group. For many children, it is also reassuring if the therapist is not too gullible. If it appears a youngster is trying to be deceptive or bend the rules, confront this issue and set appropriate limits. Even though CBT is a collaborative approach, the therapist is still the adult in the interaction and, as such, should be willing to enforce societal norms.

Strategies that facilitate learning in CBT vary depending on the child's degree of confidence or proficiency with handling a particular situation. If the situation is new to the child, start by modeling coping behavior, and encourage parents to do the same. If the child has had some exposure to the situation but lacks confidence, empathic encouragement is often helpful. This consists of a combination of validating the child's experience (for example, "I know this must be hard for you because . . . ") while expressing genuine confidence that the child can master the situation. If the child has had some exposure to the situation but is still struggling with the skills to manage it, try preparing for the situation using Socratic questions such as

"What could you say to yourself to feel better about this?" or "What could you do to handle this better?" Finally, if the child clearly has the skills to manage the situation but is reluctant to apply them, sometimes restricting the child's alternatives in the situation works best. For example, if a child can cope at school most of the time but sometimes calls a parent hoping to be taken home, the parent can tell the child that brief reassurance will usually be provided with calls, and early pick-up will only be considered if there are three or more calls in a day. As most schools do not allow in-class use of cellphones, this would involve leaving class three times, which most children would find embarrassing or at least inconvenient. Chances are, the child would try to cope rather than doing this.

Strategies to improve motivation are based on the "A.B.C. rule" provided in many texts: antecedents, behavior, consequences. Examining antecedents allows one to anticipate situations where a behavior is likely to occur and plan accordingly. For example, if providing prior warnings allows a child who tantrums in response to transitions to anticipate the transition and handle it better, provide them.

Positive and negative consequences allow one to (respectively) increase and decrease repetition of the behavior subsequently. Child CBT programs generally emphasize positive consequences, not because CBT therapists are really nice people (although we may like to think we are), but because negative consequences often draw undue attention to the behavior, thus inadvertently reinforcing it. "Praise what you like; ignore what you do not like" is thus a good rule of thumb.

Both parents and therapists can be involved in providing positive consequences, and involving both is often seen as more meaningful from the child's perspective than involving only one or the other. In therapy, every tiny effort is reinforced in an age-appropriate manner. Praise is used almost universally, and tangible reinforcements may include stars and stickers in younger children and talking time or game time in older children. In withdrawn children, sometimes even making eye contact is praised.

At home, parents can often identify what reinforcements motivate their child. If not, suggest ones that are similar to those used in therapy and beware of jealous siblings who may also need some recognition for a job well done (usually in a different area from that the client is working on). Small, frequent reinforcements that are only provided after the child attempts the desired behavior are usually more effective than lavish gifts that are either not clearly linked to behavior, or promised at some distant future date. Given young children's limited time perspective, a reward that cannot be earned in a week is often meaningless.

If the child says something that is clearly wrong during the session (for example, labeling a thought as a feeling or vice versa), be positive about the child's effort to answer (for example, "good try!") and then provide the correct response. This is especially important in perfectionistic children, who sometimes become overly preoccupied with getting answers right. "Brainstorming," where as many answers as possible are generated regardless of accuracy, is sometimes a useful addition for this group. Self-conscious children are another special group. These children may be embarrassed by praise, so simply acknowledging their work may be more helpful than lavish congratulations.

Finally, encourage children to provide themselves with positive feedback. Many child-specific manuals include self-reward, because it is helpful for most children and improves the chances they will maintain the new behavior after the therapy concludes. It is important, however, to encourage them to self-reward effort, not just successful outcomes. Some strategies need to be practiced multiple times before they become effective, so it is more encouraging to focus on attempts as well as successes. Self-reward strategies also reassure parents that they will not be expected to find creative or expensive reinforcements for their child indefinitely. Remember that CBT is hard work for the child. Therefore, self-reward is almost always deserved.

## WHAT WE YET NEED TO LEARN

Developmentally sensitive approaches to assessing children and working with them in CBT continue to be developed for various populations, and to be described in texts and review articles. Children whose chronological age, level of emotional development, and/or level of cognitive development do not correspond are among the most challenging to engage and treat with CBT; they merit further study.

## WORKING WITH CHILDREN WORKSHEET

For the child you are currently seeing, think about the child's circumstances and developmental level. Try to put yourself in the child's shoes.

List the interventions described in this chapter that might be helpful with this child:

- To develop trust and rapport.

    1. _____
    _____

    2. _____
    _____

- To address any cultural differences between yourself and the child (look back at the previous chapter if you are unsure).

    1. _____
    _____

    2. _____
    _____

- To establish "ground rules."

    1. _____
    _____

    2. _____
    _____

- To address any cognitive challenges.

    1. _____
    _____

    2. _____
    _____

- To facilitate learning CBT strategies.

    1. _____
    _____

    2. _____
    _____

- To improve motivation during sessions.

    1. _____
    _____

    2. _____
    _____

- To improve motivation at home/between sessions.

    1. _____
    _____

    2. _____
    _____

## CLINICAL CHALLENGE

Consider how you would approach this case:

Bill is a 12-year-old boy with a primary diagnosis of *dysthymic disorder* (chronic, mild depression). He has attended nine CBT sessions with you, using an age-appropriate manual focusing on depressed mood. According to his mother, he was "born unhappy." He was a very colicky baby. As a preschooler, he showed a number of sensory sensitivities (sensitive to noise, hated tags in clothing) and was easily upset by minor changes in his environment or changes in routine. At the time, these traits were thought to be due to anxiety. When he started school, he was teased by other children a couple of times. Although he had friends, he concluded, "Everybody hates me," and dwelled on this idea. If he got a low mark on a test, he labeled himself "stupid," but also accused his teacher of being unfair. At home, Bill was very resentful of his younger brother George. He angrily stormed off to his room whenever his parents said a kind word to George and often accused them of being unfair. Despite his chronic unhappiness, Bill ate and slept regularly, followed the house rules, had some goals for himself, had never been suicidal, and did not meet criteria for *major depression*.

In CBT, Bill seemed like the model client. He participated in sessions and seemed eager to learn and practice his strategies. He even offered to teach other children what he had learned. His only complaint was that his therapist occasionally deviated from what was written in the manual, and "he shouldn't do that." Outside of therapy, none of Bill's negative statements or negative behavior seemed to change.

1. What environmental factors might be interfering with Bill's progress in therapy, and how would you address these?

2. What cognitive factors might be interfering with Bill's progress in therapy, and how would you address these?

3. What aspects of the therapy itself might be hampering progress, and how would you address these?

## REFERENCES

Baer, J.S., & Peterson, P.L. (2002). Motivational interviewing with adolescents and young adults. In Miller, W.R. & Rollnick, S. (Eds.) *Motivational interviewing: Preparing people for change*. New York: Guilford Press, pp. 320–332.

Beck, A.T. (1963). Thinking and depression: I. Idiosyncratic content and cognitive distortions. *Archives of General Psychiatry, 9,* 324–333.

Butler, A.C., Chapman, J.E., Forman, E.M., & Beck, A.T. (2006). The empirical status of cognitive-behavioral therapy: A review of meta-analyses. *Clinical Psychology Review, 26,* 17–31.

Hirshfeld-Becker, D.R., Micco, J.A., Mazursky, H., Bruett, L., & Henin, A. (2011). Applying cognitive-behavioral therapy for anxiety to the younger child. *Child and Adolescent Psychiatric Clinics of North America*, 20, 349–368.

Kendall, P. (1993). Guiding theory for therapy with children and adolescents. In P. Kendall (Ed.), *Child and adolescent therapy: Cognitive behavioral procedures, Fourth edition*. New York: Guilford Press, pp. 3–26.

Manassis, K., Mendlowitz, S., Dupuis, A., Kreindler, D., Lumsden, C., Monga, S., et al. (2013). Mood assessment via animated characters: An instrument to access and evaluate emotions in young children. *Open Journal of Psychiatry*, 3(1A): 149–157.

March, J., & Mulle, K. (1998). *OCD in children and adolescents: A cognitive- behavioral treatment manual*. New York: Guilford Press.

Morris, T.L., Hirshfeld-Becker, D.R., Henin, A., & Storch, E.A. (2004). Developmentally sensitive assessment of social anxiety. *Cognitive Behavioral Practice*, 11, 13–28.

Muris, P., Meesters, C., Mayer, B., Bogie, N., Luijten, M., Geebelen, E., et al. (2003). The Koala Fear Questionnaire: A standardized self-report scale for fears and fearfulness in pre-school and primary school children. *Behavioral Research and Therapy*, 41, 597–617.

Sauter, F.M., Heyne, D., & Michiel Westenberg, P. (2009). Cognitive behavior therapy for anxious adolescents: Developmental influences on treatment design and delivery. *Clinical Child and Family Psychology Review*, 12, 310–335.

Turner, C.M. (2006). Cognitive-behavioral theory and therapy for obsessive-compulsive disorder in children and adolescents: Current status and future directions. *Clinical Psychology Review*, 26, 912–938.

# CHAPTER SEVEN

# Working with Diverse Children

This chapter provides tips on doing CBT with children who, for a variety of reasons, may merit special consideration. Comorbid conditions, particularly externalizing comorbidity, extreme withdrawal, cultural differences, and reality-based challenges, will all be considered.

## WHAT IS KNOWN

Comorbidity occurs when a child meets criteria for multiple diagnoses. Treating a child who has more than one internalizing disorder (for example, social phobia and depression; separation anxiety and generalized anxiety) is common and can be readily done by doing a thorough assessment and then prioritizing the problems (Manassis & Monga, 2001; also see Chapter 3). Treating a child with both an internalizing and an externalizing disorder (for example, anxiety disorder and attention deficit hyperactivity disorder) can be more challenging. Research findings regarding comorbidity are inconsistent, with some finding no effect on outcomes, and others finding lower diagnostic remission in comorbid cases (Kendall, Brady, & Verduin, 2001; Liber et al., 2010), but children with comorbidity in research settings may differ from those seen in community practice. Community practitioners I have supervised generally report more difficulty treating comorbid cases than those with a single diagnosis.

Comorbid oppositional behaviors can be addressed by including behavior management strategies when working with parents of children in CBT (Mendlowitz et al., 1999). Such behaviors may also be secondary to the main disorder (for example, defiance of parents in order to be allowed to withdraw from the family in depression; oppositional behavior in response to being asked to enter feared situations in anxiety). Treatment for a conduct disorder usually needs to be prioritized before pursuing CBT for anxiety or depression, given the disruptive effects of this disorder on the youth and others.

Anxiety disorders and attention deficit hyperactivity disorder (ADHD) co-occur frequently, and usually these children benefit from a combination of medication and behavioral or cognitive-behavioral treatment (Manassis, 2007). Children with this comorbidity often have difficulties with tasks that require "working memory" (the ability to simultaneously store and manipulate information) (Manassis, Tannock, Young, & Francis-John, 2007), and many verbal CBT strategies do require this ability. CBT approaches that require less working memory, such as the imagery-based modules at the end of this book, may be considered in this population. Given their distractibility, children with comorbid ADHD may also benefit more from individual than group treatment.

Extremely withdrawn children can be difficult to engage in therapy. Positively reinforcing every minor sign of engagement (for example, reinforcing eye contact with the therapist), doing exercises with or for the child and reinforcing "tagging along with the therapist," and increasing the involvement of parents or peers in therapy have all been suggested (Manassis & Young, 2001). Some withdrawn children fear criticism, so setting up "win–win" situations in therapy (situations where the child can be positively reinforced regardless of response) and ignoring mistakes can be helpful. A playful approach, with decreased emphasis on results and rewards, can be helpful for some withdrawn, self-conscious children.

A special case of withdrawal occurs in the child who is selectively mute. These children fail to speak in certain settings due to social anxiety and sometimes have language deficits or other developmental difficulties as well (Manassis, Tannock, McInnes, et al., 2007). Serotonin-specific medications are often helpful in combination with behavioral or cognitive-behavioral interventions (Manassis & Tannock, 2008). Behavioral intervention that involves the parents and school has been found helpful, and one version of this is well described in a book by McHolm, Cunningham, Vanier, and Rapee (2005). Further therapeutic ideas can be found in the paper by McInnes and Manassis (2005).

Special consideration is also needed when working with children whose mother tongue differs from that of the therapist, or who come from cultural backgrounds with healing traditions that differ from typical North American practice. Linguistic differences have been examined largely in relation to treating refugee children who have experienced trauma. Ehntholt and

Yule (2006) describe this literature, highlighting the use of interpreters; medico-legal report writing for families; and a comprehensive, culturally sensitive approach.

Ethnic minority status can adversely affect treatment outcome (Weersing & Weisz, 2002), yet when specific cultural groups are targeted in CBT studies, outcomes are generally positive (Ginsburg, Becker, Drazdowski, & Tein, 2012; Miller et al., 2011). These findings suggest that adapting CBT for cultural differences is beneficial. For example, manuals can be adapted to communicate CBT principles in culturally relevant ways. Alternatively, therapists who belong to specific cultural groups can, with supervision, develop culture-specific adaptations while ensuring treatment fidelity (Nowrouzi, Manassis, Jones, Bobinski, & Mushquash, 2015). Ignoring cultural and linguistic differences is generally not helpful.

Reality-based challenges in CBT occur when the child's negative feelings are not entirely based on cognitive distortions, but have some basis in reality. An extreme example of this occurs in posttraumatic stress disorder, and there are child CBT protocols specific to this condition (Cohen, Mannarino, & Deblinger, 2006; Scheeringa et al., 2007; Smith et al., 2007). They generally emphasize reexperiencing the traumatic event in imagination during therapy sessions (called "imaginal exposure") to allow cognitive and emotional processing of what happened, as well as overcoming avoidance of situations the child associates with the trauma. Addressing parental traumatic symptoms is important to treatment success, especially in younger children (Scheeringa et al., 2007).

Reality-based challenges also occur in children who experience life-threatening allergic conditions (called "anaphylaxis"), asthma, or other painful or frightening medical conditions. Allergic and asthmatic conditions have a higher association with childhood anxiety disorders than expected by chance (Papneja & Manassis, 2006). It is unclear whether this is due to common biological substrates or the unpredictable nature of these conditions provoking anxiety. Fostering calm, sensible management of both the medical condition and the anxiety in these cases requires sensitivity to the medical concerns and intervention with the family and school as well as the child (Monga & Manassis, 2006). Cognitive-behavioral protocols for pain have been developed for children (Sanders, Shepherd, Cleghorn, & Woolford, 1994), and some CBT strategies have been used to help children cope with chronic illnesses such as diabetes, cancer, inflammatory bowel disease, and sickle cell disease (Thompson, Delaney, Flores, & Szigethy, 2011). Developing a child's sense of mastery over the upsetting feelings in CBT (as opposed to challenging the validity of frightened/depressed thinking) is one potentially helpful approach, and is emphasized in the modules at the end of this book.

## PUTTING WHAT WE KNOW TO WORK

### The Disruptive Child

Wendy was an 11-year-old girl with a long history of inattentive behavior and school difficulties. She was also very clingy with her mother, had never fallen asleep without her mother at her side, had tantrums in the morning when it was time to go to the school bus, and reported numerous worries about her health and her family's well-being. She had never been previously assessed. She was seen by a psychiatrist who prescribed stimulant medication and referred her for CBT. Unfortunately, she was still highly inattentive despite the stimulants and dismantled the assessing therapist's office furniture while he talked to her mother. She often interrupted the adults' conversation. Wendy and her mother arrived for the appointment a half hour late, because Wendy's mother had forgotten that her daughter's school had a track and field meet at another school that day. Thus, she had to drive to two schools to retrieve her daughter and bring her to the therapist. Wendy's father suffered from an anxiety disorder, and her brother had been treated successfully for ADHD with the same stimulant Wendy was taking. Upon meeting Wendy I wondered: How likely was she to succeed in CBT?

Before addressing CBT-specific issues relevant to Wendy, it is worth examining factors that may be contributing to her presentation. First, there is clearly a family history of both anxiety (father) and ADHD (brother, possibly mother) in this case, so Wendy is genetically predisposed to both. Her family history may also affect therapeutic progress. For example, her mother's disorganization may impact Wendy's attendance at therapy appointments, and the presence of two ADHD children in the family will likely result in a somewhat chaotic home environment. Therefore, the therapist may need to assist this family in organizing themselves to support Wendy's attendance and practice of coping strategies between sessions (see next chapter). Good communication between professionals will also be important, because disorganized families are often unable to facilitate this on their children's behalf. Like many children with a combined presentation of anxiety and ADHD, Wendy does not respond as readily to stimulants as a child with ADHD alone. It is worth talking to the prescribing physician, however, because dosage adjustments and timing of doses may improve the ability to focus in therapy. For example, taking a dose of short-acting stimulant medication an hour before a therapy appointment is helpful in some children. Combined anxiety and ADHD is also often associated with underlying learning difficulties. These should be investigated through a psycho-educational assessment to optimize Wendy's academic progress. If Wendy's behavior is disruptive at school, ongoing problems there may affect everyone's motivation to address the anxiety symptoms. Externalizing behaviors often need to be contained first (using medication, behavior modification, or both) in order to allow consistent work on internalizing problems in CBT.

Assuming that all of these issues have been addressed, the therapist is still left with the challenge of working with a rather inattentive child. Sometimes, these children are also oppositional, so attention to the "ground rules" spelled out in the previous chapter is important. Having "no touch" zones in the office is often helpful. For example, I usually start by making it clear that my computer is off limits.

Some of these children, however, are truly distressed and eager to learn, but really struggle to stay on track in CBT. A single question often elicits a number of interesting stories, which are not necessarily directly relevant to the answer. Frequent redirection by the therapist is needed, but should be done gently with an empathic understanding of the child's difficulty. Pointing to the relevant question in the manual is sometimes even more effective than verbal redirection in refocusing the child. The promise of talking time at the end when the material has been covered is often very motivating. A chance to explore an interesting object or book in the office at the end can be similarly reinforcing. Breaks may be needed during the session, consistent with the child's short attention span.

Finally, problems with language and working memory in this population sometimes interfere with grasping CBT concepts. Cognitive restructuring (finding alternative, adaptive thoughts to replace maladaptive, distressing ones) is particularly challenging for children with limited verbal working memory. In these children, one must either simplify the verbal components of CBT (for example, focusing on adaptive thoughts only, without identifying and challenging maladaptive ones) or try less verbal alternatives such as the imagery-based modules in this book.

## Engaging the Withdrawn Child: Depression

Paul had always been short compared to other boys his age, but did well academically and was helpful to others and well liked. His mother had suffered from a mood disorder in the past, and his maternal grandfather had committed suicide. As he entered puberty, Paul's self-esteem began to plummet. Other boys no longer wanted to be seen with "the shrimp," so his only remaining friends were girls. This fact resulted in further name-calling, and Paul increasingly became the subject of class jokes. Paul also began to worry about what he would do with his life in the future and described feeling "weird" compared to others his age. He had difficulty motivating himself to do school work, and his grades began to drop. When he was cut from the soccer team, Paul went home to his room and refused to come out. He still ate food that was brought to him and played computer games, but did very little else. His parents could not convince him to see a doctor or therapist. He responded to their questions with a noncommittal shoulder shrug and did not make eye contact. They worried about his safety.

Like many depressed teens, Paul has a number of factors that may be contributing to his vulnerability to a mood disorder. Therefore, before focusing on the question of how to engage this young man in CBT, it is important to identify and address as many of these factors as possible. A physical examination by a pediatrician is important to rule out medical causes for both the short stature and the mood disorder. A thyroid condition, for example, could contribute to both. A screen for drug use may also be helpful, given Paul's age and the tendency for some teens to turn to such substances when desperate to improve their low mood. Incidentally, a positive finding would not rule out the possibility of CBT, but would suggest addressing substance abuse in addition to addressing depression. Paul may also be less resistant to seeing a doctor who is focusing on physical symptoms rather than emotional ones. Assuming physical problems are ruled out, the physician could then begin to consider with Paul and his parents whether or not to pursue antidepressant medication in addition to therapy.

The history of depression in Paul's mother suggests a closer look at his developmental history and the family dynamics. If his mother was depressed when Paul was an infant or toddler, for example, mother–child attachment may have been adversely affected, and this may contribute to his depressive vulnerability. If he was older at the time, role reversal (looking after his mother rather than having her look after him) or other unhealthy dynamics may have developed. Even if family relationships are optimal, Paul's parents may need some guidance and education about the nature of teen depression and how to support their son's recovery (see *Helping Your Teenager Beat Depression*, Manassis & Levac, 2004).

The current peer problems beg the question: Did this young man ever have good friendships or positive experiences with peers? If he did, it is worth resuming these friendships or activities if possible. If not, finding at least one activity that includes a peer or sibling may be helpful in overcoming depressive withdrawal. Noncompetitive activities are usually best when the young person is in the midst of a depressive episode, because difficulties with attention and energy stemming from depression will prevent most teens from doing their best. Keep the focus on activity (which can naturally improve mood) and possible enjoyment, even if the teen does not acknowledge this.

Having addressed possible contributing factors and encouraged Paul and his family to discuss antidepressant medication with their physician, the therapist's next challenge is to actually meet with Paul. Younger teens often respond to parental encouragement or parental accompaniment to the office, so these should definitely be tried. Older teens usually respond less to these efforts. Initiating contact by telephone or e-mail is sometimes a helpful place to start. This allows an introduction to the therapist at a distance, which feels less threatening to some teens. Home visits are occasionally helpful, although they may also create the mistaken impression that the therapist is functioning as an auxiliary parent. Providing information ahead of time about depression and about the nature of therapy is often reassuring. Finally, contracting for a few sessions is sometimes more helpful than expecting the young person to commit to a full course of therapy. This gives the teen a chance to try out what therapy is like and the reassurance that there is a way out if he or she is uncomfortable.

Assuming you can get Paul into the office, the next challenge is getting him to talk. Remember the comments in the previous chapter about children's essentially involuntary status, and act accordingly to gradually build trust. Provide a clear rationale for how CBT is supposed to work, because this shows that you respect his intelligence and need his participation. Next, see if you can find a personal reason for him to participate. Find out which symptoms are most distressing or bothersome for Paul, because he is likely to be most motivated to work on those. If he claims to not want to change anything, suggest that working on one or two symptoms may reduce his parents' worries, and thus get his parents to stop bothering him. Most teens agree that reducing parental nagging (or teacher nagging, or some other person bothering them) is worthwhile. Some very resistant children and teens are even encouraged by the prospect of not having to see the therapist anymore if they demonstrate progress!

One further source of resistance can be the disorder itself: Depression may create a hopeless belief that effort in therapy is not worthwhile because nothing can possibly change or improve. Challenge this belief by pointing to evidence that things are already changing or improving very slightly. For example, the young person has taken the risk of meeting a new person (usually, for the first time in a long while) by seeing you. This demonstrates courage and is therefore a sign of increasing psychological strength. Even getting out of bed that day, if this has been difficult, can be construed as a sign of progress. Then, suggest that therapy will build on this slight progress until there is momentum toward more dramatic change. If the young person does not respond to these ideas, challenge the negativity by asking gently if his statements are true "all the time, 100%," and see if he can think of even a single exception to the rule. Engaging the "thinking brain" (rather than the "emotional brain") in this way sometimes lightens the mood of the conversation, and leads naturally into discussing CBT strategies.

## Engaging the Withdrawn Child: Anxiety

Suppose you were seeing a child who was withdrawn for a different reason: lack of confidence. Positive reinforcement for every slight effort to participate is discussed below, and certainly this is worthwhile. What if the child is so fearful of a "wrong" answer, however, that no answers are provided? First, make it clear there are no wrong answers. Every person is different and has different ideas. All of those ideas count (one person's ideas are not necessarily more valid than another person's ideas), and all can be tested out to see which ones work. Thus, the more ideas are generated, the better. Most questions have several "right" answers, and the therapist does not necessarily know them all. In fact, one of the best forms of positive reinforcement in CBT is for the therapist to sincerely say to the child, "I never thought of that!"

Another way to encourage participation is "talking in the third person." Here, you ask the child, "Suppose you were giving a friend advice about how to handle this situation. What would you say?" Alternatively, if the child will not volunteer situations, ask, "What are some things your friends get nervous (or worried, or sad, and so forth) about?" Talking about friends involves less direct self-disclosure than talking in the first person and so is experienced as less threatening by the child. For the same reason, some children find it helpful to apply coping strategies to hypothetical situations suggested by the therapist, rather than ones that are really happening in their lives. "Giving a friend advice" is also an example of another helpful strategy: putting the child in the role of teacher. Many children who lack confidence blossom with this approach.

"Leading the witness" by providing Socratic questions or multiple-choice questions is also engaging and anxiety-reducing for the child who lacks confidence. Taking it a step further, I sometimes say, "You already know how to cope with this. I'm just helping you focus more on how you do it." It is also sometimes helpful to point out that anxious people handle truly dangerous situations very well, just not the anticipation of them. Thus, you can tell the child, "If you focus on what to do now, you'll surprise yourself with how well you deal with the future."

Finally, the most extreme version of anxious withdrawal is found in children who are selectively mute. These children do not speak in certain social situations, often including the therapy situation, because of extreme social anxiety and possibly other factors (see references on selective mutism). Thus, their silence does not represent defiance but rather an avoidant response to the fear of social criticism. People around the child may need to be advised of this, in order to decrease their frustration with the behavior. Selectively mute children usually need behavioral intervention at home and school in addition to therapy, in order to facilitate speech, and sometimes benefit from antidepressant medications as well. Appropriate parental involvement is very helpful and has been described by McHolm and colleagues (2005).

An approach to these children is described in more detail in the article by McInnes and Manassis (2005), but from the individual therapist's perspective there are a couple of key principles. First, these children are exquisitely self-conscious, so anything that reduces self-consciousness is helpful. Thus, lavish praise can backfire because it heightens self-consciousness, but having the child read out loud or play a character in a game rather than answer questions may help because this reduces self-consciousness. Similarly, short answers that require no self-disclosure (for example, naming the capital city of a country) are easier to elicit than longer answers or answers that require self-disclosure (for example, favorite color or show, questions about feelings). Second, steps toward speech in these children are often incrementally small. Eye contact, whispers, or nonverbal signals in a one-to-one situation are often the first behaviors to be reinforced. Bridging the speaking environment (usually, at home with immediate family) and nonspeaking environments (outside the home, or with unfamiliar people) must also be done in small steps. In general, a shorter duration of mutism and a smaller number of nonspeaking environments are associated with better chances of therapeutic success, but one can still anticipate a year or two of work before speech outside the home becomes more consistent.

### Working with Linguistic and Cultural Differences

Louis, a 12-year-old boy with generalized anxiety, was an avid participant in his CBT group, frequently volunteering answers to questions. When it came to written work, however, Louis procrastinated, excused himself to go to the bathroom, chatted with other group members, and otherwise tried to avoid the task. The therapist started to wonder if Louis might have a learning disability, but then one day Louis exclaimed, "I can't do this stupid English!" Although born in North America, Louis had been schooled entirely in French. He understood English and spoke it fluently, but written English was foreign to him. Upon recognizing this issue, his therapist allowed Louis to do his written CBT exercises in French. Louis became much more cooperative, and everyone in the group learned a little French in addition to learning CBT strategies.

This example illustrates the importance of asking children about their primary language at school as well as at home before starting CBT. Therapy can then be tailored accordingly. Moreover, questions about language should not be limited to recent immigrants to North America. Even minor language difficulties can impact successful treatment. For instance, new

English speakers sometimes mentally translate questions into their mother tongue, formulate an answer, and then translate the answers back into English. This three-step process results in a long response time. Slow responses may cause therapists to underestimate these children's abilities and may limit children's opportunity to participate, especially in groups.

Cultural differences may impact children's receptiveness to CBT content and procedures. It behooves therapists to learn about similarities and differences between CBT ideas and healing practices in a given child's culture. For example, when working with First Nations clients, therapists will find it helpful to explore how the reciprocal relationship among thoughts, feelings, and behaviors is consistent with the Medicine Wheel used in many aboriginal healing traditions. Spirituality is an additional element of the Medicine Wheel, and First Nations children may draw upon this resource to complement CBT strategies. On the other hand, animal symbols used in some CBT manuals (e.g., Coping Cat, Coping Bear, etc.) may need to be re-interpreted or changed, as they may represent different attributes or character traits in different cultures.

Different cultures may also vary in their interpretation of various emotional symptoms. For example, in some Hispanic communities physical symptoms may occur after a frightening event, and be interpreted as Susto or "soul loss" (American Psychiatric Association, 2013). This interpretation may need to be discussed with the family before launching into a CBT program focused on post-traumatic stress disorder. Otherwise, the family may not understand the rationale for this treatment.

Within-cultural differences must also be considered. Carter, Mitchell, and Sbrocco (2012) worked with African Americans in CBT. They described clients on two dimensions: racial identity and level of acculturation to the prevailing culture. Clients high on both dimensions did well in therapy, provided the therapist was able to appreciate their ethnicity. By contrast, clients high on racial identity but low on level of acculturation expressed their symptoms differently (for example, more somatic symptoms and fewer emotional symptoms) and were less trusting of therapists not of the same culture than clients high on level of acculturation. For these low-acculturation clients, taking additional time to learn about cultural differences and expectations was essential to therapeutic engagement and treatment success.

The highly structured, verbal, and individualistic nature of CBT can be problematic when working with children in certain cultural groups. Many cultures emphasize the role of the family and the community in healing to a greater degree than CBT does. In these cultures, having the child consistently attend scheduled appointments, do written exercises, and acquire coping skills that do not necessarily involve his or her family may seem rigid and perhaps incongruous with traditional ways. In some cultures, social disadvantages or historical injustices also undermine trust in the mental health system. For example, in First Nations communities where children were removed from home to attend residential schools, attempts to teach children without involving the community may be viewed with suspicion. Taking extra time to develop a trusting therapeutic relationship with the child and family, facilitating regular attendance (e.g., by providing reminders or assisting with transportation costs), and explaining the rationale for regular sessions are all important in this context. Also consider additional work with the family, including extended family members or community elders if their approval is considered important for healing to occur. De-emphasizing written exercises and learning in natural environments can also be helpful when adapting CBT to First Nations settings, where there are strong narrative traditions and well-being is rooted in the land.

Finally, it is important that children do not feel torn between the values of their culture and those of the therapist, as this may result in either dropping out of therapy or facing serious repercussions at home. In CBT, this situation is most likely to arise in relation to exposure exercises. For instance, cultures vary in the degree of independence allowed children of different ages and different genders, sometimes placing limits on behavioral activation exercises or on exposure to anxiety-provoking situations. Certain OCD-related exposures (e.g., touching bathroom fixtures, interrupting praying rituals) may also be considered inappropriate in some cultures. Discussion of exposure with parents as well as children is likely to reveal these issues, allowing for adaptations of exposure exercises so that everyone can support the child's progress.

In summary, as long as therapy focuses on CBT principles, the manner in which those principles are learned can vary in relation to the child's cultural context. Further discussion on using manuals across cultures is provided in Chapter 5.

## The Realistically Challenged Child

Joe had always had difficulty making friends. He had a nonverbal learning disability that affected his ability to read social cues, making him seem awkward around other children. Nevertheless, he had one or two good buddies every year and did not show anxious or depressive symptoms until fifth grade. That year, he suddenly developed a seizure disorder. These were dramatic, tonic-clonic seizures that many people found frightening to see. They usually happened at home in the early morning. They were infrequent since Joe had started antiseizure medication, but they still occurred occasionally.

Joe had never experienced a seizure at school, but he became preoccupied with the fear of having one there. He thought he could die if this happened, and even if he survived his remaining friends would no longer want to be seen with him. He could not concentrate because every time he experienced a mild headache or felt slightly dizzy, he feared having a seizure and went to the office to call home. Because he often hyperventilated with the anxiety, these symptoms became more frequent. Soon his mother was receiving daily calls. She in turn called the neurologist daily with questions about her son's seizure control. She wondered if she should accompany Joe to school to ensure his safety. His principal wondered whether Joe needed to attend a special school or would benefit from home instruction.

Joe is an example of a child with reality-based challenges that necessitate some modification of traditional CBT approaches for anxiety. Children with other chronic medical conditions are in the same category, particularly if the condition involves a high degree of unpredictability and a low ability to control the physical symptoms. Seizure disorders are a classic example, but the same ideas would apply to childhood asthma, inflammatory bowel disease, juvenile diabetes, juvenile rheumatoid arthritis, and other medical conditions with intermittent exacerbations. Anaphylactic conditions (life-threatening allergic reactions) are becoming increasingly common in children and often result in both realistic fears and undue anxiety (see Monga & Manassis, 2006). Potentially terminal illnesses can pose even greater emotional challenges, as children face the possibility of a foreshortened future in addition to unpredictability and loss of control.

Family reactions can require a modified approach as well. A serious medical diagnosis often triggers parental grief about losing their "normal" child, and a certain degree of overprotective behavior toward an ill child is natural, even if not ideal. Parents often feel as helpless as their children in such circumstances, yet are expected to offer reassurance to them. Anticipatory grief becomes a further family issue in the case of a child with a terminal illness. Interestingly, almost all of these reactions are mirrored in families living in unsafe neighborhoods where children may become victims of crime or (in later years) engage in criminal activity. In this case, everyone in the family is vulnerable to physical harm, but parents often focus on their children's vulnerability more than their own. Each of these topics is described in more detail in the references for this chapter.

The example highlights some common difficulties that may need to be addressed in therapy. First, many children in circumstances similar to Joe's have some preexisting emotional vulnerability. In Joe's case, his social difficulties heighten his anxiety about the seizures. Thus, it is not sufficient to simply address his health-focused fears without addressing the possible reactions of his peers. A separate set of coping strategies may be needed to address the latter issue. Some children in this position also benefit from sharing some medical information with their peers, with an adult present if they desire. Rather than being shunned, they often find their peers respond with sympathy or curiosity.

Second, these children often display an interaction of physical and emotional symptoms, where one exacerbates the other. Physical symptoms are exacerbated by anxiety or mood problems, and this exacerbation further intensifies the anxiety or low mood. Therefore, it is important not to dismiss physical symptoms as "all in the head," nor to dwell on them unduly. The experience of these symptoms is real, regardless of what caused them. Some children can be helped to see the connection between physical and emotional distress, and this should certainly be attempted. For those who cannot see the connection, a pragmatic approach focused on generally coping better is often helpful. In Joe's case, "handling the worries about seizures so that life is OK when the seizures are not happening" is a sensible goal. Arguing about the low probability of seizures at school, or about the psychosomatic nature of the headaches and dizziness, is unlikely to help. To address the hyperventilation, one could suggest, "Some kids feel less dizzy and have fewer headaches when they breathe slowly." There is no need for Joe to admit that he is breathing too fast.

Third, when the child is dealing with unpredictability and limited control, it is usually best not to emphasize probabilities. Thus, for Joe, there is no guarantee that he will ever have perfect seizure control or that he will never have a seizure at school. To try and estimate the odds of these events is therefore not helpful. However, even if Joe cannot control his seizures, he can still control how he responds to the fear of having a seizure. Controlling this fear so he can get on with his life should be the main focus of therapy. The emphasis is on handling his feelings in a more adaptive way, rather than trying to control an uncontrollable reality. The modules in this book contain further ideas on this subject. Of course, if he can do something to improve his seizure control (for example, remembering to take his medication each day) that should be encouraged.

Parents often become anxious in response to the child's anxiety, as Joe's mother did. They may become more protective than is necessary (for example, wanting to accompany Joe to school) and engage in excessive help-seeking behavior (for example, daily calls to the neurologist) to reduce their own sense of helplessness. With guidance, however, they can often contain their own anxieties and model and reinforce more adaptive coping for their children. Therefore, it is well worth spending extra time with these parents to explore, validate, and help them manage feelings about their child's illness. Many appreciate specific advice on how they can help their children cope, because this reduces their own sense of helplessness. For example, parents can reduce children's medical fears by offering simple explanations in response to their children's questions, rather than engaging their children in long discussions of every possible medical scenario whether or not the child has asked about it. Limiting exposure to graphic medical images on television programs or websites is usually helpful as well. Working with the child on safety plans that reduce risk or improve coping is another helpful parenting strategy. As parent and child both begin to cope better, many children are able to return to an age-appropriate level of independence or as close to it as the medical condition allows.

Finally, school personnel and other people outside the family are often frightened by medical illness as well. We all tend to avoid what we fear, so the reaction of Joe's principal (wanting to transfer him out of the school) is not unusual. In fact, I have sometimes encountered schools that had excellent programs for managing students with aggressive behavior, but had no consistent approach for managing highly anxious children or children with medical illnesses. Although it takes extra time, it is well worth organizing a case conference about the child with key staff. Here, one can offer education about the student's condition, empathy for the school's position, advice on managing specific behaviors (for example, having a quiet place for Joe to calm down when hyperventilating and limiting his calls to his mother), and (most reassuring for school staff) one's contact number in the event of further difficulties.

## WHAT WE YET NEED TO LEARN

Cognitive-behavioral treatments for children with comorbidity, extreme withdrawal, cultural differences, and reality-based challenges all merit further development and evaluation. Research on helping children cope with frightening medical procedures, uncertain medical prognoses, and changes in self-image associated with illness or disability is particularly scant.

## DIVERSE CHILDREN WORKSHEET

Does the child you are seeing show any externalizing problems, extreme withdrawal, cultural/linguistic differences, or reality-based challenges that might affect therapy? If so, list these and list ideas from this chapter that might help.

- Externalizing problem(s): _____

  Helpful ideas:

  1. _____
  _____

  2. _____
  _____

  3. _____
  _____

- Withdrawn behavior: _____

  Helpful ideas:

  1. _____
  _____

  2. _____
  _____

  3. _____
  _____

- Cultural/Linguistic Difference(s): _____

  Helpful ideas:

  1. _____
  _____

  2. _____
  _____

  3. _____
  _____

- Realistic challenge(s): _____

  Helpful ideas:

  1. _____
  _____

  2. _____
  _____

  3. _____
  _____

## CLINICAL CHALLENGE

Answer the following questions about Wendy, Paul, and Joe:

1. Wendy's medication is adjusted, and you provide CBT for her anxiety symptoms. Her anxiety decreases, and she appears to be coping much better. You receive a telephone call from her mother, who says, "Nothing is working. Her grades at school are as bad as ever!" How do you respond?

2. You manage to engage Paul in CBT, and he becomes more active and reconnects with his friends.

   a. After six sessions, he announces that he now has a girlfriend, is delighted, and his depression is "cured." How do you respond?

   b. He stops CBT, and you do not hear from him for three months. At that point, he calls back and says his "life is over" because his girlfriend has left him. How do you respond?

3. Joe engages readily in CBT and learns to cope with his fear of seizures at school. You do not hear from him for two years. At that point, you see him with his mother, who reports that her son is now an excellent competitive swimmer. He has been invited to a swim meet in another province, which will require a two-night stay there with his team. Joe wants to go, but his mother is worried about the possibility of him having a seizure on the trip and wants you to talk her son out of the idea. How do you respond?

## REFERENCES

American Psychiatric Association. (2013). *Diagnostic and statistical manual of mental disorders, Fifth edition (DSM-5).* Washington, DC: American Psychiatric Publishing, pp. 836–837.

Carter, M.M., Mitchell, F.E., & Sbrocco, T. (2012). Treating ethnic minority adults with anxiety disorders: Current status and future recommendations. *Journal of Anxiety Disorders*, 26, 488–501.

Cohen, J.A., Mannarino, A.P., & Deblinger, E. (2006). *Treating trauma and traumatic grief in children and adolescents.* New York: Guilford Press.

Ehntholt, K.A., & Yule, W. (2006). Practitioner review: Assessment and treatment of refugee children and adolescents who have experienced war-related trauma. *Journal of Child Psychology and Psychiatry*, 47, 1197–1210.

Ginsburg, G.S., Becker, K.D., Drazdowski, T.K., & Tein, J.Y. (2012). Treating anxiety disorders in inner city schools: Results from a pilot randomized controlled trial comparing CBT and usual care. *Child Youth Care Forum*, 41, 1–19.

Kendall, P.C., Brady, E.U., & Verduin, T.L. (2001). Comorbidity in childhood anxiety disorders and treatment outcome. *Journal of the American Academy of Child and Adolescent Psychiatry*, 40, 787–794.

Liber, J.M., van Widenfelt, B.M., van der Leeden, A.J., Goedhart, A.W., Utens, E.M., Treffers, P.D. (2010). The relation of severity and comorbidity to treatment outcome with cognitive behavioral therapy for childhood anxiety disorders. *Journal of Abnormal Child Psychology*, 38, 683–694.

Manassis, K. (2007). When ADHD co-occurs with anxiety disorders: Effects on treatment. *Expert Reviews in Neurotherapeutics*, 7, 981–988.

Manassis, K., & Levac, A.M. (2004). *Helping your teenager beat depression*. New York: Woodbine House.

Manassis, K., & Monga, S. (2001). A therapeutic approach to children and adolescents with anxiety disorders and associated comorbid conditions. *Journal of the American Academy of Child and Adolescent Psychiatry*, 40, 115–117.

Manassis, K., & Tannock, R. (2008). Comparing interventions for selective mutism: A pilot study. *Canadian Journal of Psychiatry*, 53, 700–703.

Manassis, K., Tannock, R., McInnes, A., Garland, E.J., Clark, S., & Minde, K. (2007). The sounds of silence: Language, cognition and anxiety in selective mutism. *Journal of the American Academy of Child and Adolescent Psychiatry*, 46, 1187–1195.

Manassis, K., Tannock, R., Young, A., & Francis-John, S. (2007). Cognition in anxious children with attention deficit hyperactivity disorder: A comparison with clinical and normal children. *Behavior and Brain Functions*, 3, 4.

Manassis, K., & Young, A. (2001). Modifying positive reinforcement systems in response to child temperament. *Journal of the American Academy of Child and Adolescent Psychiatry*, 40, 603–605.

McHolm, A.E., Cunningham, C.E., Vanier, M.K., & Rapee, R. (2005). *Helping your child with selective mutism*. New York: New Harbinger.

McInnes, A., & Manassis, K. (2005). When silence is not golden: An integrated approach to selective mutism. *Seminars in Speech and Language*, 26, 201–210.

Mendlowitz, S., Manassis, K., Bradley, S., Scapillato, D., Miezitis, S., & Shaw, B. (1999). Cognitive behavioral group treatments in childhood anxiety disorders: The role of parental involvement. *Journal of the American Academy of Child and Adolescent Psychiatry*, 38, 1223–1229.

Miller, L.D., Laye-Gindhu, A., Bennett, J.L., Liu, Y., Gold, S., March, J.S., et al. (2011). An effectiveness study of a culturally enriched school-based CBT anxiety prevention program. *Journal of Clinical Child & Adolescent Psychology*, 40, 618–629.

Monga, S., & Manassis, K. (2006). Treating childhood anxiety in the presence of life-threatening anaphylactic conditions. *Journal of the American Academy of Child and Adolescent Psychiatry*, 45, 1007–1010.

Nowrouzi, B., Manassis, K., Jones, E., Bobinski, T., & Mushquash, C.J. (2015). Translating anxiety-focused CBT for youth in a First Nations context in Ontario. *Journal of the Canadian Academy of Child and Adolescent Psychiatry*, 24, 33–40.

Papneja, T., & Manassis K. (2006). Characterization and treatment response of anxious children with asthma. *Canadian Journal of Psychiatry*, 51, 393–396.

Sanders, M.R., Shepherd, R.W., Cleghorn, G., & Woolford, H. (1994). The treatment of recurrent abdominal pain in children: A controlled comparison of cognitive-behavioral family intervention and standard pediatric care. *Journal of Consulting and Clinical Psychology*, 62, 306–314.

Scheeringa, M.S., Salloum, A., Arnberger, R.A., Weems, C.F., Amaya-Jackson, L., & Cohen, J.A. (2007). Feasibility and effectiveness of cognitive-behavioral therapy for posttraumatic stress disorder in preschool children: Two case reports. *Journal of Trauma and Stress*, 20, 631–636.

Smith, P., Yule, W., Perrin, S., Tranah, T., Dagleish, T., & Clark, D.M. (2007). Cognitive-behavioral treatment for PTSD in children and adolescents: A preliminary randomized controlled trial. *Journal of the American Academy of Child and Adolescent Psychiatry*, 46, 1051–1061.

Thompson, R.D., Delaney, P., Flores, I., Szigethy, E. (2011). Cognitive-behavioral therapy for children with comorbid physical illness. *Child and Adolescent Psychiatric Clinics of North America*, 20, 329–348.

Weersing, V.R., & Weisz, J.R. (2002). Community clinic treatment of depressed youth: Benchmarking usual care against CBT in clinical trials. *Journal of Consulting and Clinical Psychology*, 70, 299–310.

# CHAPTER EIGHT

# Working with Diverse Families

## WHAT IS KNOWN

Most family-related CBT studies have focused on the role of family involvement in CBT or on family-focused variations of CBT, rather than describing specific challenges in working with families (reviewed in Manassis, 2005).

In CBT for child anxiety, studies on the role of family involvement show mixed results. Girls, younger children, and children in families where parental anxiety is high seem to benefit most (Barrett, Dadds, & Rapee, 1996; Cobham, Dadds, & Spence, 1998). A recent meta-analysis also suggests that family involvement focused on contingency management and transfer of control may be particularly beneficial (Manassis et al., 2014). Family-focused CBT protocols have been developed and found efficacious for obsessive compulsive disorder (OCD) (Storch et al., 2007; Freeman et al., 2014) and non-OCD anxiety disorders (deGroot, Cobham, Leong, & McDermott, 2007; Wood, Piacentini, Southam-Gerow, Chu, & Sigman, 2006). Family functioning has also been found to predict response to CBT in one study (Crawford & Manassis, 2001). Conversely, successful child CBT may improve parental symptoms and family functioning (Keeton et al., 2013).

Fewer studies of family involvement in CBT have been done in depressed than anxious youth. Existing studies have generally found that family intervention is more helpful than waitlist control for youth depression, but not necessarily as helpful as youth-focused CBT (Brent, Holder, & Kolko, 1997; Clarke, Rhode, Lewinsohn, Hops, & Seeley, 1999). One study did find, however, that poor family functioning predicted recurrence of depression and use of additional mental health treatments over time (Birmaher, Brent, & Kolko, 2000). Another study found that the relationship between family conflict and treatment outcome appears to be bidirectional for depressed youth (Rengasamy et al., 2013). Parental involvement was also found to predict youth participation in CBT in one study (Wilansky-Traynor et al., 2010).

Beyond the research literature, there are several disorder-specific parenting books that provide additional guidance on how parents can support their child's progress in treatment. My own parenting books focus on anxious children (Manassis, 2008) and depressed teens (Manassis & Levac, 2004). Foa and Wasmer Andrews (2006) have written a book specifically for parents of anxious adolescents. March and Benton's book on obsessive compulsive disorder (2007) contains substantial information on working with families of children with this disorder. McHolm, Cunningham, Vanier, and Rapee (2005) have written a helpful book for parents of children with selective mutism.

## PUTTING WHAT WE KNOW TO WORK

In this chapter, we explore the reciprocal relationship between progress in CBT and family functioning, common family dilemmas in CBT, adaptations needed with some families, and key parenting principles that are helpful to the child in treatment regardless of disorder. To begin, however, we examine two contrasting cases.

Jeff was a 12-year-old boy from a highly conflicted family who presented with symptoms of OCD. He had several washing rituals and a high need for symmetry in his surroundings. He understood the principles of CBT, but did not apply them outside the therapist's office. His parents argued openly in front of the therapist when discussing how to support his progress. Each accused the other of undermining the therapist's work and then tried to get the therapist to agree with his or her point of view. The therapist made several attempts to get them to focus on problem-solving rather than blaming each other, but to no avail. Jeff required increasing doses of medication for his OCD and was eventually hospitalized due to a severe side effect from one medication. In the hospital, he exhibited very few OCD symptoms. His medication dosage was drastically reduced, and he appeared almost asymptomatic after several weeks. Upon discharge from the hospital, however, all of his symptoms returned and appeared unresponsive to medication. Once again, the parents blamed each other for the setback and could not work together on Jeff's behalf. Family therapy had been tried twice in the past without success. Eventually, a place was found for Jeff in a therapeutic group home where he functioned well with minimal doses of medication.

Madison also suffered from OCD. Her symptoms were so severe that she could not sleep at night due to the need to perform rituals, and she eventually threatened to harm her younger brother. At this point, she was hospitalized. Madison's parents also argued openly in front of the therapist and appeared to blame each other for her problems. The nurses attending Madison in the hospital often commented on her "dysfunctional family." Madison's symptoms continued to be severe in hospital, and she could not be discharged until a combination of three medications was found to contain them. As her symptoms improved, however, so did the apparent family dysfunction. The stress of dealing with Madison's problems, particularly the constant supervision required to ensure her brother's safety, had been exhausting for both parents. Neither had slept much for several weeks prior to her hospitalization, they felt hopeless and doubtful that she could improve, and they had difficulty supporting each other in this desperate family crisis. As they recovered from these stresses, Madison's parents became knowledgeable about OCD, became encouraged about helping their daughter, and were able to support each other's efforts to help her. Three months after Madison's hospital discharge, none of the professionals involved in the case could detect any significant family problems, and she continued to function well.

Although disguised, these two contrasting cases come from my practice and taught me a valuable lesson. The lesson is this: You cannot judge family functioning based on observations at a single point in time, especially if it is a time of psychiatric crisis for a family member. As family therapists discovered many years ago, family interactions are often circular. Thus, the worse one family member is doing, the worse the other members appear. Families often look healthier once the ill member is successfully treated. On the other hand, there are some families, like Jeff's, whose difficulties are so entrenched that no amount of treatment of individual members results in improvement. Thus, the only therapeutic options are to address the whole system or, as in this case, move the child to a more stable environment.

## How Does Family Functioning Relate to Child CBT?

Families usually bring the child to the CBT therapist, so some level of family cooperation is essential. Even the older teen who comes to therapy of his or her own volition is usually still influenced by family attitudes toward the therapy. Furthermore, the child or teen must apply new coping strategies in the family context, and family members can either facilitate or hinder this process. Thus, some degree of family involvement is necessary in child CBT. If the child is not living with a parent, involvement of a guardian or (in the case of a group home) staff member is usually helpful for the same reasons.

When thinking about family involvement in CBT, it stands to reason that (1) some family issues need to be addressed more urgently than others, and (2) addressing family issues is most important in the youngest children (Barrett et al., 1996) who are highly dependent on their family environment. In preschoolers, for example, some researchers are examining whether child-focused work is needed at all, or if parent work informed by CBT principles is sufficient.

An example of a family issue that must be urgently addressed is parental anxiety in the case of an anxious child. Recall that parental involvement particularly enhances CBT benefits when the parent is significantly anxious (Cobham et al., 1998). This finding makes sense, given the difficulty anxious parents often experience providing reassurance to their children. Similarly, any parental psychopathology that interacts with the child's symptoms needs to be addressed. For example, a depressed parent may use their child as a sounding board or feel helpless to support their child's progress, a parent with ADHD may have difficulty remembering the child's appointment times or homework materials, and a parent with a serious personality disorder may undermine the child's therapy (or therapist) in various ways.

## Where Does CBT Fit in Relation to Family Functioning?

When it is clear that there have been ongoing family problems even before the child's current difficulty, it is worth considering whether these need to be addressed prior to CBT or concurrently with CBT. In highly conflicted families like Jeff's, family therapy should probably be prioritized. In families with significant problems in one area but strengths in other areas, offering family therapy concurrently with CBT or a family-focused CBT model should be considered. For example, some families have difficulty with a particular communication style, or with dividing responsibilities fairly, but can work in the child's best interest in other areas. If combining CBT and family therapy, however, it is important to ensure that the child is not overburdened with concurrent therapies.

Separate marital therapy is another option to consider in cases where most of the conflict appears to be between spouses. In situations where there is some spousal conflict but it is limited almost entirely to disagreements about parenting, doing parenting work concurrently with CBT may be all that is needed. Some manuals routinely include this type of parenting work, which usually emphasizes constructive problem-solving (either by the parents, or by the parents together with the child) and supporting the child's new coping strategies. Parenting resources for such work are listed earlier in this chapter.

Regardless of the level of family functioning, it behooves the child CBT therapist to develop some familiarity with the family's values and culture (also see Chapters 5 & 7) because these will impact work with the child. Do not assume, for example, that English-speaking but foreign-born parents necessarily adhere to North American values and norms. They may have different ideas about the nature of mental illness, the role of the therapist, and their own role in their child's mental health than the local population does. When in doubt, ask for clarification, particularly when it comes to their beliefs and hopes regarding the child's therapy. Respect cultural etiquette (for example, shaking hands may not be considered appropriate in certain cultures), and speak to a mental health professional from the same background if needed to clarify what child behaviors are considered normative there. For example, working on reducing a "praying ritual" may not be appreciated in some cultures. In addition to being sensitive to ethnic and religious differences, it is also important to be sensitive to different family types. Families with two parents of the same gender are increasing, for example, and may have unique needs. Again, avoid making assumptions and ask for clarification if needed.

## Common Family Dilemmas in CBT

To understand why families sometimes have difficulty supporting children's progress in CBT, it is helpful to review what the family is supposed to do in this regard. As discussed previously, parents are expected to bring the child to therapy, cheer on their child's progress initially, and later support or "coach" the use of new coping strategies by the child, in a manner appropriate to the child's developmental level (that is, a parent is more directive in younger children). Siblings and other family members are usually not directly involved in facilitating child progress, but may need education about what the child is trying to learn and do and, sometimes, extra attention to reduce envy of the child's special status. Factors that can interfere with parental support of the child's progress include difficulty bringing the child to sessions consistently, difficulty deciding who should be involved in the child's therapy, difficulty recognizing and validating child progress, and difficulty consistently facilitating use of new coping strategies.

The above factors are further detailed in Table 8.1. Let us look at each in turn.

*Difficulty Bringing the Child to Sessions Consistently*—This can occur because of parental disorganization (for example, parental ADHD or other psychological problem), financial difficulties that impact travel to the therapist's

TABLE 8.1
Families' Difficulties in Child CBT

| Area of Difficulty | Common Problems |
| --- | --- |
| Attending Sessions | Disorganization |
| | Financial problems |
| | Competing demands |
| | Failure to prioritize child CBT |
| | Ambivalence about child CBT |
| Deciding Whom to Involve | Separation or divorce |
| | Reconstituted families |
| | Family conflict |
| | Parents "taking turns" |
| Encouraging Progress | Parental psychopathology |
| | Failure to recognize progress |
| | Ineffectual praise |
| Supporting Coping | Unclear or unrealistic parenting advice |
| | Assuming parents are "following the book" |
| | Frustration with the child |
| | Frustration with the therapist |
| | Parental psychopathology |
| | Inconsistency over time |
| | Inconsistency between family members |

office, too many competing demands on the parent's time (for example, single-parent household, parental career that includes frequent travel, or multiple children with after-school activities), failure to prioritize the child's CBT, ambivalence (conscious or unconscious) about the child's participation in CBT, or a combination of these.

Begin by educating the parent about the need for consistent attendance, identifying the contributing factors, and doing some problem-solving with the parent to improve the situation. For example, one can provide reminder calls to disorganized parents, or bus tokens to parents whose financial difficulties are impacting attendance. If the problem recurs, suggest that CBT may need to be postponed to a time when consistent attendance is more feasible because it cannot succeed without consistent attendance. Some parents will change their behavior in response; others will express relief that they have one less burden "on their plate"; still others will become angry. For overburdened parents, it is worth commending their efforts to help their children, offering appropriate educational resources, and offering to be available in the future when their lives become more manageable. Angry parents may benefit from some further clarification that you are not rejecting them or their child, merely stating an unfortunate reality. You are quite willing to see them again when they can ensure consistent attendance, but given the nature of CBT, you cannot help their child until then.

*Difficulty Deciding Who Should Be Involved in the Child's Therapy*—This is most common in cases of family separation, divorce, or reconstituted families. If there is any lack of clarity about child custody, CBT should probably be postponed until after this is clarified. In most jurisdictions, only the custodial parent(s) can authorize medical or psychological treatment for the child, so beginning treatment when custody is unclear can result in legal problems. Clinically, children in custody disputes are so stressed by the uncertainty of whom they are going to live with that they rarely benefit from CBT anyway. Even if custody is clear, situations of acrimonious separation or divorce should be approached with caution. I have seen parents undermine their child's CBT in various ways under these circumstances. For example, when a couple has joint custody and one parent is supportive of CBT but the other is not, the unsupportive parent almost always undermines the therapy. Other times, parents will battle for equal access to the therapist, or insist on being seen by the therapist without their former partner present, even if this results in miscommunication or impacts the therapist's time with the child. Some parents even accuse their former spouse of inducing psychiatric symptoms in the child, completely derailing CBT.

On the other hand, low-conflict families can often find a therapy arrangement that works. For example, reconstituted families may choose to have one partner from each new household (often the biological parent) involved in the child's CBT, or have one or both new partners involved as well. As long as all the adults can work together in the child's best interest, a number of different combinations of adults can work. Avoid being drawn into agreement with one or the other partner, and return to a problem-solving approach focused on the child whenever possible. This does not mean that everyone has to do the same thing with the child; they must merely agree to a clear plan that is in the child's best interest. For example, most children can adapt to having different rules in one home versus the other, as long as parents do not criticize one another's approach in front of the child.

Another question that sometimes arises in two-parent families is: Does the same parent have to come all the time with the child? Ideally, both parents should attend, but this may not be feasible for the family, so most therapists will only insist on one. In this case, it sometimes seems more equitable to have parents take turns bringing the child to sessions. Unfortunately, this is very disruptive in any case where CBT includes significant work with the parents (almost all children and young adolescents). Just as one skill builds on another in child CBT, one parenting skill also builds on another. When parents alternate their session attendance, they usually promise to communicate what is discussed to their partner, but they rarely do. As a result, the parenting component of CBT often becomes disorganized and unproductive. The one exception may be parents who tape record their time with the therapist and then share the recording with their partner so he or she can "pick up where the session left off" the following week. Even so, the rapport with the therapist usually is not quite as good when an alternating schedule is used. Thus, while having at least one parent attend consistently may seem burdensome to that parent, it usually works better in supporting the child's progress.

*Difficulty Recognizing and Validating Child Progress*—This commonly occurs when parents either are too preoccupied with their own difficulties to attend to the child's behavior (see section below on parental psychopathology) or need some guidance on what to look for and how to react. For example, parents may not realize that less frequent or less intense negative reactions to a particular situation constitute progress. They may assume that until the child is completely happy and comfortable there, no progress has occurred. Looking for behavioral change in a child is a little like looking through a microscope: You usually see nothing until someone tells you what to look for. Therapists can be very helpful in telling parents what to look for. Of course, it is helpful if the parent does not engage in too much "all or nothing" thinking and can, therefore, attend to small gains. The best parental reaction to progress seems obvious: Praise the child. Unfortunately, many parents do not know how to offer effective praise. They may say "good boy" or "good girl" without identifying for the child what exactly was done that was "good." "You couldn't do that last week, and this week you've done it twice already!" is an example of a more specific and effective type of praise. Praise also needs to be geared to the child's personality. Children who are self-conscious or easily embarrassed often do better with gentle, matter-of-fact praise, while other children may prefer a more emotional approach. Some even value a parental hug more than verbal praise.

*Difficulty Consistently Facilitating Children's Use of New Coping Strategies*—This can occur when parents do not know what to do or cannot do it; when their own emotional difficulties get in the way; or when there is inconsistency in the response to the child's behavior, either between partners or across time. Guidance from the therapist is most helpful for the first of these scenarios. Parental "homework" between sessions should be analogous to children's CBT homework. It should be clear, manageable, and involve practice of what has been done or discussed in the session. For example, providing a dozen different suggestions with no discussion of how to implement them is rarely helpful. Instead, pick one or two parenting strategies that fit easily within existing family routines and can be used consistently until the next session. Then, follow up the next week to see how easy or difficult these were to implement, and "fine-tune" them accordingly. Simple, repetitive tasks are usually best even for highly intelligent parents. Creative problem-solving on the spur of the moment is difficult for most of us at the end of a long day. For example, I often recommend a time-out system for minor misbehavior because of its clarity and simplicity, even though there are other, more sophisticated approaches.

Also, while parenting books can be very helpful in providing guidance, do not assume that they can take the place of time with the therapist. Parents who read a lot do not necessarily do a lot with what they read. Find out exactly what parents are doing if they claim to be following suggestions from a particular book or author. With parents with limited time, concentrating on one chapter from a book is often more helpful than asking them to read the whole thing. Again, see what the parents were able to glean from the chapter and what they are applying, rather than assuming they are doing what it suggests.

Emotional difficulties that get in the way can relate to parental psychopathology, or simply to frustration with the child or the therapist. When parents make multiple attempts to help their child without success, it is natural for them to become frustrated. In addition, children with internalizing problems often behave worse at home (where they feel safe) than at school (where they are more anxious or withdrawn). This fact can further contribute to parental frustration. Unfortunately, parental frustration often exacerbates the child's symptoms by paying undue attention to them, or by frightening an already anxious, withdrawn child. The exacerbation can in turn exacerbate parental frustration in a vicious cycle. It is very helpful to identify these frustration cycles in families, pointing out the benefits of interrupting them and the fact that they are nobody's fault.

Frustration with the therapist can occur because of differing treatment expectations (see Chapter 4), lack of confidence in the therapist, or general frustration with helping professionals. Examples of each include the parent who expects the therapist to "get the school on board" without understanding that there are limits to both the therapist and the school's flexibility; the parent who asks the novice therapist "How many children have you treated with CBT?" or "Since you're giving parenting advice, tell me: Do you have children yourself?" or the parent who has "fired" a series of child therapists, claiming that none were helpful and each disappointed the parent. What these examples have in common is a demanding parent who may feel entitled to more service than you can reasonably provide. Avoid becoming defensive and arguing with someone like this. Instead, point out the realistic limits of your experience and of what you can provide, but offer to do as much as you can within those limits. Indicate that you may need the parent's participation in order to succeed. Do not promise to do better than anyone else. In fact, it is often more helpful to minimize your accomplishments and indicate that you would be willing to refer the child elsewhere if the parent wishes. Parents rarely continue attacking you when faced with this attitude and may calm down enough to work with you. In some cases, they can eventually even recognize their own contribution to past therapeutic failures.

Parental psychopathology often mirrors child psychopathology. Thus, parents of anxious children often have difficulty encouraging appropriate independence and modeling nonanxious coping because they are anxious themselves. Parents of depressed children often look downcast themselves, or express helplessness or hopelessness about their ability to support therapeutic change. As mentioned above, parental ADHD is common in cases of children with this condition.

Some parents are aware of their own psychopathology and are willing to address it. This often occurs with very distressing symptoms (for example, frequent panic attacks or presence of suicidal thoughts). In this case, cheer them on and offer appropriate referrals as needed. Other parents are not aware of their own emotional problems or of the impact these may have on their child. This is a more difficult situation. After all, the child has been identified as the patient, and the parent may feel blamed if the therapist begins to express concerns about parental mental health. One approach is to point out at assessment the circular nature of many problems in families, and how the parent's emotional state may be a factor in these circles. Some parents understand this; others do not. If there is no such understanding initially, sometimes it can still develop during the course of child therapy. For example, as one discusses encouraging the child to face specific feared situations, the parent may protest that this is not possible because he or she fears the same situation. Alternatively, as one discusses increasing school attendance for a depressed, withdrawn youngster, the depressive parent may admit that he or she would miss the child's company at home. These situations provide an opportunity to revisit the issue of whether or not therapy for the parent would be helpful.

Having a consistent approach to the child's behavior is a challenge in many families. Families face many demands, and consistent behavior management rarely happens if it is not prioritized. Lack of prioritization results in the common complaint: "We've tried everything, and nothing works." Usually, these families have tried different parenting strategies for a few days or at most a week at a time, without trying any one strategy over a longer period. They are often amazed when doing one thing consistently actually results in behavioral change.

Inconsistency between family members is another common problem. Often, one parent sympathizes with the child, while the other thinks the child is "faking" or exaggerating symptoms. Parents may need the therapist's help to come to a common understanding of the child's difficulties and an approach that both parents are willing and able to implement. School personnel or members of the extended family can also sometimes contribute to inconsistent behavior management. Discussions with these people can be very helpful in ensuring greater consistency. As with parents, take a problem-focused approach. You are not there to judge their behavior, but to discuss potential solutions (sometimes pointing out what has already worked for the parents), and then to encourage them to test out the approach you agree on.

Parent groups are often very helpful in promoting healthy problem-solving on the child's behalf and consistent behavior management. Parents feel a common bond with other parents in the group and are often more inclined to listen to them than to professionals. The mutual support and positive reinforcement provided by the group is encouraging for many disheartened parents. There is also an old saying that "many heads are better than one," and this is particularly true for groups that have a problem-solving focus. I am often surprised at the number of creative and effective solutions a parent group can generate for a particular problem. Finding their own solutions is also empowering for parents. Therefore, one of the most helpful things a group therapist can say about a particular problem is often, "What do other people in the group think?" or "What would other people around the table do in that situation?" As with all parenting interventions in CBT, encourage parents to test out their ideas between sessions and report back on the results to "fine-tune," if needed, and determine what works for each child.

## Common Compromises When Working with Families

As parental involvement in child CBT has become more common, a number of manuals have been developed that highlight important parenting ideas and approaches for particular disorders. What if parents cannot agree to this degree of involvement? For example, some parents are quite willing to support their child's progress, but really cannot take time off work consistently when the therapist is available. Providing information about how to support progress either in writing or on the telephone is probably the next best thing. Discussion is preferable to just providing information, because it allows the parent to ask questions and comment about how to use the information in relation to the child.

Other parents believe that only the therapist can help the child. While one should do one's best to challenge that belief, it can be very ingrained. Some of these parents initially limit their involvement, but are reassured by the knowledge that "something is being done for the child" after several therapy sessions, and are then more willing to participate. Others never take an active part in their child's treatment. In a young child, one should probably not pursue CBT in this situation. In an adolescent, it may be possible to do some work with the young person without parental involvement, although lack of parental involvement is still a serious limitation. In these cases, I have sometimes worked with teens on strategies for coping with their parents' behavior, as well as coping with other problematic life situations.

Occasionally, parents may not be able to attend a series of sessions, but are able to glean one or two key parenting principles, either at assessment or during a single session, that allow them to be helpful to their child. For example, one mother told me that the simple advice to "stop talking" when her child began to panic and offer comfort instead dramatically altered her relationship with her child. The parents of a depressed boy recognized in a single session that the whole family engaged in "pity parties" (mutual negativity and commiseration) when any one of them began to talk negatively. By stopping this behavior, they were able to lighten the mood in the house considerably and contribute to their son's recovery.

### "Pearls for Parents" of Children in CBT

From the discussion above, it may seem that parents often contribute to difficulty working with children in CBT. Nothing could be further from the truth. In fact, parents can facilitate progress in child CBT more effectively than any other person in the child's life. Why is this? Reasons include the following:

- Parents spend more time with the child than anyone else. During the week, school takes about thirty hours, sports and other organized activities perhaps six to eight hours, therapy one hour, and the rest is up to Mom and Dad!
- Parents know what will or will not motivate their child. They have had years of experience observing their child's responses to various attempts to influence his or her behavior. If a parent says, "There's no way my son will go for that," they're probably right.
- Children often want to please their parents. They may not always admit it, but a kind or encouraging word from a mother or father means more than almost any other type of reward.
- Parents can often empathize with what the child is going through. This is particularly true when they have experienced similar difficulties to those of their child, either recently or when they were children themselves.

- Parents want to see their children do well. The child's well-being is usually more important to his or her parents than to anyone else on the planet. This means they are willing to spend extra time working on their children's problems and often advocate more vigorously for their children's well-being than anyone else.

For all of these reasons, parents are valuable allies for the child CBT therapist. Many child CBT manuals already include parent sessions or parent modules. A few behavioral principles cut across specific disorders or specific manuals, however. These "pearls for parents" include the following:

1. Practice what you preach.
2. The "less negative talk, less negative emotion" principle.
3. The principle of empathic encouragement.
4. The "P.A.S.T.E." problem-solving approach.
5. Treating the parents as the "hub of the system" around the child.
6. The need for parental respite and support.

*Practice What You Preach*—There is an old saying about children: They do not do what you say, they do what you do. It is true, and it speaks to the profound way in which children are affected by adult behavior. Whether they like it or not, parents become role models for the children they raise. As a result, time spent helping parents modify their own maladaptive behaviors is never wasted, and encouraging parents to obtain treatment for any mental health problems they have is crucial to children's progress.

Reframing these ideas positively, all parents can facilitate their children's progress in CBT by demonstrating the adaptive coping behaviors they want their children to use. Relaxation strategies for anxious children, for example, can be practiced as a family. Increasing the activity level of a depressed youngster is easier when others in the family are active too. Children use coping self-talk more consistently when they occasionally see their parents using it to deal with ordinary stress. For example, the exclamation "I'm late for work!" can be followed by "but I'll phone ahead and apologize, and join the meeting when I get there. I'm usually on time, so my boss will forgive me for having one off day." The opportunity to model healthy coping is also reassuring for some parents. For example, children who do not readily communicate their feelings may leave their parents unsure how to be helpful. As a therapist, I often tell these parents to model what they want their children to do, and some of it will eventually "rub off," even if there is little discussion of emotions. With this reassurance, parents can relax and focus on healthy strategies, rather than annoying the child with repeated futile attempts to elicit information about feelings.

*Less Negative Talk, Less Negative Emotion*—Reasoning with children and teaching them problem-solving skills have been touted as the hallmarks of modern, authoritative parenting. When children are asking for help and eager to talk, this makes sense. When they are angry, oppositional, or just not in a talking mood, it does not. Trying to explain things and reason with an angry or sullen child usually results in mutual frustration and escalating arguments. At those times, it makes sense to go back to the basic behavioral rule: If you want to see more of the same, pay attention to it; if less, ignore it.

Ignoring a distressed child may seem heartless to some parents, and others may worry that an opportunity to develop better coping skills is being missed. In the long run, however, having the child learn to soothe some upset feelings without involving others is a valuable coping skill. It is a tough way to learn, but is almost always preferable to the arguing and emotional upset that occurs when parents choose to get involved.

Ignoring is not always easy to do. Parents may need considerable practice to disengage from their children effectively. Children who are in the habit of engaging their parents in negative interactions will often behave in ways that maintain the habit. For example, parents often feel they are being unreasonable if they do not justify their actions to their children, so asking the simple question "Why?" is an easy way for the child to maintain a negative interaction. If the parent replies, "Because I say so!" he or she feels like an authoritarian Neanderthal. "We'll talk about it in the morning (or at some other time several hours hence)" is often one of the few ways to defuse the situation. I often tell parents in these dilemmas: When in doubt, stop talking and breathe slowly. Once the child learns that negativity will not result in parental attention, child behavior usually improves, and helpful interactions that foster adaptive coping become possible.

*Empathic Encouragement*—Trying something new is difficult and a little frightening for most of us. Adaptive coping skills are new to most children. Therefore, we are asking children in CBT, regardless of its diagnostic focus, to undertake difficult and potentially frightening tasks. When parents are able to understand this child perspective and empathically show the child that they understand, it makes a huge difference to the child. The child has his or her distress validated, feels cared for, and feels reassured that the parent will not make demands that go beyond what the child can handle. Children who feel this way are far more likely to attempt new tasks than those who do not. Therefore, taking time to help parents put themselves in their child's shoes is definitely a worthwhile therapeutic activity.

At the same time, children need to feel that their parents have faith in them. Parents who cannot express confidence in their children's abilities, or give mixed messages about those abilities (for example, saying "you can do this" to the child, but looking very worried and tense) have difficulty encouraging the use of new coping strategies. In working with these parents, the therapist must often repeatedly point out the child's strengths.

A good exercise for these parents is to have them observe the child closely for as many signs of competence as possible, ignoring child problems (usually the opposite of what they normally do).

When parents continue to have difficulty either empathizing with their children or expressing confidence in their children, the reasons often go back to their own past history. Attachment difficulties in relation to their own parents may be affecting the current parent–child relationship (see Manassis, 2004, for more detail). For example, people who have experienced little empathy from their own parents often have difficulty showing it to their children. Alternatively, the child may remind the parents of a particularly dysfunctional relative, or of their own childhood problems. When the therapist gently explores these possibilities, a parent may reveal (for example): "Sarah's just like Aunt Mary, who eventually went schizophrenic!" or "I quit school because of a teacher like that, and I see the same thing happening to Timmy now!" If these concerns are not extreme, reassurance and education may address them. For example, one could demonstrate how Sarah and Mary are psychologically different from each other, and how Timmy and the teacher may yet resolve their problems. If the concerns are more extreme and are significantly affecting child progress, the parent may benefit from psychodynamic psychotherapy.

"*P.A.S.T.E.*"—The acronym P.A.S.T.E. stands for: *P*ick a problem, examine *A*lternatives, *S*elect an alternative, *T*ry it out, and *E*valuate the result. There are other, similar acronyms for problem-solving, but they all follow the same basic principles. Problem-solving is helpful when parents are trying to develop more effective parenting strategies, and also when parents are working with older children and adolescents to help them develop more effective coping strategies.

Younger children often need to be provided most strategies, but as soon as the child is able to participate in problem-solving this should be encouraged. Why? If a child is taught a coping skill that is effective for a given situation, he or she will go back to the teacher of the skill to obtain more skills each time a new situation is encountered. If a child is taught problem-solving, he or she will be able to generate and test out new skills for new situations independently. Thus, reliance on parents and therapists decreases as children become better problem solvers, increasing their confidence and resilience in the face of stress.

Problem-solving can be challenging, both when used to develop parenting strategies and when used with children. Common difficulties parents encounter with each step (and therapists may need to avert) include:

- *Difficulty working on one problem at a time.* It seems very slow to some parents, but reassure them that by developing an approach to problems using a single example one usually gets further than by trying to do too many things at once.

- *Difficulty generating alternatives.* People do get set in their ways and have trouble seeing that other ways are possible, and possibly more effective. Involving a partner or a group of parents is often helpful in "brainstorming" alternative ideas. If this is not possible, the therapist may have to suggest alternatives by asking, "What would happen if you did X?" or "Have you ever thought of something like Y?" or "Some parents have told me that Z helped. What do you think?" or "What have other people suggested?"

- *Difficulty agreeing with the therapist on what alternative to try.* Sometimes, this is because parents cannot agree on what is "best." Other times, a parent may fear picking the "wrong" alternative. Lighten the mood by pointing out that, after all, it is just a trial, and what is learned from it will be useful regardless of the outcome.

- *Difficulty implementing the alternative that was selected.* Sometimes "life gets in the way," and parents do not realize how much time and effort is needed for the new alternative. Other times, the parent is ambivalent about the new strategy and so "forgets" to do it. Identify these parental reactions and normalize them (change is difficult for all of us), then explore whether there are ways to get around them.

- *Forgetting to follow up and evaluate how things went.* Most parents need to set a definite time to do this, or it does not happen. Once a time is set, make sure the evaluation is objective and covers what went well and what could have gone better. Optimists tend to see only the progress and neglect to "fine-tune" their approach if needed. Pessimists tend to see only what went wrong and throw out new approaches without giving them a chance. Neither is helpful, so aim for a balanced assessment.

Analogous problems are encountered when problem-solving with children and adolescents, often accompanied by some skepticism about whether the whole idea of problem-solving is worthwhile. Solutions are similar to those discussed above, and the best remedy for a skeptic is often to say, "You won't know until you try!" and indicate a willingness to participate in the trying.

*"The Hub of the System"*—Children are more dependent on their environment than adults, and it is important to understand this environment as a system. This means that the child interacts with a variety of people, including family members, school personnel, peers, coaches or activity leaders, professionals, and other community members, and these people often interact with each other. Each person perceives the child differently and reacts to the child differently, often making the world a rather confusing place for children.

As highlighted above, consistency is essential to shaping children's behavior. In order to get all of the people in the child's environment to work together and ensure consistency, someone has to be aware of all the people and be willing to communicate with them. The therapist can rarely take on this role without the parents' help. For example, the therapist may not even be aware of extended family members that have an important influence on the child's behavior. Furthermore, in order for the therapist to communicate with other professionals or with people outside the family, the parents' written permission is usually required. Thus, it makes sense to involve parents in both understanding the child's "system" and coordinating communication within that system. Older children and adolescents may want to have some control over information that is disclosed to others, and this should be respected whenever possible. Nevertheless, it is difficult for most young people to advocate effectively for all of their needs outside the family, so some degree of parental involvement is still usually needed.

*Support for Parents*—When children have significant mental health problems, parenting them becomes almost a full-time job. Many parents have full-time jobs outside the home as well. Parental discouragement, exhaustion, and "burnout" are therefore very common, and often detrimental to the children. As child CBT therapists, we should be aware of resources for parents in our communities that reduce these problems. Parent support groups and opportunities for parental respite (for example, having a trained individual who can mind the child for a few hours or a day) are definitely worth investigating. Some communities have programs for siblings as well, which should be pursued if available.

Some parents never take advantage of these opportunities (either because they are managing well or because they cannot find the time), but they still appreciate knowing they are there to access in the future if needed. Others participate to gather more information about their child and resources the child may be eligible for. Others participate to regain strength and encouragement from like-minded parents in a similar predicament. All benefit from knowing they are not alone and that they are not "failing" as parents if they occasionally feel overwhelmed by their child's problems.

## WHAT WE YET NEED TO LEARN

Parenting behaviors and family interactions that help or hinder progress in child CBT deserve further research attention. Similarly, parenting behaviors and family interactions that reduce or increase relapse need further study. Moreover, rather than studying whether or not parents and families should be involved in the child's care, we need to focus on *how* to involve them best. The answers will likely vary depending on child age, specific disorder, and other child and family characteristics. Given the emerging evidence for bidirectional effects between treatment outcome and family functioning, studies of CBT treatment elements that may improve family functioning are also warranted.

## DIVERSE FAMILIES WORKSHEET

Review Table 8.1. Have you encountered any of the common family-related difficulties mentioned there? List them, along with any reasons for them you are able to determine. Then list ideas from this chapter that may be helpful.

- Attendance problems: _____

  Reasons: _____

  Helpful ideas: _____

  1. _____

  2. _____


- Problems regarding whom to involve: _____

  Reasons: _____

  Helpful ideas: _____

  1. _____

  2. _____


- Problems encouraging progress: _____

  Reasons: _____

  Helpful ideas: _____

  1. _____

  2. _____

- Problems supporting coping: _____
  _____

  Reasons: _____
  _____

  Helpful ideas: _____
  _____

  1. _____
     _____
  2. _____
     _____

## CLINICAL CHALLENGE

Review the case of Madison above.

1. What family interventions described in this chapter might have been helpful while she was in the hospital?
2. What family interventions described in this chapter might have been helpful after she left the hospital?

## REFERENCES

Barrett, P.M., Dadds, M.R., & Rapee, R.M. (1996), Family treatment of childhood anxiety: A controlled trial. *Journal of Consulting and Clinical Psychology*, 64, 333–342.

Birmaher, B., Brent, D.A., & Kolko, D. (2000). Clinical outcome after short-term psychotherapy for adolescents with major depressive disorder. *Archives of General Psychiatry*, 57, 29–36.

Brent, D.A., Holder, D., & Kolko, D. (1997). A clinical psychotherapy trial for adolescent depression comparing cognitive, family, and supportive therapy. *Archives of General Psychiatry*, 54, 77–88.

Clarke, G.N., Rhode, P., Lewinsohn, P.M., Hops, H., & Seeley, J. (1999). Cognitive behavioral treatment of adolescent depression: Efficacy of acute group treatment and booster sessions. *Journal of the American Academy of Child and Adolescent Psychiatry*, 38, 272–279.

Cobham, V.E., Dadds, M.R., & Spence, S.H. (1998). The role of parental anxiety in the treatment of childhood anxiety. *Journal of Consulting and Clinical Psychology*, 66, 893–905.

Crawford, A.M., & Manassis, K. (2001). Familial predictors of treatment outcome in childhood anxiety disorders. *Journal of the American Academy of Child and Adolescent Psychiatry*, 40, 1182–1189.

deGroot, J., Cobham, V., Leong, J., & McDermott, B. (2007). Individual versus group family-focused CBT for child anxiety: Pilot randomized controlled trial. *Australia and New Zealand Journal of Psychiatry*, 41, 990–997.

Foa, E.B., & Wasmer Andrews, L. (2006). *If your adolescent has an anxiety disorder: An essential resource for parents*. London, UK: Oxford University Press.

Freeman, J., Sapyta, J., Garcia, A., Compton, S., Khanna, M., Flessner, C., et al. (2014). Family-based treatment of early childhood obsessive-compulsive disorder: The Pediatric Obsessive-Compulsive Disorder Treatment Study for Young Children (POTS Jr)—a randomized clinical trial. *Journal of the American Medical Association Psychiatry*, 71, 689–698.

Keeton, C.P., Ginsburg, G.S., Drake, K.L., Sakolsky, D., Kendall, P.C., Birmaher, B., et al. (2013). Benefits of child-focused anxiety treatments for parents and family functioning. *Depression and Anxiety*, 30, 865–872.

Manassis, K. (2004). Child–parent relations: Attachment and anxiety disorders. In Silverman, W.K. & Treffers, P.D.A. (Eds.), *Anxiety disorders in children and adolescents, Second edition*. Cambridge, UK: Cambridge University Press, pp. 280–298.

Manassis, K. (2005). Empirical data regarding the role of the family in treatment. In R. Rapee & J. Hudson (Eds.), *Psychopathology and the family*. London, UK: Elsevier Press, pp. 283–300.

Manassis, K. (2008). *Keys to parenting your anxious child* (2nd ed.). Hauppauge, NY: Barron's Educational Series, Inc.

Manassis, K., & Levac, A.M. (2004). *Helping your teenager beat depression*. New York: Woodbine House.

Manassis, K., Lee, T.C., Bennett, K., Zhao, X.Y., Mendlowitz, S., Duda, S., et al. (2014). Types of parental involvement in CBT with anxious youth: A preliminary meta-analysis. *Journal of Consulting and Clinical Psychology*, 82, 1163–1172, doi:10.1037/a0036969.

March, J.S., & Benton, C.M. (2007). *Talking back to OCD*. New York: Guilford Press.

McHolm, A.E., Cunningham, C.E., Vanier, M.K., & Rapee, R. (2005). *Helping your child with selective mutism*. New York: New Harbinger.

Rengasamy, M., Mansoor, B.M., Hilton, R., Porta, G., He, J., Emslie, G.J., et al. (2013). The bi-directional relationship between parent-child conflict and treatment outcome in treatment resistant adolescent depression. *Journal of the American Academy of Child & Adolescent Psychiatry*, 52, 370–377.

Storch, E.A., Geffken, G.R., Merlo, L.J., Mann, G., Duke, D., Munson, M., et al. (2007). Family-based CBT for pediatric OCD: Comparison of intensive versus weekly. *Journal of the American Academy of Child and Adolescent Psychiatry*, 46, 469–478.

Wilansky-Traynor, P., Manassis, K., Monga, S., Shaw, M., Merka, P., Levac, A.M., et al. (2010). Cognitive behavioural therapy for depressed youth: Predictors of attendance in a pilot study. *Journal of the Canadian Academy of Child & Adolescent Psychiatry*, 19, 81–87.

Wood, J.J., Piacentini, J.C., Southam-Gerow, M., Chu, B.C., & Sigman, M. (2006). Family CBT for child anxiety disorders. *Journal of the American Academy of Child and Adolescent Psychiatry*, 45, 314–321.

# CHAPTER NINE

# Group-Based and School-Based Child CBT

## WHAT IS KNOWN

### Group-Based Child CBT

Because most school-based CBT has been done in groups, these two topics fit well together in the same chapter. Group-based and individual child CBT for anxiety disorders were found equally efficacious in a recent meta-analysis (James, James, Cowdrey, Soler, & Choke, 2013). Group-based child CBT has also been shown to be efficacious for depression (Rohde, Clarke, Lewinsohn, Seeley, & Kaufman, 2001) and obsessive compulsive disorder (OCD) (Martin & Thienemann, 2005; Thienemann, Martin, Cregger, Thompson, & Dyer-Friedman, 2001). It may also help prevent depression in adolescents at risk due to parental depression (Clarke et al., 2001) and prevent relapse in children and adolescents with OCD (Asbahr et al., 2005). One criticism of these studies has been that most comparisons are with waitlist or minimal intervention conditions, raising the possibility of change being due to nonspecific factors unrelated to CBT.

Moreover, all of the groups studied used manuals specifically designed for groups (versus individuals), and some studies found subgroups of children that responded better to individual treatment. In particular, children with high social anxiety reported greater gains in individual than group CBT in one study (Manassis et al., 2002), possibly because participation in a mixed anxiety disorders group was more stressful for them than individual therapy. Interestingly, groups designed exclusively for socially phobic adolescents have shown very good results (Baer & Garland, 2005; Hayward et al., 2000). This discrepancy may speak to the value of aiming for relatively homogenous CBT groups whenever possible. Most studies already have a limited age range for a given group (usually three or four years at most) and include some cognitive criteria for group participation (for example, a certain minimum IQ or absence of serious learning disabilities) to ensure that children in the group can learn CBT strategies at a similar pace.

Groups for adolescents may need to include specific strategies to ensure adolescent engagement in treatment (Scapillato & Manassis, 2002). These may include cohesion-building activities, psychoeducation, exposure to peer models, opportunities for observational learning, and using the group as a safe forum for social problem-solving that mirrors the adolescents' usual social milieu (Scapillato & Manassis, 2002). Several group-specific manuals are cited below.

## Group-Specific Manuals

- Clarke, G.N., Lewinsohn, P.M., & Hops, H. (1990). *Instructors manual for the adolescent coping with depression course.* The therapist manual and the adolescent workbook may be downloaded for free from: http:www.kpchr.org/public/acwd/acwd.html
- Group-specific manuals from Dr. P. Kendall's research group for anxiety, learning and behavior problems (problem-solving focus), and depression can be obtained at www.workbookpublishing.com
- Manassis, K., Mendlowitz, S., Scapillato, D., Avery, D., Fiksenbaum, L., Freive, M., et al. (2008). *The coping bear: Group and individual cognitive behavioral therapy for children and their parents with anxiety disorders.* Los Altos, CA: CEDETA/Sociometrics Corporation.

## School-Based Child CBT

Providing CBT in schools is based on the idea that children who require care in highly specialized clinics represent the "tip of the iceberg" for many mental health conditions, including anxiety and depression. As shown in Figure 9.1, the number of children who have mild symptoms (the base of the triangle) is much larger, but these children are at risk of deteriorating and moving into the upper layers of the triangle if their difficulties are ignored. Through relatively simple, cognitive-behaviorally based interventions delivered by less specialized personnel in convenient settings, these children may develop coping skills that prevent this progression. School is

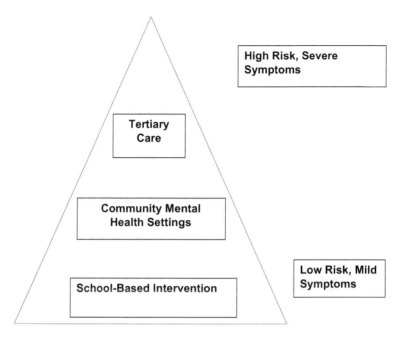

FIGURE 9.1    Intervention appropriate to child risk.

an obvious location for reaching these mildly affected but at-risk children and identifying more seriously affected children so they can be referred to appropriate treatment centers. School-based CBT interventions can be universal, meaning the intervention is provided to all students in a classroom, or targeted to specific children considered at risk for anxiety or depression-related problems.

A meta-analysis of school-based CBT for anxiety revealed significant symptom reduction in participating children for both universal and targeted interventions (Neil & Christensen, 2009). A similar analysis for school-based CBT for depression also revealed symptomatic improvement, but with greater effect sizes for interventions targeting children with elevated symptoms than universal interventions (Calear & Christensen, 2010). Studies have often compared interventions to waitlist controls. Those using well-designed active controls sometimes find control participants improving, too, at least for anxiety symptoms (Manassis et al., 2010).

Most manuals for these programs are easiest to obtain by writing to the authors. However, the school-based program that is most widely known and used internationally, the FRIENDS program for anxiety (Barrett, Farrell, Ollendick, & Dadds, 2006), also has a popular website (https://www.mcf. gov.bc.ca/mental_health/friends.htm).

## PUTTING WHAT WE KNOW TO WORK

### Case Example: A Very Sick Patient

"Where's Jenny?" asked a plaintive little voice in the child CBT group. Jenny was 11 years old and had been a real role model for the younger children. However, she felt the work they were doing was "babyish"; she told her mother, and then stopped coming to the group.

> "Jenny's not coming any more," the group leader stated matter-of-factly.
> "Maybe she didn't like the joke you made about her Halloween costume, Danny," suggested a nine-year-old boy, looking accusingly at his friend.
> "It's not my fault if she took it personally!" protested Danny.
> "Quiet children, it's time for today's coping lesson," said the group leader, ignoring their concerns.
> "My tummy hurts," said the youngest girl, who really missed Jenny.
> "Crybaby!" muttered the boy beside her, but the leader did not hear.
> "Who's got their homework done?" she asked cheerfully.
> Nobody volunteered.

Who is the sick patient referred to in the title of this example? No, it is not the youngest girl. It is the group!

When doing child CBT in groups, each participating child has needs that the therapist must address, but the group should be thought of as an additional client or "patient" that also needs attention. Without attention to the functioning of the group, what is supposed to be a positive, safe environment can quickly deteriorate, and the group can become unpleasant or even harmful for some children. Being called a "crybaby" (as in this example) is not a therapeutic experience for anyone! Moreover, an important therapeutic opportunity has been missed. If the leader had attended to the group's distress at missing Jenny, she could have not only soothed that distress but also helped the group find ways of dealing with the sadness and confusion people feel when a familiar person is lost. "Coping with loss" could have been a valuable CBT-focus that day. If this was an early session where few coping skills had been previously learned, at least the principle of acknowledging distressing feelings and talking about them (rather than blaming people or otherwise acting out) could have been illustrated.

Finally, Jenny's departure might have been anticipated. If there is a poor developmental "fit" between a particular child and the rest of the group, this is usually obvious in one or two sessions. The group leader could have acknowledged and validated her discomfort. "It must be hard to sit patiently when other people need more time than you do" or "I guess that example is different from how things happen in your grade" are examples of empathic comments that might have facilitated discussion of the issue. Ways to include Jenny that acknowledged her more "grown-up" approach to things could have been developed. For example, she could have been asked to help younger children struggling to learn the material (many children love to teach others), partnered with the next-oldest child in the group on some tasks, or been given tasks modified to better fit with her developmental needs. Talking to Jenny's parents about how she makes a valuable contribution to the group, in addition to getting benefit from it, would also have been helpful, possibly preventing her premature departure.

Differences between group and individual child CBT have been included in previous chapters, but will be reviewed here. To put them in context, however, it may be advisable to reread the relevant chapter if you are struggling with a particular issue. In brief, the two modalities differ in:

- Assessment criteria
- Treatment expectations
- Aspects of the therapeutic alliance
- Aspects of working with parents

The key aspects of each will now be reviewed.

**Assessment Criteria**

There is often pressure to run CBT groups in the community in the hope of doing more with fewer staff, but that hope may be misplaced. The organization of multiple children and families to attend consistently at the same time, the adequate assessment and preparation of all those children and families, and the need to integrate the group with other services provided by other mental health professionals all consume considerable time. Moreover, most CBT groups run better with two therapists rather than one. Two therapists allow for training, spreading the availability of CBT, and also some individualized attention (from the second therapist) for children who are struggling in the group. Cotherapists can also be valuable observers of group interactions, which are easily missed by the "lead therapist" as he or she may be focused on covering the CBT skills for that particular session. Concurrent parent groups may confer additional benefit in child CBT, and these may require one or two additional therapists. In summary, while groups are somewhat more efficient than individual therapy for teaching CBT principles, they do not reduce therapist workload in direct proportion to the number of group members. In other words, organizing and running a CBT group of seven children is not 1/7 of the work of doing seven individual cases.

Assessment for group suitability should be as rigorous as for individual CBT (see Chapter 2), and include some additional considerations. A pre-group meeting with each group-referred child is advisable to assess these additional factors and to get a sense of how various children might "fit" with each other. The factors include:

- Distractibility and behavioral problems. No more than two children with these difficulties should be included in a group, and if they are severe the child should be referred for individual treatment.
- Highly withdrawn or socially anxious children may have difficulty learning CBT concepts in this (for them) stressful setting. Mild social anxiety is sometimes alleviated through group support, but children with severe social anxiety or selective mutism have difficulty both contributing to and benefiting from groups. Individual therapy should be considered in these cases.
- Children with learning or language difficulties can be problematic in groups, depending on how far behind their academic or linguistic skills are relative to other group members. Significant delays may result in stigmatization for "slowing down" the pace of the rest of the group.
- Ages of group members should be within a three- or at most four-year range, to ensure a similar level of cognitive maturity. The older but cognitively immature child can sometimes be included, as long as he or she does not stand out from the rest of the group in another important way.
- CBT can work in single-gender or mixed-gender groups, but groups with only one member of a particular gender are inadvisable because that member often drops out.

**Treatment Expectations**

For the most part, these should resemble the treatment expectations to discuss with children and families for individual CBT (see Chapter 4). Consistent attendance is even more important in group than individual CBT, however, as sessions are not typically rescheduled, and it can be challenging for a child to catch up if more than one consecutive session has been missed. The child's contribution to the group is also missed when he or she does not attend (see example above), often to a greater degree than anyone anticipated. In addition, some common misconceptions about group treatment that may need to be addressed include:

- The child will get less out of group treatment than individual treatment. Parents often reason that if the child is getting the therapist's attention only 1/7 or 1/8 of the time, then the therapeutic benefit will be proportionately lower. This is simply not true, as children often benefit as much from group treatment as from individual treatment (see references). There are potentially additional benefits to groups, including universality (the sense of not being the only one with the problem), peer support and encouragement, and "brainstorming" (the group generating more ideas than an individual therapist could).

- The group will address the child's social skill deficits, or result in long-term friendships for an isolated child. CBT groups do not necessarily enhance social skills unless this is the primary focus of the group. If the group is focused on reducing anxiety or reducing depressive symptoms, for example, social skill gains may or may not occur. Friendships do sometimes form during CBT groups, but these are by no means guaranteed, nor are they typically facilitated by the therapist.

- The therapist will tell the parents everything that happened in the child group and everything their child did or did not say in the group. The need for some confidentiality of group information that does not pose any risk to the child or others should be explained. Parents are often given a short "briefing" of what happened in the child group, and some therapists even have children tell their parents what they learned that day, but specific examples should not be shared unless the child wants to do so. This practice ensures that children feel comfortable disclosing important information in the group, without fearing that their parents or other children's parents will hear about it.

## Aspects of the Therapeutic Alliance

Principles of working with children in a CBT group certainly resemble those for individual treatment, but require some additional thought. Therefore, it is well worth finding a group-specific manual (see resource list) for the focus of the CBT group. Whether or not a manual is available, some group-specific considerations include:

- Teaching to a variety of learning styles. Many group manuals already include a variety of exercises to appeal to visual, verbal, kinesthetic, and other ways of learning. If working without a manual, it is wise to include these.

- Having clear ground rules for group behavior, preferably developed during the initial group session or two with therapist and member participation. Important rules should address turn-taking when people speak, not criticizing others' ideas, keeping others' examples confidential outside the group, and dealing with behavior that disrupts the group.
- Having exercises that engage the whole group in a cooperative task. Having everyone contribute ideas or solutions to a particular problem is the simplest version of this idea. Group drawings, group feeling lists, or group relaxation practice are other common examples. These exercises not only facilitate learning but also increase group members' confidence in what they can achieve together.
- Encouraging group members to help each other. This works particularly well when taking up homework exercises that some group members have struggled with. The "teacher" and the child who receives help can both benefit from this approach.
- Finding rewards that appeal to the whole group. Beyond individual praise and points, groups afford the opportunity to provide social rewards. Game time or snack time at the end of the group becomes the most appealing aspect of the therapy for some children and can be highly motivating.

**Aspects of Working with Parents**

Parent groups can confer the same benefits as child groups (universality, mutual support and encouragement, brainstorming) and a few more. Because parents feel a common bond with other parents in the group, they are often more inclined to listen to them than to professionals, facilitating therapeutic change. For example, parents with significant personal psychopathology will often recognize the need for treatment much more readily when it is suggested by another parent than when suggested by a therapist. There is also a perception that other parents "know the score" when it comes to raising children, whereas therapists (especially those whose ages fall outside the typical childrearing years) may have less appreciation of today's parenting stresses. The problem-solving focus of many parent programs is often experienced as empowering for parents. Few experiences are more encouraging and empowering than reporting back to one's parent group that one's efforts to change a particular child behavior actually worked.

If available, it is certainly advisable to use a parent group manual (see references). If working without a manual, key points to remember include:

- Encouraging parents to share as much or as little as they are comfortable with about their child's difficulties with the group. In the initial sessions, this is respectful and often leads to a surprisingly rapid discovery of similar experiences among group members, and to mutual empathy and support.

- Having ground rules, analogous to those in the child groups, agreed upon in the first session or two. An important rule to add for most parent groups is "We will discuss one problem at a time." Parent groups easily become unfocused commiseration sessions without this rule.

- Encouraging feedback right from the start. Parents do not always express their dissatisfaction as readily as children do, so it is important to elicit this. "How did you think this session went?" or "Did you get something out of this session?" are sometimes good questions to ask before concluding a parent group meeting.

- Encouraging parents to find their own solutions, rather than turning to the therapist for all the answers. While certain parent-generated solutions are clearly not acceptable (for example, those that could harm the child), most are creative and based on a more detailed knowledge of the child than the therapist has. Also, if parents are to carry on solving problems after the group ends, they will need this skill. To encourage parents to find solutions for a problem, ask "What do other people in the group think?" or "What would other people around the table do in that situation?" This also encourages group members to help each other, which benefits both the helper and the recipient of the help.

- Encouraging parents to test out their ideas between sessions and report back on the results to "fine-tune," if needed, to determine what works for each child. Parents are usually more amenable to this type of homework than to a written exercise, and it is far more practical. If parents do not do this, point out that the group will have little to talk about in the next session. Formal teaching is more limited in parent than in child groups, so parents' reports are necessary "grist for the mill" of group discussions.

- Setting limits with talkers and engaging the silent types. This is the most common aspect of group dynamics that a therapist must monitor and attend to. Gentle redirection of someone who is monopolizing the conversation is an art. "That is a really good point, and we will talk more about it next week. Right now, we need to get back to . . . " is one example of redirecting a talker. Asking others in the group to comment on the issue is another. At the other end of the spectrum, some parents never speak unless spoken to. The therapist should create an opportunity for everyone to speak at least once during a session (for example, "What did you think about X, Helen?"), but respect some people's need to warm up slowly or to just listen for a while.

- Remembering that parents need positive reinforcement just as much as children do. Often, they will positively reinforce each other for contributing ideas, but if someone's contribution is not acknowledged the therapist should acknowledge it. This is often easiest to do during a problem-focused discussion by summarizing who contributed which ideas. Ideas and contributors that have not been previously acknowledged can be given additional emphasis. Positive reinforcement for attendance (for example, "Wow! You made it through that traffic mess out there!") is helpful too, especially with members who may feel less connected to the group.

**Group Dynamics**

In addition to these differences from individual CBT, one must also attend to group dynamics when working with children and parents using this modality, as illustrated in the example at the beginning of this chapter. First and foremost, children must feel safe in the group. Intervening to prevent bullying or verbal taunts is essential. The task-focused, structured nature of CBT groups also reduces anxiety and promotes a sense of safety, more so than unstructured, process-oriented groups do. For this reason, it is important to keep the group on task, as long as one does not totally ignore the members' emotional needs as the leader in the example did. Session structure is similar to individual CBT. After an introduction to the session agenda, children review homework (although with encouragement to help each other understand any concepts that they are struggling with), learn a new CBT skill until everyone can demonstrate an understanding of it, discuss homework to be practiced between sessions, and then have some social time at the end.

Members who feel alienated from the group are not only at risk for a poor therapeutic outcome themselves, but also place other members of the group, and potentially the entire group, at risk. The "ripple effect" of a single group member who is negative about the group or stops attending can impact everyone. On the other hand, too much attention to individual needs may undermine helpful group interactions. "Brainstorming," for example, is much easier when the group is focused on solving a problem rather than addressing individual difficulties.

Balancing the needs of the group and the needs of individual members can be challenging in child CBT, but it can be easier if two group therapists are present. One can be a trainee or less experienced therapist, as long as the two can work together. In this case, one therapist leads the group, keeps it focused, and ensures that CBT content is covered. The second therapist attends to group process and helps group members that may be struggling with the material, have behavioral problems, or require individual attention for other reasons. After each session, the two therapists share their experiences, including any concerns about particular members or the dynamics of the group. The problem can then be addressed promptly the next week.

Common problems include children who feel alienated from the group, have difficulty keeping up with the rest of the group, have difficulty containing their behavior in the group, attend inconsistently, or "clash" with another child, resulting in conflict. With two therapists, each child's progress is briefly reviewed each week, so these problems can be addressed. In addition, the level of cohesion or sense of "belonging" that seems to be present in the group can be gauged. This is just as important as learning CBT principles when offering CBT in this format. Emphasizing commonalities between group members, highlighting unique contributions certain members make to the group, including a social or game time at the end of each group (often with a snack), including cooperative group challenges (for example, "let's see how many words for feelings we can come up with as a group"), and encouraging children to help each other when they are "stuck" on a particular CBT task are all ways of improving cohesion. As in individual work, therapists who take a genuine interest in the children's day-to-day lives also foster a strong therapeutic alliance. Allowing children to do the same with each other, as long as it does not distract from the task at hand, also fosters allegiance to the group.

Crisis situations can arise even in the best-organized groups. This is even more likely when including children with comorbid conditions (for example, anxiety and depression). It behooves the group therapist to be aware of local emergency resources and access them promptly when the need arises. While having a group member express suicidal thoughts or lose control behaviorally (two common crises) may be upsetting to other group members, it need not be disastrous. As long as the group leader provides an explanation of what has happened and subsequent updates on how the child in crisis is doing, other children are often very sympathetic. They may, for example, want to send a get well card if the child is hospitalized or convey their continued interest in the child in some other way. Many children are reassured to see a group leader take action to prevent a group member from harming themselves or other people in the group. Parents sometimes require more reassurance than children when this occurs. They may be concerned about contagion (their own child behaving the same way as the child in crisis) or question the therapist's competence. This is one of the few situations where talking to parents about some of what is happening in the child group may be appropriate, although the children deserve to know why this is necessary. If a crisis occurs outside the group, the affected family and child usually have their own preference about how much to share with the group, and the therapist should generally respect their wishes. Many CBT groups never encounter a serious crisis. Although crises are not expected, however, preparation for them is still worthwhile.

## School-Based CBT

Several child CBT programs for schools have been developed recently. The best known is the FRIENDS program by Dr. Paula Barrett and colleagues in Australia. It has been successfully demonstrated to reduce anxiety in comparison to a waitlist control condition (no intervention), so it is now being adopted as part of the school curriculum in Australia and parts of Canada. It is available via the FRIENDS website (https://friendsprograms.com/).

Before running out to buy this program, however, it is worth considering the benefits and potential pitfalls of school-based child CBT. On the positive side, school-based child CBT provides the opportunity to reach many more anxious or depressed children who could benefit. Only about 20% of children with mental health problems typically come to clinics, but 100% of children are obliged to go to school! School-based intervention may also reduce the stigma typically associated with seeing a mental health professional in a clinic or hospital. CBT is a didactic treatment, so it is very similar to learning another school subject already on the curriculum. This makes it a "natural fit" for the school environment. Furthermore, many anxiety- or depression-related problems in children manifest during the school day, so teachers are often eager to help children manage these. Therefore, they are often very receptive to CBT-based interventions.

A note of caution is warranted, however. Studies to date have focused mainly on waitlist control conditions rather than other active interventions. When active interventions are provided, the use of well-supervised, highly structured sessions that include regular positive reinforcement of participation has been found to correlate with therapeutic change (Manassis et al., 2010). It is therefore possible that a well-supervised, structured after-school program with positive reinforcement from a caring adult (e.g., a good sports coach, drama coach, or school newspaper organizer) could also be therapeutic. One would hope that the skills learned in CBT do confer a greater benefit than one of these programs in the long term, but this possibility is still being studied.

Who are the best candidates for school-based CBT programs? Should they be provided to every child, because the skills can be helpful to everyone, or should we target children who are at risk for more serious problems to avoid wasting time, energy, and money on a program that is not necessary in many cases? As mentioned, targeted interventions seem to show greater benefit in depression (Calear & Christensen, 2010). Should children be selected based on their ability to disclose symptoms (because these children are more likely to be ready to address those symptoms) or based on others' perceptions of their symptoms? Who should be excluded from such programs? There is still debate about these questions.

Finally, how does one implement a program in a way that the school is likely to embrace it and sustain it over time? In a school setting, it is not enough to identify suitable children who could benefit from CBT. The school board, the principal, the people implementing the program (whether teachers or mental health professionals), the parents, and the child all need to be convinced of the value of the program, or it will not be adopted in the long run. This fact implies a lot of interpersonal contact and work with the schools, quite apart from just "doing child CBT."

Having run school-based CBT programs for several years, I do have a few suggestions. These include:

- Do not attempt school-based CBT until you are confident about using this modality clinically. You will not be able to "sell" it to the schools without that confidence. Then, always ask for the opportunity to present your program to parents of children attending each school, as this is essential to ensure child participation. Utilizing videotapes, brochures, or program websites can also help to publicize and market your approach.

- School personnel tend to be sensitive to the possibility of stigmatizing children attending programs with a mental health focus. Anticipate this, and find ways to reassure them. Giving your program a child-friendly, nonpsychiatric name helps. For example, we named our program "The Feelings Club" (Wilansky-Traynor & Manassis, 2004).

- Count on at least a year of planning and meeting with various school personnel before you actually start your program. Approach key leaders in mental health at the level of the school board (for example, chief psychologist, chief social worker). Try to identify a "champion" for your program among those leaders. Find out if you need a written agreement with the school and/or school board to work with the children, if your staff will need police background checks, if you need permission to be on school premises after hours (if you are running an after-school program), if you need access to clinical backup services for emergencies, and any other requirements either by the board or the local schools.

- Do not compromise on basic CBT needs such as private space for groups, timing that allows children to attend consistently (no conflicts with bus schedules or other activities they attend), and some opportunity to meet with parents to educate them about the program and enlist their support.

- Provide ongoing support to teachers or mental health personnel who are providing the program. Most schools prefer to have the "experts" do the program first to avoid liability concerns, and then are amenable to having their staff join you in implementing it later. Independent implementation by school personnel may take several years to develop.

- Leaders in implementation will prefer to have some local decision-making ability, so respect their experience and solve problems with them, rather than for them. Also, remember that the principal is vital to a program's success in a given school, so take time to get to know that person, convince him or her of the potential benefits of your program, and allay any concerns that he or she may have.

- Logistics, testimonials to your program's success in other schools, and school board approval will be important for people who are skeptical or less directly involved, often including parents. Working these issues out ahead of time will often allay their concerns.

- Expect less parental involvement than in clinical settings, but offer to meet with parents regularly. Unlike parents of clinically referred children, many parents of children identified in the school system do not realize their children struggle with anxiety or depression. Therefore, their motivation to participate in a CBT program may be reduced.

- Most educators prefer "whole-school" to targeted interventions because they avoid the risk of singling out certain children and improve the emotional climate of the school. While this is laudable, most schools will not be open to adding CBT training to their curriculum, at least not initially. Curricular requirements are already too high for many teachers to manage, so few welcome another "add-on." Demonstrating the benefits of a targeted program may, however, promote the adoption of a "whole-school" program later.

- If your program is not adopted as part of the curriculum, be clear on what types of children you are targeting. As in most child-focused CBT, the child's main problem should relate to anxiety or depression. Children with significant behavior problems may be identified by teachers as "needing help," but they rarely benefit from a child CBT program, especially if it is offered in a group.

- If you are planning a group intervention, use the same guidelines as for clinical groups, as outlined earlier in this chapter.

All of the above is possible, but only with a great deal of ongoing commitment over several years. In my experience, only the most dedicated child CBT providers attempt it.

## WHAT WE YET NEED TO LEARN

Group treatments are being developed and evaluated for more and more disorders, including some that might seem counter-intuitive (e.g., groups for children with selective mutism). Further evaluation of group- and school-based CBT relative to active (rather than waitlist) control conditions and longer-term follow-up studies are indicated. The effectiveness and cost effectiveness of universal versus targeted prevention programs, and of teacher-led programs versus those led by mental health professionals, also merit clarification.

# CBT GROUP WORKSHEET

If you are planning a child CBT group program in your setting and have the necessary support of your organization to do so:

- What logistical issues do you need to address? Think about engaging clinicians who might refer to the group, obtaining funding for minor group supplies (snacks, stickers, etc.), having a consistent and convenient time and place for the group, collating manuals and other group materials, and having a cotherapist or other peer support. If you are obtaining consultation or supervision, you may also need families' permission to record the group sessions.
Issues/tasks:

  1. _____
  2. _____
  3. _____
  4. _____
  5. _____

- What manual will be best suited to the population you hope to treat?
Manual: _____
_____

Reason: _____
_____

Cost: _____
_____

- How will you assess children for group suitability and educate referring clinicians about this issue?
Assessment procedure(s): _____
_____

Education for clinicians: _____
_____

- How will you clarify treatment expectations for the children and families?
Procedure(s): _____
_____

- How will you ensure a good therapeutic alliance with the children?

  Procedure(s): _____

  _____

- How will you ensure a good therapeutic alliance with the parents?

  Procedure(s): _____

  _____

- How will you anticipate and address potential crisis situations?

  Procedure(s): _____

  _____

## CLINICAL CHALLENGE

1. You arrive to run your first child CBT group session at a school. You are informed that you will be meeting in the library, and a rather noisy "homework club" will occur at the other end of the library. The library is an open area, and soon children who are not in the CBT program begin walking by your group on the way to the lending desk and start listening in. About 30 minutes into the group, the janitor arrives and tells you the group must move because he needs to clean the area. You move the group, but 15 minutes later he returns and tells you to wrap up because he always locks the building at that hour.

    a. What do you do at that time?

    b. What do you do the next day?

2. You are running your first group for parents of anxious children who are participating in a concurrent CBT group program. After a round of introductions, you provide a brief description of the goals of the parent group and its relationship to the child program, and ask if there are any questions. How do you respond to the following situations?

    a. A rather severe-looking gentleman in a business suit asks pointedly whether or not you have raised children yourself, and what your child CBT success rate is.

    b. A cell-phone rings loudly, one mother responds, and she spends the next five minutes instructing her daughter on how to make lasagna for dinner as all the other parents listen.

    c. Another mother volunteers that she has done CBT herself. She then describes her therapy in detail and smiles at you knowingly, monopolizing the group conversation.

    d. Near the end of the session, the parents are working on a joint problem-solving exercise, discussing alternative ways to get their children to sleep independently. One mother volunteers, "I know my son, and I can't see how any of this will help him without medication." She turns to you, "Can you recommend something?"

## REFERENCES

Asbahr, F.R., Castillo, A.R., Ito, L.M., Latorre, M.R., Moreira, M.N., & Lotufo-Neto, F. (2005). Group cognitive behavioral therapy versus sertraline for the treatment of children and adolescents with obsessive compulsive disorder. *Journal of the American Academy of Child and Adolescent Psychiatry*, 44, 1128–1136.

Baer, S., & Garland, E.J. (2005). Pilot study of community-based cognitive behavioral group therapy for adolescents with social phobia. *Journal of the American Academy of Child and Adolescent Psychiatry*, 44, 258–264.

Barrett, P.M., Farrell, L.J., Ollendick, T.H., & Dadds, M. (2006). Long-term outcomes of an Australian universal prevention trial of anxiety and depression symptoms in children and youth: An evaluation of the friends program. *Journal of Clinical Child and Adolescent Psychology*, 35, 403–411.

Calear, A.L., & Christensen, H. (2010). Systematic review of school-based prevention and early intervention programs for depression. *Journal of Adolescence*, 33, 429–438.

Clarke, G.N., Hornbrook, M., Lynch, F., Polen, M., Gale, J., Beardslee, W., et al. (2001). A randomized trial of a group cognitive intervention for preventing depression in adolescent offspring of depressed parents. *Archives of General Psychiatry*, 58, 1127–1134.

Hayward, C., Varady, S., Albano, A.M., Thienemann, M., Henderson, L., & Schatzberg, A.F. (2000). Cognitive-behavioral group therapy for social phobia in female adolescents: Results of a pilot study. *Journal of the American Academy of Child and Adolescent Psychiatry*, 39, 721–726.

James, A.C., James, G., Cowdrey, F.A., Soler, A., & Choke, A. (2013). Cognitive behavioural therapy for anxiety disorders in children and adolescents. *Cochrane Database of Systematic Reviews*, Jun 3;6:CD004690.

Manassis, K., Mendlowitz, S., Scapillato, D., Avery, D., Fiksenbaum, L., Freire, M., et al. (2002). Group and individual cognitive behavioral therapy for childhood anxiety disorders: A randomized trial. *Journal of the American Academy of Child & Adolescent Psychiatry*, 41, 1423–1430.

Manassis, K., Wilansky-Traynor, P., Farzan, N., Kleiman, V., Parker, K., & Sanford, M. (2010). The Feelings Club: A randomized controlled trial of school-based intervention for anxious and depressed children. *Depression and Anxiety*, 27, 945–952.

Martin, J.L., & Thienemann, M. (2005). Group cognitive-behavior therapy with family involvement for middle-school-age children with obsessive-compulsive disorder: A pilot study. *Child Psychiatry and Human Development*, 36, 113–127.

Neil, A.L., & Christensen, H. (2009). Efficacy and effectiveness of school-based prevention and early intervention programs for anxiety. *Clinical Psychology Review*, 29, 208–215.

Rohde, P., Clarke, G.N., Lewinsohn, P.M., Seeley, J.R., & Kaufman, N.K. (2001). Impact of comorbidity on a cognitive-behavioral group treatment for adolescent depression. *Journal of the American Academy of Child and Adolescent Psychiatry*, 40, 795–802.

Scapillato, D., & Manassis, K. (2002). Cognitive-behavioral/interpersonal group treatment for anxious adolescents. *Journal of the American Academy of Child and Adolescent Psychiatry*, 41, 739–741.

Thienemann, M., Martin, J., Cregger, B., Thompson, H.B., & Dyer-Friedman, J. (2001). Manual-driven group cognitive-behavioral therapy for adolescents with obsessive compulsive disorder: A pilot study. *Journal of the American Academy of Child and Adolescent Psychiatry*, 40, 1254–1260.

Wilansky-Traynor, P., & Manassis, K. (2004). *The Feelings Club manual*. Available from the authors, Centre for Addiction and Mental Health, Toronto, ON.

# CHAPTER TEN

# Overcoming Therapeutic Obstacles

Even the most experienced and astute therapists sometimes get "stuck" in doing child CBT. This chapter helps you anticipate and address some common difficulties encountered in child CBT.

## WHAT IS KNOWN

Lack of improvement with CBT can relate to a number of factors. Predictors of less favorable treatment outcomes that have been established in depressed youth include older age, severe depression, comorbid diagnoses, family discord, and high impairment (Emslie, Mayes, & Ruberu, 2005). Recurrence rates are high in this population, and predictors of recurrence include family history of depression, comorbid disorders, negative cognitive style, and negative life events (Birmaher, Arbelaez, & Brent, 2002).

Predictors of less favorable outcomes that have been established in anxious youth include family dysfunction (Barrett, Farrell, Dadds, & Boulter, 2005), low family cohesion (Victor, Bernat, Bernstein, & Layne, 2007), parental anxiety (Creswell & Cartwright-Hatton, 2007), high initial severity (Barrett et al., 2005; Southam-Gerow, Kendall, & Weersing, 2001), attentional bias towards threat (Manassis, Hum, Lee, Zhang, & Lewis, 2013), low child involvement in therapy (Chu & Kendall, 2004), and depressive symptoms (Southam-Gerow et al., 2001).

Many authors also emphasize the importance of careful assessment and case formulation to optimize CBT outcomes (Chorpita, 2007; Manassis,

2014). An approach to addressing therapeutic difficulties that incorporates these ideas is described in this chapter.

## PUTTING WHAT WE KNOW TO WORK

### Examples of "Getting Stuck"

I feel an adolescent girl has made good progress in managing her anxieties after fourteen sessions of CBT, but she is dissatisfied because she still occasionally feels overwhelmed. I attribute this to some remaining perfectionistic tendencies, which appear to be part of an emerging personality style. Nevertheless, I agree to arrange a consultation with a colleague. He prescribes a new medication that reduces her perfectionism and rigid thinking, and she is now amenable to a host of additional coping strategies that she was unwilling to try previously. Her episodic feelings of being overwhelmed subside, and she is now satisfied with her progress in therapy. Therapy concludes amicably a few weeks later.

An 11-year-old boy feels he has made good progress in CBT, but his parents still worry a great deal about him. Their worries prevent them from allowing their son to engage in age-appropriate independent activities. The boy does not mind being sheltered this way, but I believe he could make more progress if he had appropriate parental support and encouragement. I consult a colleague who specializes in family therapy. My colleague advises that these parents are unlikely to change anytime soon, and encourages me to "leave the door open" for the boy to come back. Three years later, he returns complaining that his parents are "nosy" and "too strict" because his evening curfew is earlier than that of his classmates. He no longer shows any anxiety symptoms. He welcomes my suggestions for negotiating greater autonomy from his parents. The parents are gradually able to allow him greater freedom as he demonstrates that he can handle it responsibly.

These examples from my own practice demonstrate a simple fact: Nobody can succeed with all of their clients all of the time without a little help. We all need to be able to turn to colleagues for advice, a different perspective on a case, additional treatment for a client, or just a shoulder to cry on.

When starting a new treatment modality, supervision is essential. Thus, when you are learning child CBT, your first couple of cases should be discussed weekly with a more experienced therapist. Audiotaping or videotaping your sessions for review with the supervisor is ideal, but taking good notes will suffice if you are honest and report the difficulties you encounter, not just the successes. Even when you no longer need supervision, however, it is wise to maintain contact with a few colleagues or mentors doing similar work to "bounce ideas off," and also some colleagues working with a similar population using other modalities (as in the examples above). Meeting regularly as a small group is helpful for many child CBT therapists for both ongoing consultation and mutual support. A yearly CBT workshop or two to hone one's skills and keep up to date on new developments is also helpful, regardless of one's level of experience. Some conferences or training centers also offer videotapes of expert therapists that can be very enlightening to watch.

Think about different ways of working with colleagues. For example, sometimes an informal question over coffee is helpful in getting a case back on track, while other times a more thorough consultation is needed. Be careful to be clear about who has responsibility for the case, however, especially if you prefer a less formal approach. If you do not have any "local experts" in a particular area, consider accessing tele-health services (Neufeld, Yellowlees, Hilty, Cobb, & Bourgeois, 2007) to obtain consultation from a colleague in another city or town.

## Consultations

If you opt for a consultation, have a clear question for the consultant. Examples might include: What additional treatment options (if any) should be considered in this case? Can this child benefit from further CBT, or is it time to try something else? What is interfering with progress in this case?

Also be clear what you hope to gain from the consultation. Some common situations where consultation may be helpful to you include:

- You want advice on how to optimize the treatment you are providing because you are dissatisfied with the rate or degree of progress.
- You want advice on how to optimize the treatment you are providing, because you are having difficulty in the therapeutic alliance with the child or with the parent.
- The child or parent wants a "second opinion," because they are dissatisfied with you or with the rate or degree of progress.
- You are unsure if you want to continue to treat the client, either because of difficulties in the therapeutic alliance or because of lack of progress.
- You want to share care with the consultant (i.e., have him or her provide treatment additional to yours if appropriate).
- You want the consultant to take over the case. In this case, be clear that you are making a referral for treatment, rather than asking for a consultation. Treatment referrals disguised as consultations are often perceived as "dumping" a case and will not endear you to your consultants.

Improving outcomes for evidence-based treatment through effective consultation has been further described by Schoenwald, Sheldow, and Letourneau (2004).

## Obstacles to Successful Child CBT

Before obtaining a consultation, or while waiting for it, consider some common obstacles to successful child CBT and address those you think may apply in your case. Leahy (2006) has described therapeutic challenges in CBT in detail. A simpler model is presented here.

A good analogy for challenges in CBT is that of a car radio. Listening to music on the car radio, there are two possible problems. One problem is the presence of weather patterns, topographical features, or other environmental sources of interference with the radio signal. These result in static, that annoying crackly sound that prevents enjoyment of the song or musical piece. A second problem relates to the strength of the signal. When one is driving around in the town where the radio station is located, this is rarely an issue, but when one is driving in the countryside there is a predictable point where the signal begins to fade, and soon the music is no longer audible.

Applying the analogy to CBT, there are two similar problems: factors in the child's life that are not amenable to CBT and may interfere with therapy (the "static") and providing CBT in a manner that is suboptimal (the "weak signal"). Most of the book so far has addressed the first of these. Therefore, if you are struggling with your client, review some of the potential factors that may be interfering with therapy. Try to contain your own frustration, and view the therapeutic impasse as a mystery to be solved. "Playing detective" is usually more fun than blaming yourself, the client, the parents, or the therapy. Ask yourself some questions about these common problems, encountered frequently in child therapy:

- Has there been a new life challenge, resulting in an exacerbation of the child's symptoms?
- Has the child experienced a recent remission in symptoms, reducing the desire to continue therapy?
- Has the child's motivation to continue therapy changed, perhaps due to embarrassment or a competing activity?
- Has parental support and participation in the therapy changed, perhaps due to discouragement or competing time demands?
- Is there a hidden child or family expectation about therapy that has not been met?

Sometimes people nod in agreement when treatment expectations are discussed, but secretly hope for something else. For example, parents may hope for a radical personality change in the client, or an improved parent–child relationship, despite agreeing to focus on reducing child mood or anxiety symptoms.

- Is the child receiving another intervention that is undermining yours?
- Is there substance use or another previously undisclosed issue in the child or family that is affecting therapy?

Also consider the possibility that there has been change in the element(s) that apply over the course of therapy. For example, a new stress or concurrent problem may have emerged, or initial treatment goals may have been forgotten or neglected. If there is a new stress or problem, reevaluate where CBT fits in the overall treatment plan. If the problem is significant, further CBT may need to be postponed until it is addressed, or the focus of CBT may need to shift to the new issue. Review of initial goals and expectations and of progress evident from baseline may be helpful for discouraged children and families.

Let us now look at the second problem: suboptimal CBT. To understand what constitutes suboptimal CBT, we must first understand what is optimal. Many problems addressed in CBT relate to facing something new, whether it is facing a fear, facing a situation where one normally engages in rituals, or just facing the day by getting out of bed (in depression). Mastering such new situations is most likely to work when they are approached in a planned, thoughtful way, and the child then engages in intensive, incremental practice. This is the common theme among various techniques that relate to approaching situations. Other problems addressed in CBT relate to stopping an undesirable behavior (for example, aggression, hair-pulling) or thought. In this case, the common theme among techniques is planning ahead, labeling the thought or impulse when it occurs, and then deliberately shifting attention to something else, usually a coping thought or an alternative activity.

In children, both approaches require certain helpful attitudes on the part of the therapist and the child's parents. These include realistic optimism about the child's ability to succeed (with empathic acknowledgment of how challenging the task may be), vigilance for and validation of every small sign of progress, calm and deliberate ignoring of setbacks, and positive reinforcement that is perceived as meaningful and encouraging by the child.

Keeping the above two themes in mind, we can now examine where things can go wrong. For handy reference, these are also listed in Table 10.1. First, both approaches require planning and intensive, repetitive practice.

TABLE 10.1
Common Trouble Spots in Child CBT

| Type of Problem | Problem with Therapy | Problem with Attitudes |
| --- | --- | --- |
| Approaching a Situation (intensive, incremental practice) | Inadequate preparation | Lack of realistic, empathic optimism (e.g., depression) |
| | Infrequent practice | Lack of attention to progress (e.g., overly busy) |
| | Short duration of practice | Lack of meaningful positive reinforcement (e.g., out of touch with child's values) |
| | Lack of repetition within or between sessions Dilution of skills Unstructured teaching Too few incremental steps | |
| Stopping a Behavior or Thought (label and shift attention) | All "approach" therapy problems | All "approach" attitude problems |
| | Impulsivity | Inability to calmly ignore setbacks |
| | Difficulty finding an acceptable substitute | |
| Any Problem | Therapeutic drift Problem in the alliance | |

Sometimes, planning is lacking and children are exposed to new situations suddenly, with inadequate preparation. They panic or feel betrayed by the adults in their lives and refuse to go back into those situations. Sometimes, practice is not intensive or repetitive enough. When people undergo rehabilitation from strokes or other brain injuries, they progress best with daily practice of an hour or more over several weeks or months (Doidge, 2007). Why should we expect children to adapt to novel situations, often quite foreign to them, with less effort? Working with highly withdrawn, depressed youngsters can certainly resemble a rehabilitative process, and benefits are few without a daily attempt to engage them in activity. In anxious children, there is a physiological need to remain in an anxiety-provoking situation until stress hormones subside in order for desensitization to occur. Twenty to thirty minutes is the minimum time needed for this process to occur. Frequency and duration of practice are both important in providing CBT that is intense enough to produce lasting change.

Moreover, the same skill or skill set must be practiced each time. Those who vary the content of CBT exercises "to make them more interesting" or add new elements to an existing therapy risk diluting the practice children need to consolidate new skills. For the same reason, teaching CBT skills in sessions that lack structure or teaching them without between-session practice rarely succeeds.

Other potential problems with approaching situations include having too few incremental steps and providing insufficient encouragement related to progress. The first problem often occurs when an adult designs a behavioral program for a child without a thorough understanding of the child's point of view. For example, a parent may think that independent sleep can be achieved by moving two feet further away from the child's bed each night, not realizing that, on the third or fourth night, this places the parent outside the child's field of vision. The child panics, and the parent either gives up or accuses the child of being uncooperative. The parent does not realize that, for the child, the difference between coping while having the parent in view and coping while not having a parent in view is huge. Having the parent talk in a soothing tone while not in view may help with this large step. Alternatively, giving the child a picture or other visual reminder of the parent may also help reduce the magnitude of this step. With a little creativity, one can always create a smaller step toward progress.

Encouragement is needed at every stage of approaching a new situation. These stages can be summarized by the acronym "A.B.C." Realistic, empathic optimism is needed most at the outset or in *Antecedents* of the situation, when children doubt their own abilities. Attention to tiny signs of progress is crucial to maintain motivation while the *Behavior* is practiced. Meaningful positive reinforcement provides a *Consequence* that increases the likelihood that the child will try the behavior again. If any of these three types of encouragement is lacking, the child may become discouraged and stop working on approaching the situation. Being depressed, and thus habitually seeing the "glass half empty," can make it difficult to be realistically optimistic about the child's chances of success. Being overly busy or preoccupied with activities that do not relate to the child can make it difficult to attend closely and consistently to the child's efforts. Being out of touch with the child's values and desires can make it hard to figure out what constitutes meaningful positive reinforcement for that child.

Potential problems with stopping an undesirable behavior or thought include difficulty labeling the undesirable behavior or thought before engaging in it, finding an acceptable substitute to attend to, and maintaining an encouraging attitude while calmly ignoring setbacks. Most children are able to find acceptable and readily recognizable labels for their difficulties, but impulsivity can prevent them from stopping the behavior or thought before it overwhelms them. Repeated practice, finding situations where the behavior is easier to control to start with, and clear sensory signals to prompt the label (for example, a visual stop sign, a snap of the fingers, a strong perfume on the wrist of a hair-puller) are all recommended in various protocols. Substitute behaviors often engage the same body parts as the original (walk away rather than kicking, knitting rather than hair-pulling, chewing gum rather than smoking or nail-biting) and usually work better if they are somewhat enjoyable for the child. Undesirable thoughts are often shifted to the task at hand or "postponed." For example, an anxious child can focus on the teacher's lesson rather than worrying about the fire alarm going off at school. Obsessive thoughts are often "postponed" to a specific time previously agreed upon with the therapist.

The most common difficulty by far in stopping undesirable behavior, however, is the need to calmly ignore setbacks. Parents and therapists both readily fall into the trap of developing a high emotional investment in the child's success. When the behavior periodically recurs (as it inevitably does, as most improvement is not completely linear), disappointment with the child is palpable and may result in discouragement or angry confrontations. With anxious parents, there can be additional negative emotions related to catastrophic thinking. In other words, the anxious parent may interpret the occasional setback as a disastrous treatment failure. Parents and therapists are both well advised to not "take it personally" when the child has a setback. Approach setbacks with curiosity, if possible ("I wonder what went wrong?"), and a calm determination to adjust your approach and persevere.

Regardless of the nature of the problem, it is possible for CBT to get off track even when you have the best of intentions. As a therapist, you may have drifted away from the highly structured session format essential to CBT or begun to incorporate ideas from other types of therapy into your work with the client. It is human nature to gravitate toward the familiar, so if CBT seems unfamiliar, you will naturally go "off course" occasionally. Consider obtaining supervision or guidance from a colleague experienced in CBT, and determine whether your current practices are flexible and appropriate to the client's needs or have drifted away from "true" CBT. Use his or her suggestions constructively, and do not be discouraged; like most things in life, CBT takes practice.

**Factors Affecting the Therapeutic Alliance**

Problems in the therapeutic alliance, either with the parent or the child, deserve some additional consideration. As mentioned, there are common factors that can interfere with this alliance, such as competing demands on people's time, ambivalence about therapy, shifting intensity of symptoms, and unexpected crises in the life of the child or family. Another possibility to consider, however, is whether some matches of therapist and child or therapist and parents are better than others. It is tempting to believe that this is a minor issue in manualized therapies where therapeutic content is standardized, but it is not. The process of therapy still requires a human touch, and working with some human beings is easier than working with others.

Some people come into therapy with a "chip on the shoulder." They have difficulty trusting the therapist and expect a negative outcome. As a result, they behave defensively and sometimes rudely, increasing the possibility of a negative outcome. Their negative expectations become a self-fulfilling prophecy. These people often have "fired" several therapists or mental health professionals, although they may initially express hope that things will be different in working with you. I am always suspicious when I am expected to succeed where others have failed, and take my time to investigate what went wrong in previous attempts at therapy before starting to work with the child and family.

Another variation on this theme occurs when parents are positive about psychotherapy but seem to involve their children in some sort of therapy continuously. Regardless of one's efforts to empower them to deal with their children's problems, they see one child therapy as a prelude to the next. The children, in turn, are given the message that they are permanently ill and in need of mental health support, even when they have many strengths and abilities that could reduce the need for that support. In this case, it may be helpful to recommend no therapy if the child has mild symptoms and would benefit from enjoying more age-appropriate activities and less therapy. If the child has moderate to severe symptoms, of course, one should offer therapy but take extra time to educate the family about its time-limited nature and the expectation that the child will function without ongoing therapy afterward.

For those with psychodynamic training, it is also helpful to keep in the back of one's mind the possibility of "transference." That is, sometimes people relate to each other or to the therapist in ways that mirror relationships within their families of origin. If this does not interfere with progress in CBT, I usually do not mention it even if it is obvious to me. If it does interfere, a short discussion of how we all tend to "repeat old patterns" in ways that are not always helpful can sometimes address the specific obstacle to CBT. For example, a parent may have had the childhood experience of a sibling always being favored by his or her own parents. If the child in therapy reminds the parent of that sibling, the parent may have competitive feelings toward that child, which interfere with doing what is in the child's best interest. Reminding oneself, "This is my child, not my sibling," when such feelings emerge is very helpful in this case. If the parent is not able to do this, or does not acknowledge the problem, the possibility of psychodynamic therapy for the parent may be gently discussed. The same ideas would apply if the parent related to me (the therapist) as though I were the sibling and this interfered with working together for the child's benefit.

Finally, we all have certain strengths and weaknesses when it comes to working with different clients. Some people relate better to adolescents, while others relate better to younger children. Some people relate better to boys, others to girls. Similar cultural background can facilitate the therapeutic alliance, while cultural differences can result in miscommunication and unintended rifts in the alliance. Some diagnostic groups are more appealing to certain therapists than others. As an introvert, for example, I find it easier to work with anxious or withdrawn children than with more boisterous or overly talkative children. While it behooves us to develop flexibility in our therapeutic style so that we can serve a diverse clientele, there are limits to that flexibility. Sometimes it is more helpful to the child and family to refer to a colleague who enjoys working with that particular population than to attempt therapy with a client to whom you know you will have difficulty relating therapeutically.

### New Approaches to "Client Resistance"

Several authors have written about enhancing motivation in adult CBT clients they consider "resistant" (Beck, 2005; Newman, 1994). Personally, I hesitate to use that term with children, as it seems to blame problems in the therapeutic relationship on the child, who is clearly the less powerful partner in the relationship. Nevertheless, there are some practical suggestions for improving treatment motivation in this recent work that can be helpful if adapted to the child's developmental level.

One, borrowed from psychodynamic approaches, has already been mentioned in relation to working with parents: identifying transference (or "*in vivo*, interpersonal overgeneralization," as some CBT therapists call it). It can also occur in working with children, however—especially children who have had negative experiences with authority figures in the past. They may come into therapy with negative expectations of the therapist and, therefore, may be minimally engaged in treatment. If the therapist responds critically to the child's lack of engagement, the child's negative expectations are confirmed, and therapy deteriorates further. Awareness of the child's developmental history and gentle interpretation of its possible effect on the relationship may be helpful.

For example, when seeing a child with a history of abuse who often responds to questions with a shoulder shrug, I might comment "It seems like telling me about situations we could work on is not easy. But then, I wouldn't trust me either if I had been treated the way you were treated by adults. Maybe we can start with one that most kids I see have found helpful.

Would that be OK?" If the child agreed, I would continue with the CBT exercise. If the child disagreed, I would explore what the child fears would happen if we continued and offer possible concerns about therapy if none were volunteered ("Some kids worry it will be upsetting to do this, or they'll get the answers wrong, or I'll tell their parents the stuff we discuss, or it just won't help. Do you worry about any of those?"). A school social worker I supervised got to this point with her client, and poignantly recalled how the child had told her she feared being punished by her parents for failing math, because sessions sometimes made her late for math class.

Another group of motivational techniques relate to showing respect for client autonomy. These may be worth considering in adolescents, who often value personal autonomy as they are engaged in the developmental struggle to develop their identities. Providing the client with choices, using Socratic questions rather than telling the client what to do, hypothesis-testing on issues where client and therapist differ, examining the pros and cons of change with the client, being transparent about the case conceptualization, and documenting helpful ideas in the client's own words have all been suggested and are further described in the article by Newman (1994).

Finally, sometimes apparent lack of motivation occurs when there is something about the therapy that is not clear to the client. Both Newman (1994) and Beck (2005) emphasize that psychoeducation is an ongoing process in CBT, not limited to the first few sessions. Explain how the tasks of CBT will achieve the overall goal of therapy, and teach any skills that the child may need to complete those tasks. For example, an anxious child who finds exposure exercises distressing may appreciate a thorough description of how desensitization works. A depressed teen who engages in very little activity may benefit from a discussion of the effects of exercise on mood and related brain chemicals (endorphins). If the child appears overwhelmed by his or her problems, break the problems into smaller parts and discuss which parts are within the child's control, or could be with additional training. When children understand how therapy can work and are reasonably hopeful about achieving their goals, motivation often improves.

## WHAT WE YET NEED TO LEARN

Although we know a number of predictors of poor outcome in CBT, it is not yet clear how to best treat children who have these predictors. For example, children with attentional bias towards threat may benefit from attention bias modification training (Lowther & Newman, 2014), but it is not yet clear whether this is best done before anxiety-focused CBT, instead of CBT, or concurrently, and the training is largely limited to research settings. Similarly, the optimal treatment of comorbidities and of family dysfunction in relation to child CBT for internalizing disorders awaits further study.

# THERAPEUTIC OBSTACLES WORKSHEET

If you have encountered difficulties during your child CBT case:

- Diagnose the problem(s) (circle):

  Is it one of the common problems listed in Table 10.1?    Yes    No
  Is it a problem related to therapeutic drift?    Yes    No
  Is it a problem related to the therapeutic alliance?    Yes    No
  Is it a problem related to client motivation?    Yes    No

  What is the likely problem? _____
  _____

- Think about how you can best address the problem.

  Choose one of the following options:

  1. Problem-solving based on what you have read in this book.

     I will address the problem by trying: _____
     _____

     a. _____
     _____

     b. _____
     _____

     c. _____
     _____

  2. Consultation with a colleague.

     I will consult: _____
     _____

     Name: _____
     _____

     Contact information: _____
     _____

  3. Referral elsewhere.

     I will refer this case to: _____
     _____

     Name: _____

     Contact information: _____
     _____

## CLINICAL CHALLENGE

Consider the following dilemma:

Nancy is eight years old and has been working successfully in CBT to address separation anxiety in relation to her mother. She is an only child and has been raised by her mother and maternal grandmother since birth. You have two sessions left in the therapy when Nancy's mother informs you that the maternal grandmother has died suddenly, and Nancy is "a mess," and none of her coping strategies are working any more. She feels the treatment has failed her daughter. What do you do?

## REFERENCES

Barrett, P., Farrell, L., Dadds, M., & Boulter, N. (2005). Cognitive-behavioral family treatment of childhood obsessive-compulsive disorder: Long-term follow-up and predictors of outcome. *Journal of the American Academy of Child and Adolescent Psychiatry*, 44, 1005–1014.

Beck, J.S. (2005). *Cognitive therapy for challenging problems: What to do when the basics don't work.* New York: Guilford Press.

Birmaher, B., Arbelaez, C., & Brent, D. (2002). Course and outcome of child and adolescent major depressive disorder. *Child and Adolescent Psychiatric Clinics of North America*, 11, 619–637.

Chorpita, B.F. (2007). *Modular cognitive behavioral therapy for childhood anxiety disorders.* New York: Guilford Press.

Chu, B.C., & Kendall, P.C. (2004). Positive association of child involvement and treatment outcome within a manual-based cognitive-behavioral treatment for children with anxiety. *Journal of Consulting and Clinical Psychology*, 72, 821–829.

Creswell, C., & Cartwright-Hatton, S. (2007). Family treatment of child anxiety: Outcomes, limitations and future directions. *Clinical Child and Family Psychology Review*, 10, 232–252.

Doidge, N. (2007). *The brain that changes itself.* New York: Viking.

Emslie, G.J., Mayes, T.L., & Ruberu, M. (2005). Continuation and maintenance therapy of early-onset major depressive disorder. *Paediatric Drugs*, 7, 203–217.

Leahy, R. (2006). *Roadblocks in cognitive-behavioral therapy: Transforming challenges into opportunities for change.* New York: Guilford Press.

Lowther, H., & Newman, E. (2014). Attention bias modification (ABM) as a treatment for child and adolescent anxiety: A systematic review. *Journal of Affective Disorders*, 168, 125–135.

Manassis, K. (2014). *Case formulation with children and adolescents.* New York: Guilford Press.

Manassis, K., Hum, K., Lee, T.C., Zhang, G., & Lewis, M.D. (2013). Threat perception predicts cognitive behavioral therapy outcomes in anxious children. *Open Journal of Psychiatry*, 3(1A), 141–148.

Neufeld, J.D., Yellowlees, P.M., Hilty, D.M., Cobb, H., & Bourgeois, J.A. (2007). The e-Mental Health Consultation Service: Providing enhanced primary mental health services through telemedicine. *Psychosomatics*, 48, 135–141.

Newman, C.F. (1994). Understanding client resistance: Methods for enhancing motivation to change. *Cognitive and Behavioral Practice*, 1, 47–69.

Schoenwald, S.K., Sheldow, A.J., & Letourneau, E.J. (2004). Toward effective quality assurance in evidence-based practice: Links between expert consultation, therapist fidelity, and child outcomes. *Journal of Clinical Child and Adolescent Psychology,* 33, 94–104.

Southam-Gerow, M.A., Kendall, P.C., & Weersing, V.R. (2001). Examining outcome variability: Correlates of treatment response in a child and adolescent anxiety clinic. *Journal of Clinical Child Psychology,* 30, 422–436.

Victor, A.M., Bernat, D.H., Bernstein, G.A., & Layne, A.E. (2007). Effects of parent and family characteristics on treatment outcome of anxious children. *Journal of Anxiety Disorders,* 21, 835–848.

# CHAPTER ELEVEN

# Concluding Therapy

## WHAT IS KNOWN

Issues pertaining to concluding therapy have traditionally received less emphasis in CBT than in psychodynamic psychotherapy (Shefler, 2000). In part, this may be due to the fact that CBT is, by definition, time limited, and the duration of therapy is usually spelled out clearly at the beginning. Even so, some children and some parents can have surprisingly strong reactions to concluding therapy.

Several authors have described the use of booster sessions. These are sessions that follow a course of CBT and are spread further apart than the weekly sessions that constitute the therapy itself. Across disorders, they are designed to review progress, review strategies, and consolidate and maintain treatment-related gains. They generally do not include new strategies for the child. In obsessive compulsive disorder, they may aid in the eventual discontinuation of medication as children learn to cope using CBT strategies alone (March, Mulle, & Herbel, 1994). In adolescent depression, there is evidence they may result in further gains beyond the acute treatment phase (Clarke, Rohde, Lewinsohn, Hops, & Seeley, 1999; Emslie, Mayes, & Ruberu, 2005). A recent meta-analysis by Gearing, Schwalbe, Lee, and Hoagwood (2013) found that studies of anxious or depressed youth that included booster sessions had larger effect sizes than those that did not, both post-treatment and at follow-up. These findings suggest that such sessions may help maintain treatment gains. This chapter describes an approach to preparing clients for the conclusion of therapy, including when to offer booster sessions.

## PUTTING WHAT WE KNOW TO WORK

I was leading a parenting group in a CBT program for anxious children, and things seemed to be progressing well. The group was clearly mutually supportive and also able to work constructively together. The parents had started turning to each other for advice, rather than always asking me for it, which is usually a good sign. They were generating solutions to their children's problems, testing them out, and reflecting on the results week by week. My job seemed to be getting easier, and I anticipated a positive conclusion to the group soon.

Then we hit a wall. I walked in, and every parent, without exception, described deterioration in their child. One child who had previously managed to sleep alone was back to nightly tantrums at bedtime. Another child whose social anxiety was improving had stormed out of a piano recital in tears. One after another, the horror stories were recounted, and angry glares became focused in my direction. After all, I was the negligent therapist who would be abandoning everyone and their children in a week's time. The resentment was palpable.

The first time this happened, I responded by reviewing progress the children had previously made, suggesting this was merely a "bump in the road," and trying to reengage the group in problem-solving. My approach was not very warmly received, but by the next week most of the children seemed to have recovered from their sudden exacerbations. After a few groups, it became evident that this pattern of apparent deterioration near the end of the group is common and predictable. My cotherapists and I even coined a term for it, "the session eleven phenomenon" (our program consists of twelve sessions). Anxiety about concluding therapy in both parent and child almost inevitably results in this pretermination crisis—unless it is anticipated. Now, whenever we run similar groups, we tell parents ahead of time to expect deterioration just before the end of the sessions, and to interpret it positively. The deterioration is really a sign that the therapy has been valuable to the child, and he or she does not want to lose it. If the parents can reassure the child that whatever symptoms emerge are manageable, with or without the therapist's help, the crisis usually resolves. In fact, sometimes getting through this difficult time becomes a sign to the child and family that they are ready to "graduate" from therapy.

The challenges of concluding therapy (sometimes called "termination") have received relatively little attention in the CBT literature. Nevertheless, they are evident in almost every therapy to a degree. Many manuals include strategies to ease termination, and these commonly fall into three categories:

1. Preparing for termination from the outset.
2. Some form of graduation ritual.

3. Approaches to gradually reducing the child and family's reliance on the therapist.

## Preparing for Termination

Child and parent should both be clear from the start that CBT is a time-limited therapy. Furthermore, that time limit is not necessarily dependent on the child's progress or lack of progress. If lack of progress inevitably resulted in an extension of therapy, this would create a considerable incentive to avoid progress, which would undermine the therapy. Part of what motivates the work of CBT is the attitude "Let's see how much we can do with the time that we have." If goals are kept realistic and modest, children often exceed them in the time allotted, which is encouraging for everyone. Moreover, because children and parents develop an approach to problems in CBT, further gains are often made after the therapy ends.

Most therapists begin talking to children and parents about these issues at the beginning of therapy, when discussing treatment expectations. People do not always remember these discussions, however, so it is important to follow up with periodic reminders during the course of therapy. "This is session five, so we have seven sessions left" is a helpful reminder for a child. "What behavior would you like to focus on most in the remaining four sessions?" may be a helpful question (and reminder) for a parent. At the latest, by the halfway point in therapy, there should be a reminder of how many sessions remain. In the last few weeks, it should probably occur weekly. If a trial of therapy is proposed because there are questions about the child or family's treatment suitability, it is essential to clearly define the duration of that trial and do a reevaluation when it is over. Three to five sessions is probably as long as a trial should continue before reevaluating treatment suitability. Allowing sessions to continue without a reevaluation can result in a therapy of indeterminate length and expectations. This is generally not helpful in CBT (see above).

Children and families may also assume that therapy will be extended if sessions are missed. This may or may not be possible, depending on the circumstances. For example, therapists that are trainees doing time-limited rotations may not be able to extend sessions beyond the end of their rotation. This fact should be clearly stated for the child and family. Missed sessions also interfere with the child and parent's ability to focus on problem situations consistently, and to build a coherent set of new coping skills. Simply put, people tend to forget what they learn when more than a week elapses between sessions. Therefore, with the exception of serious illnesses or other unforeseen crises in the family, missed sessions should be discouraged, and one way of doing this is to indicate that they will *not* result in an extension of therapy.

Even with periodic reminders, children and parents can react adversely to the prospect of termination, and they are not always aware of this issue. A child or parent who becomes increasingly demanding, needy, or impatient with the rate of progress may be experiencing anxiety about termination. As mentioned in the example, setbacks a week or two before the therapy ends are also a common sign. Labeling this anxiety and addressing it is very helpful. In child anxiety programs, dealing with anxiety about termination often provides an excellent opportunity to apply newly learned coping skills. Parents, too, can benefit from identifying this form of anxiety and reframing it as an opportunity to apply new parenting skills.

**Graduation Rituals**

Most child CBT includes some acknowledgment of the child's successful conclusion or "graduation from therapy" during the final session. In group therapies, there is often a party-like atmosphere, with extra food or extra time for games or socializing relative to the other sessions. Similar elements can be included when concluding individual work as well. Demonstrating new skills to parents is another nice way of acknowledging child progress, if this has not been previously done. Diplomas or certificates are valuable symbols of success and completion of therapy for many children. In many CBT therapies, children keep a cumulative tally of points for in-session work, homework, or both. The tallied points can be exchanged for a variety of age-appropriate rewards at the conclusion of therapy. All of these symbols of success serve to reassure the child that he or she has made an important step forward, by completing this therapy, and away from the symptoms that have been so distressing. For many children, it seems like a step toward adulthood as well, further increasing their confidence that they can now cope independently.

Having something small from the therapist's office to take home can also be a helpful symbol of success, and of the continued ability to use coping skills learned there in daily life. Parents often like to take the therapist's card for future reference. Children may prefer a small object or toy, or something specific to their work with the therapist. Sometimes, child CBT workbooks are used for this purpose. The therapist keeps the workbook for the duration of the sessions to avoid it being misplaced, but gives it to the child at the end. This gives the child a helpful source to refer back to, if coping skills need to be "refreshed," and also a reassuring, tangible reminder of all that has been accomplished. Encourage the child to find a special place at home for the book (for example, in a drawer next to his or her bed, or on the top shelf of a book case in his or her room). This symbolizes the continued prominence of CBT skills in the child's life, as well as making the book easy to find whenever it is needed.

### Reducing Reliance on the Therapist

Anxiety around termination in children and adults often relates to the fear that once therapy concludes the therapist will suddenly disappear from their lives, dropping their case like the proverbial hot potato. Telling them that reliance on the therapist will be reduced gradually and incrementally is often very reassuring. In CBT, there are several specific options for doing this.

One option is to increase the time between the final few sessions. The advantage of this approach is that a gradual tapering off of therapy time builds confidence for some people. The disadvantage is that spreading sessions too far apart may interfere with consolidating newly learned coping strategies. Therefore, tapering probably should not occur until all principles in the manual have been taught, and a couple of "just practice" sessions have been done. In most programs, this means only the final two or three sessions can be spread more than a week apart.

Another option is to plan one or more "booster sessions." In this approach, all the manual-based sessions occur weekly, but a month or so after the final manual-based session a follow-up session termed a "booster" occurs. In this session, key CBT principles are reviewed briefly, and the therapist finds out how successfully or unsuccessfully these have been applied, allowing for "fine-tuning" of the child's and parents' approach. Boosters should probably occur no more frequently than monthly, with no more than about three booster sessions in total. More booster sessions or more frequent booster sessions constitute a continuation of therapy and require a further contracting discussion (including further goal-setting) with the child and family. Occasionally in complex cases ongoing supportive therapy is needed for the child, the parent, or both, but this should be clearly described as such and not labeled CBT.

Telephone calls to "touch base" after therapy concludes can be reassuring for some children and parents. These calls should be brief, and give the caller the opportunity to report on progress. I often suggest to children that they use them as a "chance to brag a little." If problems are reported that do not respond to brief reassurance from the therapist, a further session should be scheduled. Trying to do therapy via telephone is generally not ideal, as important information (for example, the client's facial expression and body language) is not available in this medium. Some clients do not call back, but find comfort simply in having the therapist's telephone number available "just in case." Here, the therapist's number is treated as a transitional object that eases the client's separation from the therapist.

Finally, some children and parents are ready to conclude CBT when the manual-based sessions are finished, but like to know that "the door is always open." Telling them that they can return if needed, even if several years have elapsed, is often reassuring. It is important to be truthful, of course, as some settings do have age limits for their clientele. If the child is close to an age limit, discuss this with the child and family. Similarly, discuss any plans you have to retire or go on an extended leave, with information about who will assume your clients. If the child or family seems a bit needy, it is sometimes helpful to add to "the door is always open" the statement "but I won't be offended if you never walk through it again."

## Relapse Prevention

Judith S. Beck (1995) and other CBT authors have emphasized the importance of considering strategies for relapse prevention. Strategies for adults are further described in her book. When working with children, we often facilitate the continuing use of CBT strategies in various ways. These can include:

- Having the child designate a "special place" to keep his or her workbook, so it is not lost and can be accessed easily if needed.
- Having the child and parents schedule times to continue practicing relaxation or other CBT strategies so these are not neglected.
- Emphasizing the role of parents as "coaches" throughout therapy, as they learn more about supporting their child's progress. When therapy ends, they continue coaching their child in the use of CBT strategies, picking up where the therapist left off.
- Anticipating times of high stress (for example, starting a new school year, moving to a new house) and encouraging parent–child communication and review of coping strategies at such times. The family can then decide whether or not the review of strategies is sufficient to manage the stress. If not, they are advised to call back for a "booster" session, preferably before the child feels overwhelmed.

## Returning for More CBT

Children do sometimes need to come back for a further course of CBT, either because of a new life challenge or a new developmental stage. Societal expectations of independent behavior increase as children get older, and coping strategies that are helpful for younger children are not necessarily appropriate for adolescents. If this happens, find out first what new challenges are contributing to the child's symptoms, and address any unnecessary stresses or need for added support. For example, if the family has recently separated, a support group for children of separated or divorced parents may be more appropriate than further CBT. If the child is anxious about having lunch at school, but has been taunted or bullied in the lunchroom, ensure better supervision there to reduce this stress. After these common-sense interventions, see if the symptoms resolve or remain, and proceed with further therapy only if symptoms remain.

To address remaining symptoms, begin with a review of coping strategies the child has previously learned or previously used. Determine why these are insufficient or no longer effective. Sometimes, the child no longer remembers how to do them properly (for example, remembering to breathe deeply, but doing it too quickly for relaxation to occur). Sometimes, the strategies need to be updated. Cognitive strategies learned at elementary school age are often no longer effective in adolescence, as the young person begins to reason in more abstract ways than previously. A more sophisticated approach is needed and often welcome at this age.

It is important not to see children who resurface in your office as therapeutic failures. Few children have a perfectly smooth developmental course after CBT. In many cases, parents can help them master the occasional setback. In some cases, a session or two with the therapist to review previously learned skills is enough to get the child and parents back "on track." If more is needed, contract for a further course of therapy. There is no shame in offering a "refresher course" to those who are still struggling.

Remember also that there is a cognitive bias inherent to doing therapy: people who get better stop seeing us, so eventually we see mainly those who do not get better. As a result, we get the biased impression that few of our clients are improving and begin to doubt ourselves. Correct the bias once in a while; you have probably forgotten most of the people out there you have helped!

## WHAT WE YET NEED TO LEARN

Further studies are needed on the best ways to prevent relapse following CBT for various disorders. Finding ways to ensure continued use of coping strategies by CBT 'graduates' is likely to be an important element of this work.

# CONCLUDING THERAPY WORKSHEET

- Preparation:

  Have you recently reminded the child and parent of how many sessions are left?

  Yes          No

  If not, do so and address any concerns they may have in relation to this prospect.

  Client concern(s): _____
  _____

  Plan to address concerns:_____
  _____

  Other preparation: _____
  _____

- Graduation:

  Check the manual you are using for any "graduation exercises" or other interventions to aid successful conclusion of therapy.

  Present          Absent

  If present, reiterate: _____
  _____

  If absent, will do: _____
  _____

  (See suggestions in this chapter)

- Reducing reliance on the therapist:

  Plan: _____
  _____

- Relapse prevention:

  Plan: _____
  _____

## CLINICAL CHALLENGE

You have been working with Nicholas, a 12-year-old boy with social anxiety, for the past 11 weeks, and he has made excellent progress. Concurrently, you have worked with his parents on different strategies for increasing their son's exposure to and mastery of social situations with good effect. You remember (and your progress notes confirm this) that you discussed the timing and conclusion of therapy at least three times with Nicholas' parents at various points in the therapy, including the previous week. At that time, everyone agreed that nothing further was needed, apart from additional "real-world practice," which the parents would facilitate. The parents agreed to only call back in the event of a setback. This is your final session, and Nicholas says he is looking forward to inviting a friend over to play his new video game, the reward he has earned by working so hard over the previous three months. Nicholas' mother turns to you and says, "So, when would you like to see us again?" How do you respond?

## REFERENCES

Beck, J.S. (1995). *Cognitive therapy: Basics and beyond.* New York: Guilford Press.

Clarke, G.N., Rohde, P., Lewinsohn, P.M., Hops, H., & Seeley, J.R. (1999). Cognitive behavioral treatment of adolescent depression: Efficacy of acute group treatment and booster sessions. *Journal of the American Academy of Child and Adolescent Psychiatry,* 38, 272–279.

Emslie, G.J., Mayes, T.L., & Ruberu, M. (2005). Continuation and maintenance therapy of early-onset major depressive disorder. *Paediatric Drugs,* 7, 203–217.

Gearing, R.E., Schwalbe, C.S., Lee, R., & Hoagwood, K.E. (2013). The effectiveness of booster sessions in CBT for child and adolescent mood and anxiety disorders. *Depression & Anxiety,* 30, 800–808.

March, J.S., Mulle, K., & Herbel, B. (1994). Behavioral psychotherapy for children and adolescents with obsessive compulsive disorder: An open trial of a new protocol-driven treatment package. *Journal of the American Academy of Child and Adolescent Psychiatry,* 33, 333–341.

Shefler, G. (2000). Time-limited psychotherapy with adolescents. *Journal of Psychotherapy Practice and Research,* 9, 88–99.

# CHAPTER TWELVE

# Training Others in Child CBT

## WHAT IS KNOWN

After successfully treating several cases, many CBT therapists express a desire to train colleagues in this modality. So-called train the trainer programs have been developed to address their needs and to disseminate CBT more widely in the community.

Dissemination is not a simple process, however. Rather, it involves knowledge of best practices for a given disorder, competence in CBT for that disorder, and an understanding of the application of CBT to the developing child (Sburlati, Schniering, Lyneham, & Rapee, 2011). Furthermore, there are barriers to such dissemination at the client, therapist, and organizational levels. For example, clients may have difficulty committing to the weekly appointments needed for CBT if they live in an area that is distant from the therapist. Therapists may have difficulty adapting CBT materials to the characteristics of local clients if these differ from typical research clients for whom the materials were developed. Organizations may expect therapists to attend to emergencies or other responsibilities that conflict with regular CBT sessions. For these reasons, studies suggest that effective training programs educate both the therapist and organization on principles and best practices, use active learning styles, encourage flexibility within treatment, and establish a support system for both the therapist and the organization (Bennett-Levy, McManus, Westling, & Fennell, 2009; Herschell, Kolko, Baumann, & Davis, 2010; Manassis et al., 2009; Rakovshik & McManus, 2010).

There is general agreement that training in child CBT should include experiential as well as didactic elements (Bennett-Levy et al., 2009; Herschell et al., 2010; Manassis et al., 2009; Rakovshik & McManus, 2010). In other words, it is not enough to read about child CBT or listen to lectures on the topic—to learn, you must actually do it! Experiential aspects usually include ongoing case supervision, which is described further in this chapter.

Training models for CBT have also highlighted the need to include general therapeutic competencies (e.g., thorough assessment, understanding child and adolescent development, ability to form a positive therapeutic relationship) and general CBT competencies (e.g., understanding relevant CBT principles and research, devising a CBT-related case formulation and treatment plan) in addition to specific CBT techniques (Sburlati et al., 2011). These general competencies may be especially relevant when adapting a specific program to certain youth characteristics or parameters of practice, as community practitioners often do.

In summary, the challenge of simultaneously learning and adapting CBT to one's clientele (as community practitioners often do) can be formidable, and is therefore further addressed in this chapter.

## PUTTING WHAT WE KNOW TO WORK

### Preparing to Train Others

Before attempting to train others in child CBT, it is wise to reflect upon those aspects of training one personally found helpful. List specific topics and specific adaptations to local clients and practice conditions that should be emphasized with your trainee(s). One sample list of topics is provided at the end of the chapter, but this should be adapted based on your local child CBT experiences.

Next, reflect upon the relationship you had with your trainer or supervisor. What trainer attitudes and what aspects of the supervisory relationship were particularly helpful? What could the supervisor have done differently to make training more effective? Ensuring that supervision sessions occur consistently and respecting trainees' existing knowledge and therapeutic experience are universally helpful, but other aspects of training may vary depending on local circumstances. For instance, use of certain types of humor may work well in less formal settings but be frowned upon in more formal ones. A trainer preparation sheet is provided at the end of the chapter to record your ideas.

When preparing to train others in child CBT, also consider the pros and cons of working with a single trainee versus a supervision group. Groups can be more challenging to organize and may allow less time for discussion of individual clients than one-to-one supervision. Trainees may experience a heightened fear of embarrassment in a group, sometimes resulting in reluctance to share problems they are encountering in therapy. On the other hand, groups can often generate more helpful ideas than a single supervisor can, and feedback from peers is a powerful learning tool for participants. Peer supervision groups can also offer participants ongoing support and guidance around CBT cases regardless of the availability of a particular supervisor. Whether training is done in an individual or group format, certain key aspects of the supervision process should be borne in mind. These are discussed further below.

### Supervisory Process with Individual Trainees

Consistent with current supervision models, training should begin with an evaluation of the trainee's background knowledge and experience regarding general principles of child therapy, general principles of CBT, and specific CBT techniques. An understanding of what behaviors and challenges are normative in children and adolescents of different ages is important too. Discussing each of these areas at the outset is informative for the trainer and conveys to the trainee that the supervisor is interested in tailoring teaching to his or her specific needs. The supervisor should also discuss what to expect in supervision and allay any trainee fears or concerns about the process. Emphasis should be placed on starting with a simple case, reading manuals and other relevant materials before using them with clients, and attending both therapy sessions and supervision sessions consistently.

During training, supervisors should provide didactic teaching in areas where the trainee knows little, Socratic questions and discussion in areas where the trainee has some knowledge, and brief summaries of key ideas in areas where trainee knowledge is substantial. Thus, as training progresses, supervision can usually shift from mainly didactic teaching and coaching in specific therapeutic skills to a more Socratic approach. For example, the supervisor can increasingly respond to trainee questions by asking, "What do you think?" or "Have you dealt with a similar situation before?" Good supervisors also adapt their style to the trainee's level of experience. For instance, micromanaging an experienced therapist can undermine his or her confidence, so it should be avoided, but a trainee with limited experience may appreciate specific directions and experience anxiety without them.

When supervising, it is often helpful to put oneself in the trainee's shoes at various stages of training. What were you anxious or confused about at the start of CBT? What do you wish your supervisor had said or not said at the time? Use the insights you recorded on the supervisor preparation sheet. Also, don't forget to reinforce correct answers to questions and evidence of good clinical judgment in your supervisee. Adults in supervision often need as much or more encouragement than children doing CBT! Try to alleviate anxiety about negative evaluation by emphasizing that supervision is intended to be a collaborative search for what works rather than a performance evaluation. Then, act accordingly.

After an introductory session or two with the trainee, CBT supervision usually benefits from a predictable session structure. Organizational matters (e.g., scheduling and other practical matters) are best dealt with early so they do not distract trainees from discussions of topics and cases later. Next, it is helpful to focus on a topic related to child CBT. Usually, the topic is relevant to the stage of therapy the supervisee is engaged in. Thus, discussions of engaging children in therapy or setting realistic treatment goals would constitute early topics, specific strategies for teaching relaxation or cognitive restructuring would come later, and discussions of termination and relapse prevention later still. As mentioned, the more experienced the trainee the more Socratic the approach to the topic can be.

Then, the bulk of the session should focus on case discussion. In some settings, trainee sessions are audiotaped or videotaped (with client consent, of course) and the supervisory discussion follows a viewing of the tape or parts of the tape. If available, this is an excellent format for learning. In many settings, however, supervisors rely on trainee reports. In this case, it is often helpful to have the trainee use a fidelity checklist (Manassis & Mendlowitz, 2011) and to explicitly encourage him or her to report struggles encountered in therapy sessions, not just successes, to optimize learning. Remember to ask not only about the child's behavior in therapy but also about parental responses to the child's therapy and parental willingness to support child progress. Pay particular attention to situations where an adaptation or minor deviation from the CBT manual used may be indicated. Distinguishing between helpful therapeutic flexibility in the use of manuals and unhelpful loss of treatment fidelity can be a particular challenge for inexperienced therapists. The case discussion usually concludes with a summary of take-home points for future therapy sessions and any related reading or exercises for the trainee to do in the coming week.

Providing constructive feedback to trainees and eliciting feedback from them can sometimes seem awkward in supervision. Both are important, however, in order to facilitate learning, ensure a positive supervision experience, and avoid having trainees drop out of supervision. Many supervisors use the "sandwich technique" when providing feedback. That is, they tell the trainee what he or she did well, then point out what could have been done better, and then reiterate what was done well. Thus, the areas for improvement are clearly stated but are placed in the context of trainee strengths. In most cases, this is an effective way to communicate feedback while minimizing trainee shame or embarrassment. Rarely, trainees engage in unprofessional or potentially dangerous actions that require firmer corrective action.

Eliciting feedback is usually easiest to do if introduced as a routine practice at the beginning. For example, the supervisor can say, "Every couple of weeks I will ask you how helpful you are finding these sessions and anything we can do to make them more helpful." Requests for feedback then become an expected part of the supervisory process. In addition, it is helpful to ask for feedback any time the supervisee seems persistently anxious, negative, angry, or otherwise uncomfortable. Label the trainee's affect, and gently explore what is causing the discomfort. It may relate to the client, the setting, a behavior in the supervisor, or something about the supervisory process that is upsetting and which the trainee may or may not be fully aware of. Also, pay attention to your own feelings as a supervisor. If the process is not interesting or not fun, what is the reason? Does it relate to the client being described, the setting, a behavior in the trainee, or something else? If it is not clear, gently explore with the trainee what is happening when you meet next.

## Supervisory Process with Supervision Groups

Group supervision should rely upon the same principles as individual supervision. Consistent attendance, however, is even more important in supervision groups as members contribute to one another's learning, and group dynamics change when one or more members is missing. As in individual supervision, teaching becomes gradually more Socratic over time. For example, the supervisor may ask, "Does anyone else in the group have thoughts about this issue?" or "Has anyone had a similar experience?" Pointing out common themes in the group also encourages members to help each other with clinical learning challenges. Eventually, members value each other's ideas as much or more than those of the supervisor. As a result, members engage in peer supervision rather than relying on the 'expert' by the end of the group and can continue to learn and support each other's practice of CBT regardless of the availability of the supervisor.

A few additional points to keep in mind when supervising groups include:

- Make sure each member of the group has a case discussed at least every other week.
- Notice those who participate a lot versus a little: Try to draw out quieter members and politely set limits on those who tend to monopolize the group.

- Discourage members from communicating with the supervisor outside the group unless absolutely necessary, as it can adversely affect group dynamics (e.g., making one member seem like a "teacher's pet") and deprive other group members from learning from the experience that is shared privately with the supervisor.
- If there are obvious divisions in the group, identify these and look for common ground; if divisions are present but less obvious, wonder aloud about the tension in the room and explore the reasons.
- If the group becomes overly negative, identify this problem and try to redirect members to a problem-solving focus.
- If the group becomes overly competitive, encourage stronger participants to help those who are struggling rather than gloat.
- Point out the strengths of the group as well as those of individual members.
- Encourage gentle, constructive feedback (i.e., "sandwich technique") among members as well as providing and eliciting feedback regularly.

Finally, regardless of the number or type of trainees you see, remember to convey some of your own enthusiasm for child CBT. After all, CBT represents one of the few opportunities we have as therapists to make a difference in a child's emotional adjustment in a relatively short period of time while actually having fun!

## WHAT WE YET NEED TO LEARN

Training models for community-based CBT are evolving as new technologies become available. For example, we have successfully trained a number of practitioners in child CBT using tele-psychiatry methods (Manassis et al., 2009). Use of technology in distance training, however, merits further evaluation. Balancing the need for fidelity to CBT principles with the need to adapt CBT training to local clientele and local conditions of practice is an ongoing challenge that also warrants further study.

# SAMPLE TOPICS LIST

- Overview of child CBT principles
- Introduction to supervisory process
- Case selection
- Integration of CBT into a treatment plan
- Contracting with children and families
- Rapport-building with children and families
- Engaging children when working with a manual
- Helping children improve feeling recognition in themselves
- Helping children improve feeling recognition in others
- Teaching relaxation
- Behavioral activation
- Developing constructive parental involvement in therapy
- Dealing with schools and supporting children/parents dealing with schools
- Teaching children to identify adaptive and maladaptive thoughts
- Teaching cognitive restructuring
- Teaching problem-solving
- Encouraging self-reward
- Encouraging independent use of strategies and generalization beyond the office
- Developing exposure hierarchies
- Supporting exposures
- Anticipating termination of therapy
- Relapse prevention
- Training others

Notes: 1) Specific types of challenging children and challenging families vary from setting to setting and are addressed largely during case supervision, but a frequent challenge may also be discussed as a topic. 2) The order of topics is flexible after the first few sessions, and is designed to best meet trainee needs. 3) All topics are discussed with reference to various ages/developmental stages of the children being treated.

## TRAINER PREPARATION SHEET

Important Topics: _____

_____

_____

_____

_____

Important Local Adaptations: _____

_____

_____

_____

_____

Supervisory 'Pearls': _____

_____

_____

_____

_____

Supervisory Pitfalls to Avoid: _____

_____

_____

_____

_____

Supervision Time and Place (Book them to ensure consistent availability!)

_____

_____

_____

_____

_____

## CLINICAL CHALLENGE: BRAD

A supervisee describes working with a 13-year-old socially anxious boy (Brad) who says very little in sessions, usually appears uncomfortable, and breathes a deep sigh of relief when allowed to leave. When describing this client, the supervisee speaks briefly and appears very uncomfortable. He appears relieved when the supervision session ends. As the supervisor, what do you do?

## REFERENCES

Bennett-Levy, J., McManus, F., Westling, B.E., & Fennell, M. (2009). Acquiring and refining CBT skills and competencies: Which training methods are perceived to be most effective? *Behavioral and Cognitive Psychotherapy*, 37, 571–583.

Herschell, A.D., Kolko, D.J., Baumann, B.L., & Davis, A.C. (2010). The role of therapist training in the implementation of psychosocial treatments: A review and critique with recommendations. *Clinical Psychology Review*, 30, 448–466.

Manassis, K., Ickowicz, A., Picard, E., Antle, B., McNeill, T., Chahauver, A., et al. (2009). An innovative child CBT training model for community mental health practitioners in Ontario. *Academic Psychiatry*, 33, 394–399.

Manassis, K., & Mendlowitz, S. (2011). *Child CBT Fidelity Checklist*. Toronto, ON: University of Toronto.

Rakovshik, S., & McManus, F. (2010). Establishing evidence-based training in cognitive behavioral therapy: A review of current empirical findings and theoretical guidance. *Clinical Psychology Review*, 30, 496–516.

Sburlati, E.S., Schniering, C.A., Lyneham, H.J., & Rapee, R.M. (2011). A model of therapist competencies for the empirically supported cognitive behavioral treatment of child and adolescent anxiety and depressive disorders. *Clinical Child and Family Psychology Review*, 14, 89–109.

# APPENDIX I

# Possible Answers to Clinical Challenges

The answers below are labeled "possible," because there is usually more than one way to arrive at a good clinical outcome. That way may vary depending on your training, circumstances of practice, and other factors. Therefore, do not be too concerned if your answer is different from mine, as long as you understand the reasons for your approach.

## CHAPTER 1: VICKY

1. Whether they are aware of it or not, Vicky's parents are undermining efforts to help her. Therefore, I would begin by having a frank discussion with them about Vicky's poor long-term prognosis and the inability of any professional to help her if she does not cooperate. Vicky's parents are in the best position to insist on that cooperation, but only if they realize that the alternative is a continuing inexorable decline in her functioning. They can begin by insisting she take the medication, insisting she attend school at least part of the day, or both. Another therapist might be helpful too, but only if they accept that no therapist will understand their daughter perfectly. The choice is theirs. If they cannot insist on one of these interventions, I must bid them adieu. At this point, some parents anxiously describe the reasons for their inability to be firm with their children, often leading to a referral for treatment of their own anxieties and a greater desire to do what is in the child's best interest. Other parents will move on to the next professional, unrealistically hoping for an easy answer to their child's problems.

2. Once Vicky's parents are more cooperative, I would pursue a gradual, behavioral approach to school reentry. There is some evidence that this is more likely to succeed if she concurrently takes an antidepressant-type medication to reduce her anxiety (Bernstein et al., 2000), so I would pursue this as well. I would contact Vicky's teacher and any other adults involved at the school to explain the rationale for this approach and elicit their cooperation in implementing it. Note: While suicidal threats should never be dismissed, Vicky's appear to be designed to manipulate her parents, as she has no other evidence of depression and a rather active social life at the mall. Therefore, I would matter-of-factly indicate that gradual school reentry will occur regardless, and have her escorted there if needed.

3. Vicky is ready for CBT when she is making a daily attempt to attend school (leaving the house and approaching the school building at minimum), and is genuinely motivated to conquer her fears and reestablish regular school attendance. Motivational interviewing techniques are sometimes a helpful prelude to CBT in these cases. Vicky's parents must be able to support the treatment plan, as discussed above.

### CHAPTER 2: TOM

1. Most impairing problem: Based on the case description, I am fairly certain that Tom's main problem relates to anxiety or to depression. His lifelong anxious temperament, distress about being "different" from his peers, and lack of behavior problems are all very consistent with an anxiety disorder. Before interviewing Tom, I might have also thought about an Autism Spectrum diagnosis, given the degree of his social isolation. His appropriate responses to other children, good eye contact, desire for more friends, and painful awareness of being "different," however, make an Autism Spectrum diagnosis unlikely. Note that difficulty responding to open-ended questions is quite common among socially anxious children.

2. Contextual factors: Although his medical history appears noncontributory, I would still like Tom to have a physical checkup with his family doctor if this has not been done recently. Even children with a lifelong history of anxiety sometimes experience exacerbations in response to illness or medication. I would also inquire about any caffeine consumption, exercise routines, and sleep routines and provide appropriate advice about these. From Tom I would want to know if there have been any other recent stresses at school or in his family apart from the bullying and ridicule by peers, so these can be addressed. Family

history of anxiety and the degree of family cohesion or conflict are also important, because they will all influence the family's ability to support Tom's treatment. For example, if Tom's mother is herself anxious and disagrees with her husband's no-nonsense approach to his problems, this parental inconsistency could make it difficult for them to encourage appropriate social exposure for Tom. On the positive side, Tom's intelligence, awareness of his feelings, and good relationships with adults are all favorable prognostic signs.

3. Key situations: Tom's symptoms seem to "flare up" when people try to push him into social situations he is not ready for. It happened when the teacher tried to push him into a group situation, but likely also happens at home when his father tries to push him to contact his peers on weekends. Instead of pushing, his father could work with Tom to facilitate social contact by, for example, inviting his friend over using a telephone call that Tom contributes to (doing the whole call independently would likely be too big a step). Similarly, rather than pushing Tom into a peer group, his teacher could encourage another child (preferably one with similar temperament) to play with Tom at recess to gradually increase his socialization and decrease his risk of victimization by bullies.

4. Either a MASC (March, 1998) or a standardized measure specific to social anxiety (for example, the SASC; LaGreca & Stone, 1993) could be used to monitor progress, because Tom is quite aware of his symptoms. In addition, I would consider having at least one behavioral measure of progress (for example, working on using the telephone or talking to his "friend" in the school cafeteria or another nonclassroom situation) both to corroborate the standardized scale and to show Tom's father that his son is making an effort to work on his problem.

5.–6. "Ideal" characteristics: Tom is almost an ideal case for CBT. He has all of the characteristics in Table 2.1, and his family has most of these as well. The interpersonal conflict between Tom and his father is the only apparent problematic issue, and this can probably be addressed through psychoeducation and appropriate parenting advice.

7. Additional interventions: Tom might benefit from social skills training, because social skills are often lost with prolonged social avoidance. Role-plays of appropriate ways to approach peers could be part of CBT. If difficulties persisted in other social situations, further training could be provided subsequently.

8.–9. Given his age and lack of learning problems, Tom does not require a modified CBT approach or nonverbal strategies.

10. Individual CBT would be preferable to start, because Tom's high social anxiety might make a group seem overwhelming and, thus, make it difficult to learn CBT strategies in a group environment.

11. There are no contraindications to CBT in this case.

## CHAPTER 3: JERRY

1. Some people would say that Jerry's obsessive compulsive disorder (OCD) is the most impairing problem, because it results in a potentially serious medical problem: skin breakdown on his hands. One might also consider the degree of family conflict the most impairing problem, however, because it is threatening to derail existing treatment and is likely making Jerry more anxious and thus exacerbating his OCD. Furthermore, because Jerry is not of age, medical decisions will be made by his custodial parent. Until custody is clear, one cannot change much in the management of this case. Finally, the family conflict is making it very difficult to ascertain the truth: Does Jerry really have the diagnoses his mother says he has?

2. There are no easy or quick fixes in this case. A first step, however, might be to locate a practitioner with expertise in custody and access assessments. To assist this practitioner, one could obtain further history regarding Jerry's symptoms, particularly from people outside the family who might have witnessed them (for example, school teachers or previous doctors), and regarding previous treatment. It is not always possible to determine the truth with certainty in these cases, but a good history is a necessary prerequisite for any treatment, even if that treatment must be delayed until custody is clear.

3. While awaiting the result of the custody assessment, one could begin some supportive therapy with Jerry, as long as it was clear that this would have no bearing on the custody issue. Jerry is struggling with teasing, sexuality concerns, and other early adolescent issues in addition to his horrible family situation. He could use a good listener. Establishing a good therapeutic relationship may also make him more amenable to CBT in the future, if this is indicated.

4. Everyone in this family is motivated to start somewhere else, as everyone has a different perspective on what the "real" problem is. As mentioned, I would vote for starting with Jerry's concerns until the parental conflict is resolved. The only caveat would be to maintain a good relationship with Jerry's family doctor to ensure that the skin damage to his hands is treated appropriately until a more definitive treatment is decided upon.

## CHAPTER 4: JOSH

1. I would ignore the "useless" comment, but indicate that, since we are spending the hour together anyway, we might as well discuss some things that interest him. If it would make him more comfortable, we can minimize "feelings talk," although I cannot promise to eliminate it entirely (I sometimes joke that it is one of my "bad habits"). Let us start with, what does he enjoy about "Dungeons of Doom"? I would listen intently and try to understand the game as best I can. If I could connect the game to some other aspect of life that he values, I would. If not, I might ask if Josh has experienced the kind of enjoyment he gets from the game anywhere else (perhaps before the "lousy year at school")? Could he see himself getting back to that enjoyment, or some part of it? How does he think that could happen? What would he need to do? What would his parents need to do? What would I need to do? If possible, I would begin to formulate some treatment goals focused on his answers. Behavioral activation is an important aspect of recovery from depression, so I would not mind beginning with concrete, behavioral goals and avoiding extensive discussion of thoughts and feelings for now. Hopefully by the end of the session we can agree on one behavioral goal, or at least on meeting again to discuss his goals further. Later, probably in a subsequent session, we can discuss the connections between thoughts, feelings, and behaviors (the basic principles of CBT), but in the context of trying to reach his goals. If paying attention to his feelings and thoughts can help him cope in a situation he previously enjoyed, Josh is less likely to consider this a "useless" exercise than in his previous therapy.

2. The discussion with Josh's parents would follow the outline in this chapter on CBT treatment expectations, but with a cautionary note. Their son is very defensive, and it is not yet clear whether he will engage in this therapy. Nevertheless, you will try to engage him in therapy. If he continues to see you, they must recognize that a few initial sessions may be needed to develop rapport with him and find treatment goals that he can agree to before actually doing CBT. Thus, the time frame for therapy may be slightly longer than usual. The limits of confidentiality are also important to emphasize in this case, because you want the option of involving the parents if Josh is at risk (for example, if he becomes suicidal), but otherwise allow much of the therapy content to remain private to increase Josh's level of trust.

## CHAPTER 5: JENNY

1. Since Jenny is a 10-year-old with generalized anxiety disorder and no other significant diagnoses, I would use the *Coping Cat* CBT manual for anxious children or a local adaptation of it. She could do either individual or group CBT.

2. Assuming Jenny has no significant learning disabilities, the manual could be used without modification.

3. Given that an initial educational session with Mrs. Smith is unlikely to dispel all of her misconceptions about CBT, I would plan to see her weekly before or after Jenny's session (or in a CBT-focused parenting group, if this is offered) to help her support Jenny's therapeutic progress. The book *Keys to Parenting Your Anxious Child* can be used to guide the content of the parenting sessions. If Jenny's father is involved in her life, I would invite him to participate in this parenting intervention as well, so the parents can work together consistently for their daughter's benefit. Such intervention would also provide the opportunity to further observe and discuss any parental anxiety or other parental mental health issues that might require additional treatment.

4. If Jenny had not yet started *Coping Cat*, I might consider starting her with the needle phobia–focused manual, assuming it followed CBT principles and came from a reputable source. At this point, however, she is already at the midpoint of her treatment, so a switch would be inadvisable. Fortunately, exposure to a variety of anxiety-provoking situations is an integral component of *Coping Cat*, and some of the same strategies that Jenny is learning for her anxiety can readily be applied to her needle phobia. I would provide this information to Mrs. Smith, write the school a note indicating that treatment for the needle phobia is in progress and request patience for a few weeks, and make sure that obtaining an immunization is one of the anxious situations Jenny focuses on mastering in CBT.

## CHAPTER 6: BILL

1. Bill's lack of progress could relate to environmental factors, cognitive factors, other aspects of the therapy, or a combination of these. Although it sounds like Bill has a rather difficult temperament, the statement by his mother that he was "born unhappy" suggests she has rather low expectations of his potential for improvement. Those

expectations may become self-fulfilling if she reacts only to Bill's behaviors that confirm her expectations and ignores those that do not. Encourage her to look for and validate her son's strengths. He has friends, makes an effort academically, tries to follow the rules, and even participates in therapy without complaint. Over time, he may also show subtle signs of progress in tolerating change or reducing his negativity, and she should attend to those. Sibling rivalry is also a problem in the family. Currently, the family seems to be blaming Bill for it, but George may be playing a part as well. Advice to the parents on managing sibling situations would be helpful. Also check with Bill if the teasing at school is continuing, because most teasing and bullying is never witnessed by adults. Address this issue with the school if needed.

2. Cognitively, Bill's age and level of development suggest he should benefit from CBT. However, his rigid emphasis on "fairness" and rules may be a clue to some nonverbal learning difficulties. If these are present, they may make it difficult for him to apply strategies he learns in the office to real-world situations. They may also pose some academic challenges at school as he progresses into higher grades. A thorough psychoeducational assessment would be helpful. Some people would argue that a diagnostic reassessment would be worthwhile, because Bill's moodiness and explosiveness might suggest a bipolar condition that could be medicated. Given that Bill is still functioning relatively well, however, my own preference would be to complete a good trial of CBT first.

3. One possibility, not uncommon in young adolescents, is that Bill sees CBT as an intellectual exercise. He is manipulating his thoughts in therapy, but is not really connecting them to his feelings. Until he does so, progress will be limited. In this case, reduce the amount of material presented in sessions until Bill shows evidence of making the thought–feeling connection. Another possibility is that the therapy has been targeting a variety of negative thoughts so far, without focusing on the ones that are most troublesome to Bill: thoughts of being treated unfairly by others. Help Bill to identify situations that seem unfair to him whenever they occur, and develop consistent things he can say to himself and things he can do in those situations. If he questions this approach, point out that he is already coping with one "unfair" situation: the fact that you occasionally deviate from the manual! Finally, there may be no problem with the therapy at all, except for the need for a few more sessions. Some children do not show gains outside the office until the end of therapy, because it takes time to learn and apply new skills.

## CHAPTER 7: WENDY, PAUL, AND JOE

1. Wendy's mother has made a mistaken assumption about her treatments: that they will improve her academic performance. Unfortunately, neither medications for ADHD nor CBT are designed to do this. ADHD medications can help the child focus, but this may or may not improve her grades. Academic success requires more than the ability to focus: Learning skills may need to be developed that the child has missed due to her inattention, motivation and study habits may need to be addressed, and so on. CBT in this case has targeted anxiety, not school performance. In some cases, school performance actually worsens with successful anxiety-focused CBT because the child may be less anxious about the consequences of school failure. I would gently explain these issues to Wendy's mother. Then, I would arrange a meeting with the parents and the school to examine what factors might be affecting academic success and do some problem-solving to address these. If not done previously, I would also obtain a psychoeducational assessment because many children with ADHD and anxiety also have learning disabilities that can interfere with school success.

2a. Although I would certainly share Paul's excitement about the girl-friend, I would caution him that six sessions of CBT rarely "cures" depression, and he should complete his treatment to reduce the risk of relapse and future depressive episodes.

2b. I would definitely resist the temptation to say "I told you so" to Paul. Instead, I would empathically listen to his concerns about losing the girlfriend and acknowledge that this is a major stressor that would be very upsetting for anyone. Nevertheless, I would challenge his assumption that his "life is over" and encourage him to think about what he still enjoys or used to enjoy before he found the girlfriend. After taking a few sessions to address this crisis and ensure Paul is no longer having suicidal thoughts (note: I would consider "life is over" a passive suicidal thought), I would suggest resuming CBT to improve his ability to manage his moods now and in the future. Some teens are quite reluctant to engage in CBT in this situation because "thinking about one's thinking" seems less relevant to them than the interpersonal issues they are struggling with. If this were the case, I might consider referring Paul to a colleague with training in interpersonal therapy (IPT), a structured therapy that has also received some evaluation in this population. My preference would be to re-engage in CBT if possible, however, because (a) it is usually easier to complete a therapy that was already underway than start a new one; (b) switching therapists might be perceived as a further loss by Paul, placing him at risk of a depressive exacerbation.

3. I would not attempt to dissuade Joe from going to the meet. Instead, I would empathize with his mother's anxiety about her son, because it is natural given his seizure history. However, I would tell her that it is important for her son to participate as fully as he can in activities he enjoys, and there are probably ways of ensuring this happens safely. I would suggest she talk with the coach about Joe's seizures and how they are managed. She can suggest that either the coach or another adult supervises his medications on the trip. If there is a change of time zones involved in the trip, timing of medication doses may also need to be adjusted, but this is not difficult if planned in advance. A note from the neurologist outlining the medications Joe takes would also be helpful, to avoid any concerns by airport personnel about him transporting pills (sometimes mistakenly thought to be drugs). A Medic-Alert bracelet may be helpful in the unlikely event Joe has a seizure. With these sensible precautions, Joe should be able to enjoy his trip and see it as an encouraging step toward greater independence. If Joe's mother is uncomfortable with these suggestions, I would offer to meet with her, Joe, and the coach to do some problem-solving about the trip.

## CHAPTER 8: MADISON'S FAMILY

1. When Madison is hospitalized, it is at a time of family crisis, and all family members seem overwhelmed. One cannot expect the family to do much creative problem-solving in this state. Instead, it is probably best to give them concrete advice. For example, encourage the parents to limit displays of negative emotion in front of their children as much as possible. Also, ensure Madison's younger brother is safe, and reassure him that his sister is getting treatment for her problems and will not harm him. Start to locate community resources that the family can access after Madison leaves the hospital, including any respite care available, and help the parents make a plan for how they will cope when Madison comes home. If one or both parents have a history of personal mental health problems, make sure appropriate community professionals are involved to address these. Make sure there is a follow-up appointment for the family before Madison is discharged from hospital.

2. When Madison returns home, she will likely need a combination of medical treatment and CBT. Madison's parents should be involved in the CBT to support her progress using (1) empathic encouragement

to practice her CBT strategies and (2) problem-solving to consistently limit her OCD behaviors at home. As the crisis resolves and the parents return to their usual level of functioning, they can also model appropriate coping strategies for Madison.

## CHAPTER 9: GROUPS

1a. At the time, I would try to compromise with the janitor. For example, I might explain that it is important to complete the group but offer to lock the building for him, if he can show me how to do so. Alternatively, I might offer him a coffee and snack (since most child groups include a snack at the end) for staying the extra time, and promise to address the issue with the principal the next day to avoid future problems.

1b. The next day, I would request an urgent meeting with the principal. At the meeting, I would calmly but accurately describe the problems encountered and review the group parameters (which should be shared with all participating principals before starting a school-based CBT program). In particular, I would indicate that privacy is essential so children can freely share their concerns, a quiet area is needed so children can focus on learning the material, and the full time is required for each group session. Then, I would engage in a problem-solving discussion with the principal. I would ask whether there is a location other than the library where the group could occur and how the group could fit with the usual routines at his or her school building. If the janitorial routine cannot be changed, perhaps holding the group over the lunch hour might be considered. Alternatively, having the children miss a few minutes of class time at the end of the day so the group can begin earlier than previously might be acceptable. The principal might have some suggestions as well, assuming he or she is motivated to continue the program at that school. Logistical problems are to be expected when working in the school environment, but with patience, mutual respect, and flexibility, they can often be solved.

2a. Before answering these questions, I take a deep breath and remind myself that this fellow's rather intimidating style likely reflects anxiety about how the CBT group will affect his child. Then, I answer honestly, but provide the appropriate context. For example, if I do not have children, I say so but indicate that I have seen children in psychotherapy for several years (so he is reassured that I am not totally inexperienced) and have learned that parents can often provide valuable insights about their children (so he is reassured that his point of view will be validated and taken into consideration in the group). Similarly, I admit that a "success rate" is difficult to provide because it depends on how success is defined, but reassure him that we are using a manualized program that has been internationally evaluated. In these evaluations, most children showed improvement, and many were diagnosis-free after treatment. If he is interested, I can refer him to the literature on these studies. Finally, I ask him if he has concerns about the program, as others in the group may share them. At this point, he will likely reveal what he is anxious about, and as before, I would try to address this in an honest but reassuring manner.

2b. Because this is the first session, I would not be too hard on this mother, but I would make it clear that this type of distraction cannot occur in the group. If the mother seems nonchalant about the incident, I might jokingly offer a cooking suggestion or reference to an alternative recipe. If she seems anxious about feeding her child, I would make an empathic comment about how busy everyone gets and how it can be difficult to fit another activity (like the CBT parent group) into one's routine. Either way, I would then indicate to the group that all cell phones and electronic devices must be turned off or at least set to vibrate during the group, and if an urgent call must be taken, the parent should step out of the group room to do so. The group can only be helpful if participants can give it their full attention.

2c. I would gently interrupt this mother and indicate that, although it is great to hear how helpful CBT was for her, we need to get back to talking about the children. I would then ask what specific aspects of her CBT experience have been helpful in addressing her child's anxiety and invite other parents to comment on what they do to help address their children's anxiety. This approach reengages the other members of the group and redirects the discussion to a relevant topic. Often, the "monopolizer" responds to this, and nothing else is needed. However, if this mother tended to monopolize conversation repeatedly or repeatedly behaved as though she were my cotherapist, I would take her aside for a few minutes after the group to explain why these behaviors are not helpful, and suggest more helpful ways of participating in the group.

2d. This question sometimes arises when one of the group leaders is a physician. I usually answer it by indicating that I wear several "hats," and as group leader I am wearing my "CBT hat." I am happy to book an appointment to discuss medication issues related to her child, but the parent group is not the place to discuss them. Many parent groups do include a session providing general information on psychotropic medication, but it is not designed to provide medication consultations for individual children. For nonphysicians, the "multiple hats" problem can also arise. For example, if you are providing psychotherapy to a family member who is not participating in the CBT program, parents sometimes try to obtain advice regarding that family member during the group. The response should be the same, as discussion of these issues distracts from the main focus of the group.

## CHAPTER 10: NANCY

First, I would ask Nancy's mother how she is coping, as she has just lost her own mother and is likely overwhelmed with grief, funeral arrangements, and other matters in addition to dealing with her distraught daughter. I would listen empathically, whatever the response. If Nancy's mother was interested in some counseling or a support group for herself, I would facilitate a referral, but if not, I would respect her choice. Chances are, the better Nancy's mother copes, the better Nancy will cope.

When the conversation returns to Nancy, I would gently explain that her daughter has every reason to be "a mess" under these circumstances, because she has just lost a close family member, who was probably also a significant attachment figure to her. Under these circumstances, I would expect Nancy to regress and show more separation anxiety, regardless of prior treatment: Her worst separation fears have just been realized! I would encourage Nancy's mother to accept and validate Nancy's feelings about the loss as best she can. It will also be important to reassure Nancy that her mother is in good health and will not leave her or die as her grandmother has.

Fortunately, if she can be supported through this difficult time, Nancy may yet return to a better level of functioning. Children are sometimes remarkably resilient. I would not necessarily continue with CBT, however, nor would I conclude therapy after two more sessions because this would likely be perceived as a further loss (loss of therapist). Instead, I would explore Nancy's feelings and thoughts about her grandmother's death, but also allow her to talk about other topics if she wishes. Children do not all have the same way of coping with a loss, and pushing them to talk about it sometimes does more harm than good. Nancy will likely need some less structured, more supportive sessions before returning to a more structured CBT format. The strategies she has learned so far are not irrelevant, they are just not sufficient to deal with the magnitude of this event. They will become useful again eventually, once Nancy has had a chance to emotionally and cognitively process what has happened.

## CHAPTER 11: NICHOLAS' MOTHER

In response to the question, "When would you like to see us again?" it is tempting to simply answer, "I don't." It is frustrating to most therapists when, after carefully preparing everyone for the conclusion of therapy, they are confronted with this comment, which implies a wish for more sessions.

Rather than being curt or rude, however, it is usually more helpful to explore the reasons for the comment. I might say something like, "I always *like* to see you folks, but I don't think I *need* to see you anymore. Nicholas is doing so well. What concerns do you still have about him?" At that point, you will either:

1. Hear about remaining problems Nicholas faces and be able to address these, even if it takes another session or two.
2. Have the parent acknowledge that Nicholas is doing well, but the parent is anxious about possible future problems. In this case, take the remainder of the session to reassure the parent's anxiety and go over strategies for relapse prevention from the chapter. Conclude therapy as planned. If the parent is still uncomfortable with leaving, make a further session to meet *only* with the parent to offer further reassurance and/or gently explore the possibility of treatment for the parent's anxiety.

## CHAPTER 12: BRAD

Interactions in supervisor-supervisee relationships sometimes mirror interactions in therapist-client relationships. In this case, the client's minimal participation in sessions, likely related to his social anxiety, results in the supervisee having little to discuss in supervision sessions. As a result, the supervisee feels self-conscious about his inability to provide more details about the therapy sessions, resulting in discomfort and awkward silences in the supervision session.

Identifying this issue for the supervisee can be very helpful. Point out that similarities between therapist/client and supervisor/supervisee relationships are common, and that the supervisee's behavior is to be expected under the circumstances. Then, see if the supervisee's experience can help him empathize with the client. Finally, try to use these experiences to find ways of making both therapy and supervision more relaxed and enjoyable.

## REFERENCES

Bernstein, G.A., Borchardt, C.M., Perwien, A.R., Crosby, R.D., Kushner, M.G., Thuras, P.D., et al. (2000). Imipramine plus cognitive behavioral therapy in the treatment of school refusal. *Journal of the American Academy of Child and Adolescent Psychiatry*, 39, 276–283.

LaGreca, A.M., & Stone, W.L. (1993). Social Anxiety Scale for children–Revised: Factor structure and concurrent validity. *Journal of Clinical Child Psychology*, 22, 17–27.

March, J. (1998). *Manual for the Multidemensional Anxiety Scale for children*. Toronto, ON: Multihealth Systems.

# Fear-Masters Modules

## CLINICIAN GUIDELINES

These guidelines provide a rationale for and review of the basic structure of Fear-Masters, a cognitive-behavioral program to reduce anxiety in certain children who may struggle with other CBT approaches (see below).

### Why Not Use a Traditional Cognitive Behavior Therapy Approach for All Anxious Children?

In many cases, "traditional" CBT (as described, for example, in Philip Kendall's *Coping Cat*) works very well. There are numerous randomized controlled trials around the globe attesting to its efficacy. Although community effectiveness is still being tested, there are undoubtedly many children for whom this is the optimal psychological intervention for anxiety.

Nevertheless, there are a significant number of children for whom this approach is problematic. These may include:

- Medically ill children, who may face realistic dangers. Traditional CBT's emphasis on probabilistic thinking may not be helpful here. These children need more emphasis on their own ability to cope with whatever comes—even if it is uncertain.

- Children with nonverbal learning disabilities (NVLD) or Asperger's. These children often don't generalize coping plans and other cognitive techniques across situations. They may need a consistent response for ANY anxiety state.

- Children with attention deficit disorder (ADD) or verbal learning disabilities (LD) may not have the verbal working memory to master cognitive restructuring or other sophisticated cognitive techniques and may therefore need a simpler, less verbal approach to coping with anxiety.

All of the above suggested to me that what was needed was a less verbal approach to CBT for childhood anxiety, which emphasizes personal mastery over anxious states, regardless of the specific situation. Each time an anxious situation occurs, the child is encouraged to deal with the fear response in the same way, which has been developed jointly with his or her therapist. Thus, there is little need to think "on the spot," and repetition builds confidence.

Repetition also, potentially, creates a conditioned response. In a conditioned response, a stimulus that evokes a particular reaction is repeatedly paired with a second stimulus, until the second stimulus also evokes that reaction. The classic example is Pavlov's dog experiment, where food, which elicits salivation, is paired with a bell until the sound of the bell also elicits salivation. In our case, a relaxed state is induced in therapy sessions using cognitive and behavioral techniques. Concurrently, a concrete and/or imagery-based reminder of those techniques is provided. Eventually, the image or the concrete reminder elicits a relaxed state, even without using the techniques. The need to think in anxious situations is reduced further, and the image or reminder is readily transportable from one anxious situation to another.

Why is it important to avoid the need to think in anxious situations? I will refer here to a rather old psychological finding: the Yerkes-Dodson curve. In this experiment, cognitive performance was measured in relation to state anxiety. The relationship was curvilinear. In other words, low anxiety states and high anxiety states both had adverse effects on cognitive performance, but mildly anxious states resulted in optimal performance. Most children facing their fears encounter a highly anxious state doing so. To expect them to use sophisticated cognitive techniques in such a state is simply not realistic. We often tell parents of anxious children, "don't talk, hug," when the child's anxiety is extreme. Reassurance is no longer effective once cognitive processes are overwhelmed by anxiety.

## What Would an Alternative Approach Look Like?

There are several good candidates for a less verbal approach to CBT. The first, as mentioned above, is use of imagery and concrete reminders to an even greater degree than traditional child CBT. A picture "speaks a thousand words," and if the same picture can be used for multiple situations, the cognitive demands in each situation are minimal, and a conditioned, anxiety-reducing response can develop upon presentation of the picture over time.

The second candidate is development of the capacity for self-observation. Again, this is not unique to the present program because it occurs implicitly in many child CBT programs, but it is somewhat more explicit in Fear-Masters. The capacity for self-observation tackles the vexing problem of helping children deal with real threats, not just imagined ones. If reality is threatening, substituting realistic thinking for anxious thinking doesn't work. What is needed is a heightened confidence in one's own ability to handle threat regardless of how realistic or unrealistic it may be.

Given children's often limited cognitive abilities, mindfulness meditation (the "gold standard" for developing the ability to stand back from one's internal states and nonjudgmentally observe them, which is used increasingly in adult anxiety management programs) may not be feasible. However, externalization has been shown to be beneficial in helping children manage both pain and uncomfortable emotional states.

Externalization is a concrete way of developing the capacity for self-observation by conceptualizing distressing emotions as separate from oneself. By implication, the child's self is "more than" the distressing emotions. Thus, one provides the suggestion that the child has cognitive resources for coping with the distressing emotions, even if these have not been previously used. In this way, externalization increases the child's confidence in coping with distressing emotions, regardless of their source.

In this program, fear is externalized. That is, fear is labeled as a problem that the child can tackle, rather than being considered an intrinsic aspect of the child. By implication, there is a "fearless" part of the child that can stand back and observe the fear and choose how to respond to it. The response that is encouraged, whenever possible, is to focus on a task the child must do at that moment (for example, attend to the teacher at school) or a perception of something in the environment that is interesting (for example, "forgetting" a mild fear of heights by focusing on the beautiful view). If this response is not possible, a reminder card of the child's favorite reassuring image is pulled out, which also contains the simple instruction "breathe." Finally, imagery-based meditation can be used in children to further strengthen both the capacity for self-observation and confidence in handling fear-inducing situations. Practiced initially at calm times, the same image can later induce the meditative state (or at least a more calm state) in anxiety-provoking situations. It becomes a conditioned response. Finding the image that is most comforting to a particular child can be a challenge, but guidelines on how to do so are provided along with several examples of child-friendly meditations.

What about exposure to feared stimuli? The program certainly encourages exposure, but works with the parent to implement it. In younger children, parents attend their children's sessions and observe in the background. Thus, they develop a sense of when their child is ready to tackle feared situations, and which ones to tackle first. Homework exercises further prompt children to think about when they are ready to tackle their fears and to share this information with their parents. Thus, exposure can begin at any point in the program when parent and child are confident about trying it. In older children or teens, parents may not attend all of the session, but join the child and therapist at the end to discuss and help implement any exposures the child feels ready to try. If exposure doesn't occur until the very end, additional follow-up sessions are used to ensure consolidation of coping skills and application to feared situations.

Despite the differences in content from traditional CBT, the directive therapeutic stance, session structure, use of a manual, emphasis on work between sessions, and other procedural elements of CBT are retained, as all of these clearly serve to reduce anxiety and facilitate mastery. In other words, this program is still done within the framework of traditional CBT, but the specific content has been adjusted to meet the needs of the children described above. Because the core skills are presented in separate modules, it is also possible to extract a particular module and use it to supplement another program, or to combine this program with another modular approach.

## Sessions with Children

Therapy sessions should focus on teaching skills and developing an individualized plan for each child for using helpful imagery, relaxation, and meditation techniques. Sessions are child-focused, with parent(s) either sitting in the background (with younger children) or joining at the end (with older children or teens). *No reading or writing is expected of the child, unless he or she wants to "fill in the blanks" in the manual.* Either parent or therapist can "scribe," and any participation by the child is positively reinforced (with gentle redirection if the child is really "off the mark"). Prioritize engaging the child in the session and ensuring he or she learns the key concepts, even if you don't read every word in the manual. Children with short attention spans in particular may benefit from condensing some of the information.

Throughout the child modules, there are references in parentheses to specific images that may be helpful in illustrating certain concepts or stimulating the imagination. Such images can be obtained for personal use with a particular client from a number of websites (for example, Google Images) and software programs (for example, Microsoft PowerPoint), although they should not be distributed further to avoid violating copyright laws. Using different images for different clients allows one to select a style of image that is most relevant to a child's particular background or age group, often enhancing engagement in therapy.

The manual is designed for a child of early school age (age 7 to 11) with or without some cognitive limitations, but can be adapted for teens with some rewording by the therapist. The title "Fear-Masters" emphasizes mastery over anxious states and evokes the image of a master teacher or wizard, but can be modified to fit with current popular culture. With adolescents, the therapist may have to use more "grown-up" imagery and provide a more detailed rationale for the program because they may be skeptical. For example, I sometimes draw the Yerkes-Dodson curve for teens to illustrate why the techniques are repeated across situations. An example of "grown-up" imagery might be to meditate upon a quiet place within oneself rather than a wave or other pictorial image. Adolescents may also need to assert their autonomy from the therapist, for example, wanting more choices regarding what techniques to use and a chance to tell you what works or doesn't work for them. Respect this need, but continue to offer gentle guidance when it's needed.

### Involving Parents

Given the challenges faced by children using this approach, parental participation is even more important than in traditional CBT. Parents help in the design of the child's plan during sessions, and between sessions they find ways to support their children in (a) recognizing anxiety states and (b) using the plan consistently. The information in the parent module can be handed out to parents and then reviewed with the therapist, or discussed with the therapist only. The latter allows more adaptation to match a particular family's culture, education level, treatment expectations, etc.

Parents are encouraged to see the child as we see him or her: as capable of managing fearful feelings regardless of their source. The feelings are a problem that the child can learn to manage, rather than an intrinsic aspect of the child that represents a defect or shortcoming. We emphasize children's need to feel they are fine and capable and whole just as they are, if they are to risk trying new behaviors.

We also work with parents to emphasize the general parenting principles of less talk/emotion, empathic encouragement, modeling, praise, and problem-solving around particular behavioral difficulties. Addressing personal anxiety about the child is often an important topic.

Positive reinforcement of parents is important in therapy, just as it is with the children (but using a more adult manner, of course). Parents often need encouragement and help recognizing small steps forward in themselves and their children. In particular, any work done between sessions is praised, because this work represents the main way of ensuring that material learned by parents and children generalizes to the "real world." Unlike traditional CBT, we do not encourage parents to use Socratic questions with their children, because (a) the plan is quite formulaic and is "fine-tuned" during therapy sessions, and (b) we try to reduce the need for children to think when in an anxious state.

**Course Structure (Assumes about 45-Minute Sessions)**

1. *Parent Module*: Two sessions at the beginning on supporting the child's use of Fear-Masters; one or two problem-solving follow-up sessions (after the child is seen).
2. *Child Modules*: One to three sessions each, depending on the child's pace.

   a. Recognizing Fear
   b. Mastering Fear through Imagery
   c. Imagery-Based Relaxation and Meditation
   d. Being a Fear-Master in Real Life

### REFERENCES FOR CLINICIANS AND PARENTS

Curtis, C.M., & Aldrich, C. (1994). *All I see is part of me.* Bellevue, WA: Illumination Arts.
Garth, M. (1991). *Starbright: Meditations for children.* New York: HarperCollins.
Kendall, P.C. (2006). *Coping Cat workbook* (3rd ed.). Philadelphia, PA: Workbook Publishing.
Manassis, K. (2008). *Keys to parenting your anxious child* (2nd ed.). Hauppauge, NY: Barron's Educational Series, Inc.
Murdock, M. (1987). *Spinning inward: Using guided imagery with children.* Boston, MA: Shambhala Publications.

In addition, parents may wish to make audio recordings of specific exercises for their children at home, and "Fear-Master" cards will also be designed with the children during the course.

## FEAR-MASTERS—PARENT MODULE: PART I

### What Is This Program About?

*Welcome to "Fear-Masters"!*—This is a short course to teach you how to help your children recognize and deal with fear, wherever it comes from, whatever the situation, whatever their age or ability. I call it fear instead of anxiety, because anxiety implies that you don't have a good reason to be afraid, or that your fear is exaggerated, and sometimes it's not. Sometimes children have reasons to be afraid. Fear is also simpler and more closely tied to the universal physiological response we will be talking about: the fight or flight response. This is a very healthy response by our body when we are faced with real danger; it helps us survive! Unfortunately, it causes unpleasant feelings of tension or panic when it happens at times when we are not in danger, and those are the times when we want to manage it.

In summary, everyone experiences fear, and everyone deals with it. Fear is a way of feeling, nothing more. What we need to help children recognize is this: They are more than their fearful feelings! Therefore, they can master fearful feelings.

While emphasizing mastery over anxious states, the title also evokes images of wizards or master teachers that are appealing to many children. If we want children to be able to deal with fear, what better way to do it than using their imagination? Imagery comes naturally to many children for whom words and explanations fail to reassure. Imagery also allows us to externalize fear. This means that children develop the ability to see fear as something separate from themselves, like a ghost or a monster. Seeing fear this way implies two things: (1) that fear is a state of mind they can choose to accept or reject; (2) that they have many personal resources to deal with that state of mind. Thus, fear becomes something "out there" and within their control, rather than an unchangeable aspect of their personality.

Notice, however, that we do not expect children to eliminate their fear. A certain amount of fear is natural and can even be adaptive in certain circumstances. Instead, we ask children to label their fear and think about how they can do things that are important to them despite fear. Trying too hard not to be afraid can be a little bit like trying not to think about pink elephants: It makes you self-conscious and exacerbates the problem. Therefore, the goal is not to eliminate fear, but to reduce its interference with what matters in life.

**What Are the Benefits?**

What happens when you develop the ability to deal with your fear?

- You think better. People whose minds are muddled with worries can't concentrate, and their ability to think deteriorates. Studies have shown that people do best on academic tests when they are just a little bit nervous. If it's more than a little bit, they start to go blank, and they cannot think and reason. That's also why (as many of you have experienced) children don't listen to reason when they are really fearful. Reasoning only works when fear is manageable, so that's what we are aiming for.
- You feel better. When you are often fearful, you have high levels of adrenaline, a stress hormone, in your system all the time. Adrenaline makes you feel tense and irritable. That's one reason fearful children are sometimes so miserable. Adrenaline-related tension can also give you headaches, stomachaches, or other tension-related pains. It can make your heart race. It can make you hyperventilate and feel dizzy, weak, or lightheaded. When the adrenaline goes down, breathing and heart rate normalize, tension decreases, and body and mind return to a much more comfortable state.
- You do better. People who are less fearful face their problems and try to solve them. People who are more fearful run away to avoid their problems, and studies have shown that avoidance makes anxiety worse. As we deal with our fear, we get better at confronting problems and solving them. Conversely, dealing with problematic situations despite fear can also reduce fear. It works either way.

**Why Develop Another Program?**

The idea for this program came from our research in cognitive behavioral therapy, or "CBT," a treatment that is helpful to many anxious or fearful children. Studies in many different centers have shown that many anxious children benefit from this treatment. Unfortunately, not all of the children benefit. Why? For some the treatment is too complicated and relies too heavily on verbal reasoning—on words. It also requires a longer attention span than many children have, and a lot of talking and thinking. Others are able to memorize the words beautifully, and they really "talk the talk." Unfortunately, they can't "walk the walk": They have difficulty applying what they learn in the real world. For others, real life is anxiety provoking. They face medical illnesses, unsafe neighborhoods, or other challenges that can't be easily reassured. "It's gonna be fine," for example, sounds pretty hollow when you have an illness with only a 50/50 chance of survival.

The final reason for this program came more from real-life experience than from research. You see, when we are afraid, most of us adults say things to ourselves like, "There's a million-to-one chance that this thing I'm worried about will happen," or "Chances are, it won't be nearly as bad as I think." We tell our children that too: "Johnny, you've studied hard so you should do fine on the test," or "Mommy is a very safe driver, so she won't get into a crash." CBT also uses these types of probabilistic statements and teaches children to use them too.

Usually, these statements are true. The particular thing you worry about probably won't happen. The big problem is: Something else might! There are a huge number of unexpected, unpredictable, rare but awful events that can happen to people that you probably have never thought of. Any one of them is extremely unlikely to happen, but there are so many of them that, at some point in your life, one of them probably will. Some events are simply beyond our control.

Now that last paragraph may have made you really anxious, and you probably want to leave. It's not all bad, though. The good news is this: We do have a choice. We're not helpless. We can't always choose our circumstances, but we can choose how to respond to them. We can teach our children how to respond as well, so they can develop the ability to master their fear. Furthermore, the response to fear doesn't have to be complicated. It can be very simple, as long as it's meaningful to the child.

From my description of children who don't benefit from traditional CBT, it's obvious that what we needed was something simple, which works in any anxiety-provoking situation, and that emphasizes one's own ability to cope with the situation regardless of how it turns out. Therefore, this program:

- Emphasizes mastery of fearful feelings rather than predictions and probability
- Uses fewer words and more imagery
- Externalizes fear (i.e., makes fear the villain), so it seems less a part of the child
- Uses a single plan for all situations
- Uses parents to help construct and implement the plan

Now let's get started!

## What Does Being a "Fear-Master" Mean?

All of us, when we're afraid, tend to respond by running away, by gasping for air, or by seeing the problem as gigantic and impossible. When we become Fear-Masters, we handle those tendencies in ourselves. We say,

"Oh dear, it's fear again," but then we remember that we've dealt with fear before, and we can deal with it again. We do what needs to be done in spite of fear. We don't let fear stop us from doing what's important and what we like to do. It doesn't matter any more that we can't predict the future, because we *can* predict our own ability to respond to it. We can trust our ability to cope, whatever happens. That's the ability we want to help your children develop, starting today.

How do we help children develop this ability? Paradoxically, we help by accepting them as they are. If children see themselves as defective and anxiety prone, they are unlikely to have the confidence to change their anxious behaviors. If they see themselves as fine and capable and whole just as they are, they just might. Anxiety is then seen as a problem to be mastered (as our title implies) rather than an essential aspect of the child's personality.

The value of acceptance is not just a theory: It's been demonstrated. Children who feel unconditionally accepted (called secure attachment) are less vulnerable to anxiety as adolescents than children who have never felt this way. We all need to feel accepted as we are in order to risk change. Doing something different in relation to anxiety is a big change for your children. Help them take the risk!

How do we understand our own and our children's ability to deal with frightening situations? We look at three areas: thoughts, feelings, and behaviors. Regardless of the specific thing in the situation that is provoking or triggering anxiety, the helpful response always involves those three areas. We'll see in a minute how you can support your child in developing each of these areas. Incidentally, these are the same three areas targeted by traditional CBT, but the strategies are a little different.

**Why Are Parents Important to Success?**

We think this approach can work, but we can't get your children to use it without your help. *You are crucial to this process.* You need to do the following:

- Understand your child's anxiety—what you are doing today!
- Encourage your child, with empathy: "I know it seems hard, but you can do it." Why is this important? Children need to feel understood before they can try to deal with their fear, so don't dismiss or ridicule their fear. At the same time, they need you to believe they are capable of success if they are to believe it themselves. For these reasons, the apparent "double message" of "I know it seems hard, but you can do it" works remarkably well.

- Support your child's use of new coping strategies—we will learn about those together with the children.
- Serve as models of calm, healthy coping yourselves—for most of us parents, that's easier said than done, but always worth the effort.

What will those new coping strategies be? Here's a quick preview of what the children will learn:

- Identifying their anxiety: the Fear Signal
- Externalizing anxiety and using reassuring imagery: being a Fear-Master
- Relaxation and meditation: strengthening the calm self
- Being a Fear-Master in real life

Your child does not have to be good at all of them. Some children will gravitate more toward one or another of these. The important thing is that they use the one(s) they like repeatedly.

Why are parents better than therapists at doing these things?

- They spend more time with their children.
- They know their children from birth, rather than seeing them at a single point in time.
- They have a stronger relationship with the child.
- Their empathetic encouragement of the child is more powerful.
- They are often better at motivating the child.
- The parent practicing skills with the child is often the best way to apply skills beyond the therapist's office!

*At Home*—Think of at least three specific situations where your child was fearful, and you were able to respond in a way that reduced the anxiety. Even if the child was still fearful, give yourself credit if you did something that helped a little bit. If you cannot remember any situations, observe your interactions with your child this week in one or two situations where your child is anxious.

1.
2.
3.

Do you calmly and quickly help your child come up with a plan for coping? Are you then able to offer empathic encouragement? That's probably the ideal approach, but few of us do it consistently.

**Common Mistakes**

Do you tend to use too many words and reasons for your child to hear? Do you get overly emotional (for example, anxious yourself, frustrated, inclined to blame someone, discouraged)? Do you get "drawn into" your child's anxiety or distress? Do you try to minimize your child's anxiety or distress? Next time, we will look at thoughts, feelings, and actions more deliberately, to see how you can help your child in each of these three areas.

## FEAR-MASTERS—PARENT MODULE: PART II

How did you try to reduce your child's anxiety this week, or in the past? What were some helpful responses you used? Make sure you recorded these, and use them again! Are there any responses that were not helpful, or reminded you of the "common mistakes" we reviewed last time? Make a mental note to change these.

Now, let's get back to thoughts, feelings, and actions related to fear. We'll understand them first in relation to ourselves, and then in relation to our children.

### Thoughts

How do we all *think* when we are fearful or anxious?

How do we see ourselves? _____

_____

How do we see the situation? _____

_____

What do we anticipate? _____

_____

Our children think this way when they are fearful. Whenever you get frustrated with your child's fearful behavior, put yourself in the child's shoes by imagining the situation from a fearful child's point of view. Remember that the child is underestimating his or her own ability to cope, overestimating the risks of the situation, and anticipating the worst. Does the fear-related behavior make more sense now?

Here are some common behaviors that relate to fearful thinking:

- Endless "what if" questions
- Not reassured by any explanation
- Perfectionism: one little thing can ruin the whole day
- Poor concentration (worrying takes up mental energy)
- Clinging or lack of independence
- Stubborn refusal to do things that are new or potentially frightening

If you saw the world the way a fearful child does, you might do these things too!

How can you help?

- Model realistic thinking—deal with your own fear, and show how you do it!
- Empathize—recognize where fearful behavior is coming from, to avoid getting frustrated.
- Point out situations where the child has demonstrated some ability to master fear or to cope with something other children might find frightening, even if the child initially denies these. This will strengthen the child's awareness of his or her resources for overcoming fear, or the "self that can deal with the fear."
- Reassure, and repeat the reassuring statement once, then stop talking. This avoids arguments and escalation of the child's anxiety.
- Help your child identify fear and encourage using the strategies from this program.
- When anxiety is overwhelming, stop talking and offer quiet comfort (note: some children do better if you are in the room but not too close; others prefer a hug). Children cannot think in this state, so trying to reason with them at this time makes the anxiety worse!

Pay special attention to your own anxious or negative thoughts about your child. If you tend to get anxious about your child or underestimate his or her ability to cope, practice:

- Giving your child the benefit of the doubt, whenever possible.
- Focusing on your child's abilities, rather than disabilities.
- Resisting the urge to do things for your child before the child has had a chance to try them on his or her own.
- "Scaffolding" new learning, by solving only part of a new challenge for your child, and letting him or her do the rest.
- Believing in your child's potential to improve with time and maturation.
- Allowing your child to make some mistakes, even if it is hard to watch.
- Trying not to overreact when your child cannot do something.
- Remembering that tomorrow is another day and telling your child this too.

When it comes to anxious children, remember: They are stronger than you think. They are stronger than they think. Show confidence in their strength, and they will surprise you, whether or not they learn anything new in this course.

If you tend to think negatively about your child, or tend to see continuing problems more readily than his or her progress, practice:

- Reframing some of his or her characteristics positively (for example, think of him or her as sensitive or imaginative, rather than anxiety prone).
- Noticing even the tiniest positive step (for example, looking someone in the eye, even if he or she is too shy to speak to them; staying in the room rather than running away, even if he or she is too shy to look them in the eye).
- Finding or creating structured situations that set up your child to succeed and experience mastery (for example, encouraging doing drama with a script for a child who cannot handle unstructured social situations; having your child teach another child something he or she has just learned).
- Emphasizing what your child CAN do, rather than cannot do, at every opportunity.

### Feelings

How do we *feel* when we are afraid? What physical symptoms do we notice in our bodies? We see those same symptoms in children, and we eventually get them to recognize the most prominent one(s) as their Fear Signal. The two common types are:

1. Panic symptoms (hyperventilation, racing heart, sweating, cold hands, nausea, dizziness, feeling out of control)
2. Tension symptoms (headache, stomachache, insomnia, urinary frequency)

How can you help?

- Validate the feeling: It is real pain, even if it is due to tension.
- Encourage relaxation or meditation, especially at bedtime.
- De-catastrophize the symptom: A night without sleep is not the end of the world; pain will not last forever.
- Encourage regular aerobic exercise.
- Ensure regular health routines (sleeping routines, eating regular meals, and so forth).
- Have the child avoid caffeine products; these can exacerbate symptoms.

**Behaviors**

What do we all *do* when we are fearful? Most often, we fight or flee. There-fore, naturally, fearful children will either:

- *Fight:* Become oppositional when you try to make them do things they fear.
- *Flee:* Avoid certain situations or activities.

These behaviors are difficult for fearful children to change, so your tough-est work as a parent will be in this area. How can you help?

- Do not get drawn into power struggles. Fearful children can rarely be convinced to do something through parental persuasion. Enforce what is necessary (for example, school attendance), and build up to the rest in small steps.
- Less talking, less negative emotion.
- Be consistent: (1) from day to day; (2) with your partner.
- Time out either the child or yourself, or both, if things are escalating.
- Offer warnings ahead of time for new situations or changes in routine.
- Plan ahead with the child for new events if possible. Surprising him or her on the day of the event robs the child of the opportunity to prepare and use his or her coping strategies.

To encourage facing what is feared, offer empathic encouragement as follows:

- I know this must seem hard.
- But you can do it.

Then, proceed to:

- Devise small steps that can be practiced frequently (daily is best), for at least 20 minutes at a time.
- Praise progress (with or without charting for points and prizes).
- Ignore setbacks (it is not a test); praise every attempt.
- Start with something that's not too hard. It is best if the child is already occasionally doing it, so you can reward increased frequency.
- Expect the child's progress to go "two steps forward and one step back."
- Start with something the child would like to work on.

- Set up the child to succeed, even if you must accompany him or her initially (and if so, add points for doing it unaccompanied).

- Make it a win–win outcome: For example, if they panic, say, "Wow, you got through it!"

Do not expect your child to feel less anxious and then do more. Usually, it works the other way around. If your child really values a particular activity, he or she will do it (with your encouragement) despite fear. Therefore, focus on how much better life will be once the situation is mastered, not on how much less distressing it will be. Success comes first; calmer feelings come later. Remember that being brave does not mean being fearless; it means doing what's important in spite of fear. More detailed strategies can be found in the book *Keys to Parenting Your Anxious Child* (see references).

Which of the three areas that we have talked about (thoughts, feelings, or behaviors) is most challenging in relation to your child? Take a moment to look at the alternative ways of responding to your child that may help for that area. You do not have to implement the whole list. Just pick one or two alternatives that you think are worth a try.

*At Home*—Try out a different way of responding to your child this week. If you don't feel you need to respond differently in any way, take the week to observe some of your own anxious thoughts about your child. We all have some of these. By becoming aware of them, we can prevent them from getting in the way of effective encouragement.

The next few sessions will be spent together with your child, gradually making a plan to help him or her face anxiety-provoking situations.

**Follow-Up Session(s) for Parents after Child Modules**

Today is a problem-solving session, to look at what is working well from the program and what is not working so well. First, tell us what is working well.

Now, what is not going so well? Let's try a common problem-solving approach to address that issue. Here it is:

**P.A.S.T.E.**

- **P**ick a problem.
- **A**lternative solutions.
- **S**elect one solution after weighing the pros and cons.
- **T**ry it out.
- **E**valuate the result and change or "fine-tune."

Fill in the steps for your issue:

**P** = _____

**A** = _____

_____

_____

**S** = _____

**T** = _____

**E** = _____

When in doubt, go back to what the child learned. Which module do you think the child needs to practice more? Help him or her review it and/or use it more consistently. Don't forget that personal feelings can interfere with effective encouragement. Are any of them getting in the way? Now that we've "tuned up" the plan, try it this week. Tell us how it went next time!

If things are going well, are there any problems related to fear that you anticipate for your child in the near future? Can you prepare for these, or is it better to just cope with your own anxiety about them? What makes sense?

**Pointers for Planning Ahead**

- Anxiety and fear go up and down, as we cope with change in our lives.
- Anticipate anxiety if a change is coming (for example, a new school year).
- Remember: Flare-ups do not need to be disasters, just go back to what worked before.
- Keep your materials and review/reuse.
- Focus on your child's strengths.
- Advocate for your child if some accommodation is needed (for example, at school).
- Ask for more professional help if he or she is deteriorating quickly or getting depressed.
- Manage you own anxiety and fear well, so you can model healthy coping!

Finally, regularly give yourself and your child credit for tackling fear: one of the most disturbing emotions human beings can encounter. It's simple to react to life's challenges by blaming oneself and becoming depressed, or blaming others and becoming angry. It's harder to know that life is unpredictable, that it's not always within anyone's control, that the only constant is change, and to cope with the inevitable anxiety that comes from that knowledge. That is what you, and your children, are learning to do. Be proud of it.

## CHILD MODULE 1: RECOGNIZING FEAR

(Image 1: Wizard)

**Welcome to "Fear-Masters!"**

This is a short course to teach you how to recognize and deal with fear, wherever it comes from, whatever the situation, whatever your age or ability. Everyone experiences fear, and everyone can live life fully in spite of it. Fear is a way of feeling. That's all. What you need to remember is: You are more than your fearful feelings! In fact, you can become a "Fear-Master": an expert at finding and handling fear! Fear often looks a lot scarier than it really is, and it goes away when you confront it and do things in spite of it.

What happens when you become a "Fear-Master?"

- You think better because your mind is not muddled up with worries.
- You do better because you solve problems instead of running away from them.
- You feel better because you are not tensed up with stress all the time, wanting to fight or wanting to run away.
- You are calm. At first, you will not be perfectly calm, but with practice you will gradually get there. You need to do the things you are afraid of in spite of fear. Doing things comes first; feeling calm about it comes later.

**Let's Get Started!**

Fear makes us afraid, worried, or nervous sometimes. Those times happen to everyone. Think of a time when you were afraid, worried, or nervous. What happened? How did you react?

Time: _____

_____

Reaction: _____

_____

When most of us are afraid, worried, or nervous, we react by running away, by gasping for air, or by seeing the problem as gigantic and impossible. Sometimes we cry or feel like giving up. Did you know there's a different way to react?

Let's daydream for a moment. Think of a person or character you admire, someone who is a hero or role model to you. It could be a cartoon, a movie character, or a real person.

*Draw a picture of your hero or role model handling the time you just described.*

(Image 2: Superhero)

My hero or role model: _____

_____

How would he or she react at that time?

Reaction: _____

_____

You could react that way too! That's how you can start to become a Fear-Master.

The neat thing is, you do not have to be invincible to do this. Remember, every superhero has a weakness. What is the weakness your hero or role model has?

_____

_____

Does that stop him or her from managing fear, and doing the right thing? No way! Everybody has weaknesses, but that is OK. It does not have to stop you from being a Fear-Master. Brave people are not fearless; they just do things in spite of their fear.

When you manage fear, you think, act, feel, and most importantly, respond to your situation from a calm base. You find ways of cuing your mind and body to return to that calm base again and again. It is the same response every time, no matter how you get there or what the situation; it's the relaxation response. The more often you trigger it, the more effective it becomes, and the more automatic it becomes. It is just like exercising your muscles; they get stronger with practice. In the same way, your ability to relax gets stronger with practice.

*Here are three things that can help you relax:*

1. Know your Fear Signal.
2. Imagine yourself as a "Fear-Master."
3. Practice meditating, to strengthen your natural, calm self.

We will talk about each of these things in detail. You may use one, two, or all of them. We will try to figure out which ones work best for you.

**Know Your Fear Signal**

Let's start to practice. First, we have to know what we are looking for. What does fear feel like? The last time you were afraid, worried, or nervous what happened? What did your body do? If you cannot remember, think of someone you saw who was afraid. What did their body do? What happens to someone when she thinks she sees a ghost? What happens to someone when he's really embarrassed? Embarrassment is another kind of fear. Let's see how many parts of the body can show fear. How many can you count? Draw arrows to those body parts on the picture of the girl doing karate. What would she look like if she was afraid?

Which body part do you notice most when you experience fear? Circle it on the picture! If you are not sure, ask your parents which one they notice themselves, or notice in you. If you notice several things in your body, pick the one that happens most often when you are afraid. Got it? That's your *Fear Signal*. Watch for it! That's the signal that tells you to become a Fear-Master! We will explain how to do that in a moment. For now, let's make sure we remember our fear signal.

My Fear Signal is:

_____

_____

Examples might be: "My stomach starts squeezing and churning and feeling weird," "I feel like I want to sink into my chair," "I start to breathe fast," or "I get all shaky."

(Image 3: Girl doing Karate)

This week, tell your mom or dad whenever you notice your fear signal. They will give you a point every time you do, and we will track those until the end of the course. Tell yourself, "It's just my fear acting up," and try to focus on something that is not connected to the fear, like an activity or game, something you can see or hear around you, or something you have to do at the time. Do not try to fight the fear, just see if you can focus on something else, even for a short while.

Parents, try responding to the situation in a way that is consistent with what you learned last week. If children do not raise any situations, ask at the end of the day (but not more than once a day) if they noticed their "fear signal." Similarly, if you see a situation where they clearly are worried or afraid, ask them, "What did you notice in your body when that happened?" This allows you to revise the "fear signal" if there is another bodily reaction that is even more common for your child than the one we discussed today. Most importantly, do not nag or persist if the child does not want to talk about fear or worry. We will review how things went next time, and do some problem-solving if needed.

*"Fear Signal" Situation (Write or Draw; Bonus Points for Extra Situations):*

## CHILD MODULE 2: FEAR-MASTER IMAGERY

**Fear-Master Imagery (Introduction)**

*Fear-Signal Review*—When did you notice your fear signal this week? What happened? Were you able to tell yourself, "It's just my fear acting up?" Parents, can you think of a situation where you noticed the fear signal in your child? Let's talk about that situation(s) until we're all clear on how to detect the fear signal.

Now, let's take the next step to becoming a Fear-Master. Think about a situation that makes some children nervous that you handle really well. Having trouble thinking of one? Ask your mom and dad if they have noticed any. Everyone has at least one of these situations, because no two people are afraid of exactly the same things. Some people are really shy and nervous when they meet new people, but they handle roller coasters with no problem. Other people are not shy, but they worry about doing well on projects. Still other people get worried when they are away from home, but they do their projects calmly and don't worry about the grade they will get. Some people are terrified of spiders, but like being around dogs. Other people panic when they see a dog, but see spiders as "no big deal." Write or draw the situation you already handle well:

Now, let's figure out what strategy you use in that situation that helps you handle the fear. Some people just tell themselves, "It's no big deal." Other people remember that they've handled the situation before, so they can do it again. Other people remind themselves that they are not alone: Other people will help out if needed. Some people take their mind off the scary parts of the situation and focus on the parts that are not scary. Some people remind themselves that they are smart enough (or brave enough, or strong enough, or good enough) to get through the situation. Some people just breathe slowly or imagine how good they will feel when it is over. Have you done any of these things? You have probably done at least one, even if you were not aware of it.

My Fear-Master strategy for this situation is:

_____

_____

Can you think of a second strategy you ever used (in this situation or other situations)? Can you think of a third strategy? Let's see how many you can come up with in five minutes. I will jot down all the ones you mention. Ready? Go!

1. _____
   _____
   _____

2. _____
   _____

3. _____
   _____
   _____
   _____
   _____

Wow! That was impressive.

*Imagining*—Now let's do something with all those ideas. See if you can imagine doing all of them at once. What sort of person or creature would you have to be to do them all? Would you be a wizard that casts different spells to make fears disappear? Would you be a cook who dissolves fears in a boiling pot? Would you be a computer expert who switches to a different program or website when something scary comes up? Would you be a knight in metal armor that deflects any frightening arrow or bullet that might come your way? Would you be the karate girl you saw earlier, who uses clever moves to fool fear and stop it from hurting her? Would you be the conductor of a train who is in control and will not let fearful thoughts run away with her? Would you be a Boy Scout who is always prepared and has a whole troop of people to support him?

Take a few minutes to decide on the best image for you.

My Fear-Master looks like:

_____

_____

Draw Your Fear-Master, cut it out, and paste it on a pocket-size card. Print or have your parent print the word "Breathe" in big letters at the bottom, because that's always a healthy thing to do, and we will learn more about that later.

Now, think about some situations that are hard for you, like the ones where you noticed your fear signal last week. I will jot them down:

1. _____
   _____
   _____

2. _____
   _____

3. _____

What would happen if you focused on your Fear-Master Image in those situations and acted like that person or creature? OK, so maybe it would not work for all of them, but let's start with just one. Is there even one "Fear Signal" situation where this would be worth a try? See if there's one coming up in the next week or so where the Fear-Master Image might work.

Situation to try my Fear-Master Image:

_____

_____

This week, keep noticing your "Fear Signal," and try the Fear-Master Image in the situation you described. Carry the card in your pocket to use as a reminder.

## Fear-Master Imagery (Continued)

How did it go this week? Did you use your Fear-Master Image? Did it seem to help even a little bit? If yes, keep using it! See if you can apply it to other situations this week. If no, what do you think got in the way?

Sometimes, using your Fear-Master Image works right away, and you don't need to learn any of the ideas in the next few pages. Sometimes, things get in the way. Some of those things can be solved by preparing better for the situation, asking for help, or relaxing yourself (and we will talk more about that next time). Do you think one of those solutions would help? Which one? Try it out this week!

If you do not think any of those ideas would help, it may be that your fear is "playing tricks" with your thinking, and that is getting in the way of your coping. Today, we will talk about some common tricks fear can play, and see if you've noticed any in yourself. If there is one Fear Trick that gets in your way a lot, you may be able to recognize it and stop fear from fooling you this way. You can also make a card with a picture of that Fear Trick and show your Fear-Master Image defeating it. Then, whenever you get your Fear Signal, you can glance at this new card and relax. Once you get some practice at doing this, fear will not stand a chance!

If you do not recognize any Fear Tricks, keep using the card from last week because "practice makes perfect."

_Fear Trick 1: The Gambler_

(Image 4: Gambler)

In this trick, fear tries to convince us that we can predict the future. Fear comes disguised as a gambler and says: "Place your bet and let me deal you some cards! You can figure out how to win! If you think hard enough, you can predict the order of those cards, and you can make sure you get a winning hand! Don't stop thinking, though, or you won't predict all the possible combinations of cards. Then you won't win."

Of course, that is nonsense. The cards cannot be predicted or controlled no matter how clever you are, which is why gamblers usually lose. Life's like that too. The future cannot be predicted and cannot be controlled completely, no matter how much you think or worry about it. If you prepare for every possible thing that could go wrong, something else bad could still happen, or something good could happen instead. You never know. You can make some sensible preparations to cope better, but the only thing you can predict or control completely is your own reaction to what happens, whatever it is.

So what should you do instead of thinking and worrying? You need to become a Fear-Master. You need to expose the gambler's lies. Imagine that your worries are like the gambler's cards. Picture yourself throwing them in the air. You do not know how they will land, but it does not matter. You can toss them away. They predict nothing. You can handle whatever happens regardless of those worries, because you're not controlled by fear.

*Fear Trick 2: The World Is a Stage*

(Image 5: Girl or boy onstage)

This trick happens a lot to people who get shy or embarrassed. For this trick, fear tries to convince you that you live on a stage in the spotlight. Fear says, "Everyone can see what you look like, and every tiny imperfect thing about your looks. Everyone is watching what you do and will laugh if you slip or fall or drop something. Everyone can hear what you say, and you might get that funny squeak in your voice, or that tongue-tied feeling like you can't say anything right, or you might have to cough or even throw up, and everyone will hear and see it all. The only way to be safe is to perform perfectly all the time, so you impress people and they don't think bad things about you."

That's nonsense too. You don't live on a stage; you live on earth. On earth, people are usually too busy to sit around judging other people. Besides, the people who care about you will forgive you if you make a mistake once in a while. You don't have to impress them. They like you and love you anyway. And as for the people who do not care about you, who cares what they think? Let them have their opinion, whatever it is. You don't have to get them to like you or admire you.

In truth, nobody is liked and admired by everyone, yet most people are still liked and loved by their friends and family. If that's you, you are just like everyone else. You're not the worst, and you're not the best, but that's OK. There's only one of you, so that makes you special, just as you are. See yourself as a Fear-Master, taking a bow, closing the curtains, turning off the spotlight, and jumping off that stage to join the human race. We don't live on stage. We live with each other, and we belong with each other, just as we are.

*Fear Trick 3: Being Alone Means Being Helpless*

(Image 6: Television set and converter)

This trick happens to people who are afraid to be alone. For this trick, fear tries to convince you that you are weak, and you can't cope without your parents. Then, fear turns off all the good memories and the good things you've learned from your parents. Instead, fear sends your mind all kinds of scary movies about car accidents, or about people dying, or about getting kidnapped and taken away, or about ghosts in you room, all kinds of scary things!

In truth, you are never that weak. Your parents would not leave you alone in a situation if you could not handle it, or they would be in serious trouble with the authorities. They're not allowed to leave you alone unless they know you're safe. They've taught you everything you need to cope in that situation, even if you don't know exactly when they are coming back for you. And as you know, they always do come back!

So now, as a Fear-Master, what do you have to do? As a Fear-Master, you have to turn off the scary movie, and turn on the movie of good memories that you have of your family. Tell yourself, "It's not real," and imagine yourself changing the channel. That's all you have to do. Now, on the new channel, you see your parents right there by your side. Watch that channel in your mind as long as you're afraid, and before long your parents will arrive. If you need help remembering them, bring along a picture or a favorite thing from home to remind you. If it's still hard, try imagining something that you remember from a favorite show. Then, enjoy the new show.

*Fear Trick 4: If One Little Thing Goes Wrong, the Sky Will Fall*

(Image 7: Chick or small chicken)

I call this trick the "chicken little" trick. Chicken Little was a character in a story who got hit on the head by a tiny little acorn and was convinced that a piece of the sky had hit him. He ran around saying, "The sky is falling, the sky is falling!" Pretty soon, he had a lot of other people convinced the sky was falling too. That wasn't very smart. With the Chicken Little trick, fear says, "If I make just one mistake, if I'm five or ten minutes late, if I don't get to my next level in swimming lessons, if I don't understand my homework one night, if just one little thing goes wrong . . . the sky will fall." Then, you don't just become fearful, but you become angry because it seems like everyone else is making things go wrong! They are screwing up, it seems, and you will pay the price!

Of course, there is no price. The sky does not fall. We all make mistakes, we all have families that make mistakes, and most of us somehow still muddle through to learn how to swim eventually, and graduate from school eventually, and have pretty good lives. The fear of making mistakes can stop us from making decisions, which can really slow us down, but the mistakes themselves are not such a disaster. In fact, if it weren't for mistakes, we wouldn't learn much. Check it out. The question you got wrong on your test is the one you'll know for sure on your final exam. Mistakes teach us important lessons, so it's important we let ourselves make them, and others make them too. The only way to avoid mistakes completely is to never do anything, and that's the biggest mistake of all! Coping when things aren't perfect is something to be proud of. It's an important skill. The most successful people are usually ones who have learned "not to sweat the small stuff." So, what should a Fear-Master do for Chicken Little? Do you have any ideas? No, we're not going to make him into chicken soup. How about tucking him into his nest and reminding him that the sky is still there, and if he gives himself some time to calm down and rest, he can enjoy a beautiful sunrise tomorrow morning. You can too, no matter how many hassles, mistakes, and awful situations you have to deal with today. You will survive today, and you always have another chance to get it right, tomorrow. And guess what? No matter how bad it seems right now, chances are by tomorrow it will just be like the acorn that hit Chicken Little: no big deal.

Now, imagine tomorrow's sunrise.

(Image 8: Sunrise)

*Fear Trick 5: You Are as Helpless as a Mouse*

(Image 9: Mouse)

In this trick, fear tries to convince you you're a mouse. This often happens when facing a situation that involves some real risks. In this case, fear tries to say, "When something scary happens, all you can do is scurry away and hide. You're just a helpless little mouse!"

Isn't that silly? You're not a mouse. You're a smart, strong, brave boy or girl. You can do all kinds of things to prepare for the scary situation and to cope when you're in it. If you're afraid of tests, you can study. If you're afraid of something really dangerous, like an operation, you can learn about it or ask your parents about it. That way, you'll be in great shape to get through it!

There's always something you can do about what you fear, no matter how awful it seems. In the next session, we'll talk about your "calm self," which will help you stop fear from taking over, whatever the situation. For now, just remember: You're not a mouse; you're a person, so use that marvelous human brain you have, and do something to prepare for what's ahead! Then, once you have done all you can do, try some of the "calm self" exercises. Here's a picture of some people whose motto is "Be Prepared," and they usually are!

(Image 10: Boy Scout & Girl Scout)

*Which Fear Trick Happens a Lot to YOU?*—Imagine what a Fear-Master would do. Go back to your Fear-Master Image. What would he or she do?

A Fear Trick I have noticed is:_____

_____

A Fear-Master Image does this: _____

_____

Draw your Fear-Master Image doing that action, and paste it on a card. Print or have your parent print the word "Breathe" at the bottom. It's a really good reminder to help you relax, and we all need oxygen! Pull out that card and look at it each time you notice your Fear Signal this week.

*Fear-Master Image Defeating Fear (Draw)*—What if none of the fear tricks seem familiar? Maybe fear is tricking you another way. For example, one boy told me, "My imagination keeps running away with me." That was his way of being tricked by fear. He drew a runaway train on his fear card. Then, he drew himself as the conductor, getting that train to slow down and stay on the track. That was his way of being a Fear-Master. After practicing with his card, he could get his mind to slow down and stay focused on what was going on. His imagination didn't run away with him any more. A girl told me, "My thoughts keep snowballing." She drew a picture of herself holding the snowball back from rolling down a hill, so it would not increase in size. Whenever she caught "snowballing thoughts," she labeled them and tried to concentrate on whatever task was in front of her.

The specific image or name you find for the problem is not as important as *giving it a name or image*. Once you have a name or image that means something to you and is easy to remember, then you can tell when fear is tricking you, stop the trick with your Fear-Master Image, and get refocused on whatever is happening in your life at that moment. If you are still struggling with this, see if your mom or dad can help find a way fear tricks you, a way to be a Fear-Master, and a way to show it on a card.

This week, practice using the new card when you notice your fear signal. Some people find they do school work more quickly because they are more focused. Others find they enjoy time with their friends more as they get more interested in people and less interested in their own worries. Even if no big changes like that happen, you can always find something else to focus on besides your fear, and that feels good.

## CHILD MODULE 3: IMAGERY-BASED MEDITATION

### Imagery-Based Meditation (Introduction)

Did you use your Fear-Master card this week? How did it work? Was it hard to remember to use it? Let's see if we need to do anything different this week. It is OK if we need to redesign the card too. It can take a while to find the best Fear-Master Image for you.

Today, we will shift to talking about your Calm Self. To get us in the mood, I'd like to start with a short story. This story is called "The Helicopter Ride."

(Image 11: Helicopter)

*The Helicopter Ride*—Ben was feeling pretty down. One day, his parents arranged for him to go on a helicopter ride with his aunt Serena to cheer him up.

Serena greeted him warmly with, "How's my special boy?"

Ben replied, "I'm not special. I haven't done anything great. I get picked on at school. My sister pushes me around. Sometimes I don't think I matter to anyone."

"I'm not so sure," said Serena, "Let's see how things look from up there." She pointed to the sky.

Once they were in the air, she pointed down. "Look!" she encouraged him.

Ben looked puzzled. "I don't understand."

Serena explained, "There, you left some footprints in the deep snow. A little girl stepped into them so she could walk. She missed her bus from school today and was worried she couldn't get home. Now she can."

She continued, "There, you whistled a tune on the bus. It reminded that man of his mother. He decided to visit her in the nursing home today. It made her very happy."

"There, you wore a bright shirt as you walked to your swimming lessons. A woman who was very sad saw the shirt. She was reminded that spring is coming soon. She smiled, and felt much better."

"You didn't try to change those people's lives, but you did. Just by being near them, you made a difference. You do it every day. We all do. We affect the rest of the world without even knowing it, just by being there."

Ben nodded. He understood, "Just by being there, we belong."

The helicopter touched down, he thanked his aunt, and he continued to be, happily.

*Relaxation*—Today, we will focus on "being." The story introduces the idea that being is important, regardless of what you do or accomplish. That is why it's OK to take time once a day to just be.

In case that sounds strange, let me tell you that people have been doing it for thousands of years. It is relaxing, it calms your mind when it's racing all over the place, it reduces your blood pressure, it reduces anxiety, it can help prevent depression, and it has no nasty side effects. The fancy term for it is meditation, but sometimes people think that sounds a little strange. Really, it's just taking time to be.

It helps if you have something to focus on while you're being, and that's why some people use certain words or images when they meditate. We are going to use images today.

(Image 12: Balloon)

When you meditate, it helps if you're breathing slowly. When you breathe fast you get tense and dizzy, and sometimes you even get a feeling of pins and needles in your hands. When you breathe slowly, you trigger the body's own natural relaxation response. The dizziness and other funny feelings subside, and you become calm.

Let's see if we can do it. Count to four every time you breathe in, one Mississippi, two Mississippi, three Mississippi, four Mississippi, then breathe out. If that's easy, try a count of five or even six. If you keep your back straight and your shoulders down, that helps. Breathe in through the nose and out through the mouth.

Balloon breathing can also help. To do that, put your hand on your tummy. See if you can make your tummy into a balloon that pushes your hand as you breathe in. That helps the air get right to the bottom of your lungs.

Are you sometimes up to a count of five or six with every breath? That's even better. Are you feeling dizzy? If you are, stop doing the balloon breathing and just try to slow down. However you do it, slowing down your breathing will help keep you calm.

Don't be discouraged it you have not got it yet. Some people have to practice once a day for weeks before they get the hang of it. Other people do it automatically, without thinking about it. On average, we grownups tend to need more practice than you do. If you're getting frustrated, take a break and see if the breathing improves as we start to add some imagery. Over time and with practice, the breathing and imagery will allow you to become calm more easily.

(Image 13: Waves and seashore)

One of my favorite images is of the ocean near the seashore on a warm, sunny day. I imagine myself as a wave on that ocean. It's an image I've found helpful in dealing with my own fear and anxiety. Like many meditations, it can also be interpreted on a more spiritual level, but it does not have to be. As I talk through it, let's take a few minutes to imagine ourselves as waves.

*The Wave*—Sit in a relaxed, comfortable posture. Close your eyes if you like. Let's take a few slow, deep breaths. Feel the air pushing against the hand on your tummy. Let's count slowly on the in-breath: One, two, three, four, and exhale. Wait a moment, and count again: One, two, three, four, and exhale. Continue breathing slowly.

Let's imagine listening to the steady, timeless rhythm of the waves

As they roll toward a warm, sandy shore.
Hear the seagulls above
Feel the warmth of the sun
Now, imagine becoming one of those waves
Your body is fluid and supple
As you gently bob in the breeze
The tension melts as your arms and legs
Roll up and down with the tide
You are a wave on the ocean of life
A tiny bundle of energy
That surges up, then forward, and then subsides
As waves have always been doing
Waves have nothing to fear
And as a wave, neither do you

You are joined to all the other waves moving around you
To all the waves that came before you
And will come after you
You are connected to them
You share their strength
And the strength of the ocean
Beneath all waves
So you are never really alone.
And if you worry about rocks ahead
That could crash into you
Remember that they could also push you in a new direction
Toward a new place you never imagined
Or turn out not to be rocks at all
You can't really tell
They're too far away
And if you worry about impressing people
Think how silly that is to a wave
As a wave it doesn't matter
How you look or what people think,
Whether you're a small wave or a big wave,
Whether you're perfectly clear, or have some debris inside
All that matters is how you use your energy
Whether you push a small bottle
So someone finds a message hidden inside
Or carry a mighty ship
With cargo for a distant land
Whether you rise up and show other waves how to move
Or push forward gently to lend them your strength
Only your energy counts
Nothing else
And the clutter and worries in your mind
Settle out like so much sand
Drifting to the bottom of the ocean
Freeing you to just be
And as a wave is warmed by the sun
And refreshed by the breeze
As it feels itself surging ahead
So you can feel alive as you go through each day
And enjoy the experience, wherever it leads
And although you eventually break apart
Into droplets of foam
As you roll onto the shore
You don't disappear:

The tide pulls you back
To join the ocean again
As it has since the beginning of time

Let's count to 10 slowly, as we leave the seashore and return to this room. Take one or two more slow breaths, and then open your eyes.

-----

Some people do not find the image of water as soothing as others, so there are other meditation images. Sometimes a more personal image helps, especially if you worry about being separated from parents or family members. Next is a meditation focusing on a comforting companion made of light. Sometimes the image of home or a familiar place can be very relaxing, so there is also a meditation focusing on that.

*The Being of Light*—Sit in a relaxed, comfortable position. Close your eyes if you like. Let's take a few slow, deep breaths. Feel the air pushing against the hand on your tummy. Let's count slowly on the in-breath: One, two, three, four, and exhale. Wait a moment, and count again: One, two, three, four, and exhale. Continue breathing slowly.

Now, imagine you have a companion
Made completely of light
A human form that is with you
Accompanying you always
But consisting only of light
You turn to face this being
And the light is gentle
It does not sting your eyes
Yet it is intense
Warming your body completely
The light is wise
Shining into every dark corner of your mind
Showing you what is there
But not saying if it's good or bad
Just clearing the confusion
So that you can see what is needed
In each moment of your life
You can play with this being
Poking at it, laughing with it
And it will dodge around
Joining in your game
You can be yourself with this being
You don't need to impress it with your deeds
Or pretend to be something you're not

It will be there for you regardless
Never judging you
Or putting you down
You can cry with this being
And it will cry with you
Feeling what you feel
Yet embracing you with warmth
It would never hurt you
And you can't hurt it
For light cannot be destroyed
It would never leave you
Or let you be hurt
Shining in the eyes of anyone who would harm you
It is always there for you
Always caring for you
Whether you're aware of it or not
Now and forever

Let's count to 10 slowly, as we return to this room. Take one or two more slow breaths, and then open your eyes.

*Home*

Sit in a relaxed, comfortable position. Close your eyes if you like. Let's take a few slow, deep breaths. Feel the air pushing against the hand on your tummy. Let's count slowly on the in-breath: One, two, three, four, and exhale. Wait a moment, and count again: One, two, three, four, and exhale. Continue breathing slowly.

I am home
Surrounded by everyone I care about
Holding me like a human hammock
Rocking me gently in the breeze
Keeping me perfectly safe
Never critical of me, or of each other
Accepting me as I am
I am home
I smell warm, familiar smells
I taste my favorite food
I hear my favorite music
I squeeze my favorite toy
Everything is familiar and good
I am home
I am loved

I am content
I am refreshed
I am strong again
I am home
And I can carry the memory of home
Wherever I go
So it's never far away
I see the people I love
Feel the familiar feelings
Know I am safe and strong
Everywhere I travel
Each time I close my eyes
I am home

Let's count to 10 slowly, as we return to this room. Take one or two more slow breaths, and then open your eyes.

*Parents*—The above are among my favorite images, but there are many others that can be helpful. If your child does not respond to the images above, look at some of the books in the references for an image that appeals to your child. For older children or children who are auditory learners, it sometimes helps to focus on a sound or word rather than an image when meditating. "Om" is traditional in some forms of Eastern meditation, but "One" (alluding to the unity of all beings, to one Divine Being, or to being united with and supported by the universe, depending on one's beliefs), "Home" (as in the meditation above), and "Now" (alluding to the here and now; no concerns about the past or future) are some nice words to focus on too.

A mindfulness approach may also be helpful for older children and teens, particularly for those who recognize that they "can't turn off the mind," and this is their key problem. Note that mindfulness exercises do not prescribe a specific form of breathing control, but rather encourage observation of the breathing process. Most people's breathing naturally slows down as they do so, however.

The focus on breathing, a physical sensation, can be very grounding for all of us. For children who often experience physical discomfort, it may be particularly helpful, providing an alternative physical focus that allows them to "observe pain" and thus experience less distress. The meditation below may be worth trying with these children as well. Jon Kabat-Zinn has written extensively on the use of mindfulness in pain syndromes in adults, and his ideas are worth a closer look if coping with pain is a key issue for the child.

*A Possible Mindfulness Script:*
Sit in a relaxed, comfortable posture.
Close your eyes if you like.

Now, pay attention to your breath.
Feel it going into your nostrils
Filling your lungs
Pushing against your ribs and belly
And escaping out of your mouth
Where do you notice it most?
Focus on that spot
Whether it's in your nose,
Your throat, your lungs, your belly
Or some other part of your body
You will come back to this spot again and again.
Now notice the feelings in other parts of your body
Whether they're tense or relaxed
Comfortable, uncomfortable
Or even itchy or painful
Don't try to make the feelings go away,
Just notice them becoming stronger, or weaker,
And return to your breath when you are able
Pay attention to how your legs feel
And return to the breath
Pay attention to how your arms feel
And return to the breath
Pay attention to how your chest and abdomen feel
And return to the breath
Pay attention to how your head feels
And return to the breath
Thoughts are just like those feelings:
They come and go,
Becoming stronger and weaker
Entering your mind and leaving it again
Like actors crossing a stage
You don't have to push them away
They'll go on their own eventually
You don't have to follow them
They're not that important
They can't help you or hurt you
They're just thoughts
And you are more than those thoughts
Watch them come and go
And return to the breath
And more may come and go
And again you return to the breath
And don't put yourself down if you follow them

Or start trying to fight them
We all do that
Just catch yourself when you can
And return to the breath
Finally remember that feelings are just like those thoughts
Nervous feelings, sad feelings, frustrated feelings
They're all just part of the scenery of life
They come and go
Become stronger and then weaker
Never defining you completely
Because you're more than those feelings
You can watch those feelings
Coming and going
Ebbing and flowing
As you return to the breath
Noticing your body, your mind, and your feelings
But always coming back to the breath
To that peaceful, quiet spot inside
Take a few more breaths
Give yourself another minute or two
Then slowly open your eyes.

*Suggest to Parents*—There are several books of children's meditations in the references that may be helpful, and you may wish to try out a few to determine what your child finds most reassuring. *Spinning Inward* by Maureen Murdock contains several meditations that may be relevant to different types of anxiety and is worth a look if the meditations I've provided here are not appealing to your child. *Starbright* by Maureen Garth contains a number of relaxing images for younger children, and I particularly liked her "Star Prelude," which encourages children to hang their worries on a "Worry Tree" before mentally entering a more relaxing place. Guidance is also provided on how to encourage meditation and use it most effectively with children. A more spiritual meditation similar to "The Wave" can be found in *All I See Is Part of Me* by Curtis and Aldrich. Older children may prefer these, because they may find some of the more concrete images (animals, teachers, etc.) a bit too juvenile. Children's preferences vary, though, so it's worth trying a few different meditations.

Try a couple of meditations with your child this week. Some children find a tape of a parent's voice comforting. If this is true for your child, either read or make an audio recording in your own voice of the meditation that your child finds most comforting, and use it consistently. Start with balloon breathing for a couple of minutes to slow everyone down, and then slowly talk through the meditation you picked. If you're calm as you do it, you'll find the pitch of your voice drops slightly from the normal conversational tone as your vocal cords relax. If nothing seems to appeal to your child, pick the meditation that you find most comforting yourself, talk through it slowly, and see if your child eventually joins you.

Most people find it easiest to set aside a few minutes at bedtime to do meditation. Be careful not to interfere with other bedtime routines, though. Some children are very attached to these. Instead, make it a nice addition to the routine that represents a little extra time with Mommy or Daddy.

If your child claims to be bored doing meditation during the first week, there's probably something that's making meditation uncomfortable for him or her. Maybe the siblings are teasing about it, or maybe it's interfering with another activity. Try to address the source of the discomfort, whatever it is. If your child claims to be bored and has been doing the same meditation for more than a week, maybe it's legitimate boredom. Try using another meditation or varying the content a bit.

Once you have found a comfortable form of meditation, have your child respond to this:

To become calm, my favorite meditation is:

_____

_____

Suggest to the child:

Give meditation a try. It only takes ten minutes or so at bedtime, and you may find it relaxing or it may make you sleepy. The worst thing that can happen is you'll get bored, and ten minutes of boredom isn't so bad. Besides, you'll get another point each time you do it. Keep noticing your Fear Signal and using your Fear-Master card too!

**Imagery-Based Meditation (Continued)**

Did you use your meditation this week? What got in the way of doing it? What helped you remember to do it? Did you start to notice yourself becoming calm? Did you notice anything else? Let's figure out how to make it easier to do, and make it seem like a good part of your routine. One common problem is that people have trouble focusing on their meditation image, and then they get frustrated because they think they're not doing what they're "supposed to."

*The Wandering Mind*

If you find your mind wandering, that's OK. That's natural. Everyone has different thoughts and ideas that come into their head. Sometimes we even have very strange thoughts or ideas. Don't be too hard on yourself if this happens. It's not your fault. We all have thoughts and ideas without meaning to.

Don't worry if you think you're a "bad meditator." There's no such thing! We all get distracted, and we can all come back to our focus. Even if you only stay with your focus for a second or two, that's fine. It will still be there when you return to it. It's kind of like tasting a sip of water on a hot day: It's there to refresh you. Nobody would go around worrying, "I'm not a good water-taster!" That would sound silly. They would just enjoy it! Give yourself a chance to enjoy your meditation too.

Remember: Distracting thoughts, whatever they are, are just thoughts. They can't hurt you or make you do things you don't want to do. They're not that powerful, and they always eventually go away. Watch them come and go. Wave them good-bye if you like.

Then, focus again on your meditation image. Even if you have a thousand distracting thoughts, that's OK. You're used to thinking and doing things. It takes practice to just be. Most people find if they observe the distracting thoughts coming and going, and don't get too upset about them, they eventually have less of them. They focus more on the meditation image, and they find it easier to become calm.

*Letting Go*

Some people find it very hard to let go of certain distracting thoughts or worries. If this happens to you, try writing down or drawing the thought or worry, then return to the meditation exercise. Writing or drawing gives us the sense of having done something about the issue, and then we can let it go. Afterward, you can choose to either act on what you've written or drawn (if it was a really good idea), or rip up the paper. Most of the time when people do this, they find they rip up the paper. Really good ideas rarely come out of a worried, distracted mind.

If writing or drawing is hard when you're stressed, imagine instead that you take the worries and hang them on a tree in the park. Then walk away. The tree will hold your worries, leaving you free to focus on more relaxing thoughts and images.

Of course, if you really have a good reason to be worried, like a science project you haven't finished, stop meditating and just do it! Always do what you can to solve the problem first, but when you've done all you can, give yourself a break. That's the time to return to your calm self.

Want to know a secret? Nervous feelings are just like distracting thoughts. They come and go as well. You can't be really fearful for more than a few minutes. After that, your body runs out of adrenaline, the chemical that makes you tense, and fear stops. Fearful thoughts and feelings come and go. They're temporary. Unless you really focus on them, they don't last. Then, you return to being calm. Being calm is actually your natural way of being. Fear interferes with it for a short time, but then it leaves. Then you go back to being who you really are: Your calm self returns.

As you practice your meditation for one more week, do not fight thoughts and feelings that intrude, but don't chase after them, either. They are not part of your calm self. Recognize them, observe them as if from a distance, and watch them go as you return to focusing on your meditation image.

## CHILD MODULE 4: MASTERING FEAR IN REAL LIFE

### Becoming Calm during the Day

You might wonder: How does meditating at night help with fear during the day? The answer is: it doesn't automatically. What can happen, though, is that when people are stressed they start to remember, "It's my fear acting up," and then go to the special image or special place they go to when they meditate. It becomes a way of dealing with whatever stress is faced at that moment, and makes that stress seem more manageable. It's yet another way of being a "Fear-Master." Then, they can return to the "calm self" that is strengthened each night when they meditate. Some people even like to draw their favorite meditation image on a card and use it instead of or in addition to their "Fear-Master Card." After learning to use meditation at bedtime, try using your image during the day. Remember your meditation image the next time you notice your Fear Signal, and take a few slow breaths. Then, remind yourself that whatever you fear, all you have to do is get through that moment. You can't change the past or predict the future. What you *can* do is get through that moment. It may be a frightening moment, but if you focus on your meditation image, it doesn't have to be an impossible moment to get through. You can get through it. Focus on your meditation image, and trust yourself to become calm again. Your calm self is your natural self, and it's not controlled by fear. It recognizes fear and fear tricks, but it does not get caught by them. It watches them come and go. Before you know it, you have survived that frightening moment. Fear hasn't stopped you. That's how practicing meditation can help you day and night!

When I notice my fear signal, I will take a few slow breaths and focus on:

_____

_____

This will strengthen my calm self, so I can return to it day or night.

### Combining Strategies

We can now review how to combine strategies. The combinations that are usually the most powerful are:

1. Recognize your Fear Signal, and focus on something you must do, on an activity, or on something you can see or hear.
2. Recognize your Fear Signal, and pull out your Fear-Master Card.
3. Recognize your Fear Signal, and use your meditation image to become calm.

What do they have in common? They all start with recognizing, "It's my fear acting up," and then doing something about it. Labeling fear is often the most important step! It's a way of reassuring yourself that you're not helpless or crazy: It's just fear, and fear may be a nuisance but you know how to handle it.

Any of these combinations can also help you face what you fear. If you're not sure you can handle a situation, just do 1, 2, or 3, and stay where you are. You may not be able to solve the problem with it right away, but at least you won't panic at that moment, and you won't run away.

If you've handled the situation before, or you think it's not too bad, definitely go into it once you've done 1, 2, or 3. Anything you've done before, you can do again, if you remember you are a Fear-Master. What about things that are just a little bit frightening? They often turn into adventures once you try them!

**Making a Plan: The Treasure Map**

Think about what you will do when you're no longer controlled by fear. What would you like to do that fear is stopping you from doing? Take a moment to imagine yourself doing it. Picture it in detail. Include smells, sounds, and feelings you might experience as well. Before long, you will be doing just that! Throughout this course, you have strengthened your calm self, so you can cope with that situation in spite of fear. Fear can't win! How will you begin to do it this week? Do you have any ideas? See if Mom or Dad can help.

Another nice way to think about your strategies is to imagine them as buried treasure. You decide where to bury it, and what your treasure map will look like. Find a spot to keep your Fear-Master card, your favorite meditation recording, and any other reminders that help you use your strategies. You could even get a box for them, and decorate it like a treasure chest. Then, draw a map of your house and put a big "X" on each spot where you keep your reminders. Just like on a real treasure map, X marks the spot! Add some people to your map. They are your treasure-hunting team! All the people who help you use your strategies are on the team. Start with your parents, and then think about other people who could help and add them. By the time you are finished, you will be leading a whole expedition!

*Draw Your Treasure Map Here:*

*Draw What You Will Do When You Master Your Fear:*

Parents, think about fearful situations your child often struggles with. Talk to your child about what strategies he or she can or would like to use to deal with those situations. Some children like to start with just one approach. Some children use all the strategies right away. People need a chance to do things at their own pace, and in a manner that works for them. Work out a plan that you and your child will use consistently in fearful situations. Whatever you choose to do, find a time and place to apply it. Agree on how much you will do, and how much your child will do. Put the ideas together with the treasure map described above.

**Questions to Help You Make a Plan**

*Fear Signal:* What is the best Fear Signal for your child? Will you help identify the Fear Signal for the child, or will the child tell you when they are afraid?

*Fear-Master:* Will your child keep the Fear-Master card in their pocket, or in their room? Will your child use the card showing the Fear-Master Image on its own or the one showing it defeating Fear Tricks? How will the Fear-Master Image help with facing the fears we talked about in the parent session at the beginning? Which situations is the child ready to work on now? Which situations should wait until he or she is more confident?

*Calm Self:* Will you meditate together? Will other family members join in? Where and when will you meditate? Will you make a recording of a favorite meditation, or read it to your child? Will your child begin using meditation during the day, and for what situations?

Be as concrete and as specific as you can about what you will try. Then, tell us your plan (or have the child tell us). We'll troubleshoot a bit and then see how it went at our follow-up meeting. Remember to be positive about even minimal participation by the child in this exercise. It's not easy to try something new like this!

Parent will:

_____

_____

_____

Child will:

_____

_____

_____

**Example Plans**

1. Parent will ask child about times when fear signal was noticed periodically, and do meditation at bedtime together. Lots of praise will be offered for noticing fear signal and trying to cope, regardless of outcome. Child will carry the Fear-Master card in school backpack and use whenever fear signal noticed.

2. Coping with nightmares (where child has almost no control over fear): Once he or she wakes up and goes to mother's bed (as most children do), mother will offer a comforting reminder that it's just a dream and can't hurt you, and do a meditation together with the child. The second or third time it happens, she'll see if child can do at least part of the meditation himself or herself, working toward greater independence, with praise for becoming calm and brave. If the same nightmare repeats (e.g., falling down stairs in a child with poor coordination), child will be encouraged to practice coping with that fear during the day (e.g., walking down steps alternating feet until confident doing so).

**Point Bank**

Award one point for each homework example or time a strategy was used during the week (note: multiple strategies earn multiple points, even for the same situation) and one point for each in-session example. Double the point value if the child actually stays in the feared situation! Facing fear is the key to overcoming it, regardless of how you do it.

*Module 1 Point Tally:* _____

_____

(Recognizing Fear Signal; "It's just my fear acting up")

Parent response was: _____

_____

Any fearful situations you'd like to do more work on? Tell your parents!

*Module 2 Point Tally:* _____

_____

(Any of: Fear Signal, Fear-Master Card)

Parent response was: _____

_____

Any fearful situations you'd like to do more work on? Tell your parents!

*Module 3 Point Tally:* _____

_____

(Any of: Fear Signal, Fear-Master Card, Calming Meditation)

Parent response was: _____

_____

_____

Any fearful situations you'd like to do more work on? Tell your parents!

*Module 4 Point Tally:* _____

_____

_____

(Any of: Fear Signal, Fear-Master Card, Calming Meditation)

Parent response was: _____

_____

_____

Any fearful situations you'd like to do more work on? Tell your parents!

Total Points: _____

_____

_____

Congratulations, you did it!!!

# Glossary

**A.B.C.**   A common acronym used in behavior modification that stands for Antecedents, Behavior, and Consequences.

**All-or-nothing thinking**   Thinking style that focuses on extremes (for example, "if the problem is not completely gone, the treatment has failed").

**Anaphylaxis**   Life-threatening allergic reaction.

**Baseline**   A measure of a specific problem or symptom before intervention, with the goal of observing change in that problem or symptom as intervention proceeds.

**Behavioral activation**   Systematic approach to helping a child or adolescent increase daily activities, especially enjoyable ones; an important element of CBT for depression.

**Booster sessions**   Additional session(s) after CBT formally concludes that are designed to consolidate treatment gains; typically spaced several weeks apart and focused on review, rather than introducing new CBT strategies.

**Brainstorming**   Generating as many ideas as possible about a particular question or problem before deciding which one(s) to act upon.

**CBT**   Cognitive behavioral therapy: a form of brief, structured psychotherapy based on the premise that thoughts, feelings, and behaviors affect each other in reciprocal ways.

**Circular interactions**   When two people interact in ways that reinforce each other's behavior, thus perpetuating the interaction; by implication, neither is at fault because it is impossible to tell where the pattern began.

**Cognitive restructuring**   Finding alternative, adaptive thoughts to replace maladaptive, distressing ones.

**Cohesion**   Sense of loyalty to a group and desire to work together with other members.

**Comorbidity**   Having more than one psychiatric disorder at the same time.

**Concurrent therapies**   Therapies that are provided to the child or family at the same time.

**Conditioned response**   A response that occurs when a stimulus that evokes a particular reaction is repeatedly paired with a second stimulus, until the second stimulus evokes the same reaction.

**Contagion**   Children picking up negative behaviors from other children, especially in groups; it is rare in well-run groups but is commonly feared by parents.

**Didactic**   An approach to therapy that is based on direct teaching.

**Effectiveness**   Treatment benefit in usual community practice.

**Efficacy**   Treatment benefit in research environments.

**Empathic encouragement**   Validating the child's feelings while expressing genuine confidence in his or her ability to master a given situation.

**Externalization**   Finding a concrete symbol for emotional symptoms, so that the child can see the symptoms as external to himself or herself and, therefore, not overwhelming.

**Externalizing disorder**   Psychiatric diagnosis characterized mainly by disruptive behavior (for example, oppositional defiant disorder or attention deficit hyperactivity disorder).

**Functional analysis**   A detailed examination of the main behaviors targeted in a child's treatment.

**Ground rules**   Basic behavioral limits for the child that are spelled out at the beginning of therapy.

**Hidden agenda**   Covert wish about therapy harbored by the child or parent but not explicitly stated as a goal of therapy.

**Imaginal exposure**   Facing a feared situation in imagination (for example, by recreating a traumatic event in one's mind to overcome posttraumatic stress).

**Internalizing disorder**   Psychiatric diagnosis characterized mainly by child feeling distressed (for example, mood disorder or anxiety disorder).

**Mastery**   A sense of personal competence that results in the ability to manage certain situations or feeling states.

**Mediator**   A factor or mechanism that may account for therapeutic change.

**Moderator**   A factor that influences the degree of therapeutic change in a child.

**Module**   Therapy unit focused on a particular CBT concept or skill.

**P.A.S.T.E.**   A common problem-solving acronym that represents the following steps: pick a problem, look at alternatives, select an alternative, try it out, and evaluate the result.

**Probabilistic thinking**   Focusing on how likely or unlikely certain events are, usually in order to reassure oneself and reduce anxiety.

**Resilience**  The ability to cope despite encountering adverse circumstances or events.

**Selective mutism**  A condition related to social anxiety in which children speak normally at home with close family but are silent in certain environments and with certain people.

**Self-esteem**  A sense of being a competent and loveable person.

**Sequential therapies**  When one therapy is provided to the child or family after another therapy, rather than providing both at the same time.

**Serotonin-specific medication**  Medication that targets the brain chemical serotonin, thought to be involved in anxiety and depression. Also termed "selective serotonin reuptake inhibitors," these medications include fluoxetine, fluvoxamine, sertraline, paroxetine, and citalopram. (Note: These are the generic names.)

**Socratic questions**  Therapist questions designed to elicit a particular answer or answers that may be helpful to the client.

**Stimulants or stimulant medication**  Medications designed to improve attention. Methylphenidate and dextroamphetamine are the most common ones. (Note: These are the generic names.)

**Termination**  Conclusion or ending of therapy, which sometimes provokes anxiety in the client or his or her parents.

**Therapeutic alliance**  Ability of the client (child or parent) and therapist to work together collaboratively to achieve the goals of therapy.

**Therapeutic flexibility**  Individualizing the use of manuals by selecting those strategies or exercises that will aid the therapist in achieving goals with a given child.

**Transference**  The tendency to transfer feelings we had in relationships in the past into current relationships.

**Treatment adherence**  Degree to which the therapist follows the treatment as prescribed in a manual or text; also termed "treatment fidelity."

**Universality**  The sense of not being the only one affected by a certain problem; often develops in group treatment.

**Verbal working memory**  The ability to simultaneously store and manipulate verbal information, an important cognitive ability when doing CBT.

**Vicious cycles**  Circular interactions that result in mutual frustration and upset.

**Yerkes-Dodson curve**  The finding that low-anxiety states and high-anxiety states both have adverse effects on cognitive performance, but mildly anxious states result in optimal performance.

# Index

Note: figures and tables are denoted with italicized page numbers.